PENNSYLVANIA
BREWERIES

PENNSYLVANIA BREWERIES

LEW BRYSON

STACKPOLE BOOKS

Published by
STACKPOLE BOOKS
5067 Ritter Road
Mechanicsburg, PA 17055
www.stackpolebooks.com

Printed in the United States of America

10 9 8 7 6 5 4 3 2

FIRST EDITION

Cover design by Caroline Stover
Labels and logos used with permission of the breweries.

The author and the publisher encourage all readers to visit the breweries and sample their beers
and recommend that those who consume alcoholic beverages travel with a nondrinking driver.

Library of Congress Cataloging-in-Publication Data

Bryson, Lew.
    Pennsylvania breweries / Lew Bryson. — 1st ed.
        p.   cm.
    Includes index.
    ISBN 0–8117–2789–X
    1. Bars (Drinking establishments)—Pennsylvania—Guidebooks. 2. Microbreweries—
Pennsylvania—Guidebooks. 3. Breweries—Pennsylvania—Guidebooks. I. Title.
TX950.57.P4B79 1998
647.95748—dc21   98–12060
                                                                                                        CIP

CONTENTS

FOREWORD

In less than fifteen years a beer renaissance has occurred in Pennsylvania. Lew Bryson has documented this rebirth in a whirlwind tour through the state's many new breweries as well as the six old ones.

Beer has always been important to Pennsylvanians. The English brought their ales and the Germans brought their lagers when they settled in William Penn's colony. None of us knows how these beers tasted, but history books have recorded accounts of marvelous brews, reminiscent of the European beers, produced in small towns, villages, and cities. By the nineteenth century, Pennsylvania became one of America's major brewing centers, but a long struggle for survival came with Prohibition in 1920.

During Prohibition, a few breweries produced beer in secret places and pumped it through pipes to the taverns that were willing to risk serving it. Most breweries, however, were forced to close their plants forever. Prohibition was repealed in 1933, but surviving breweries were nearly devastated by the Great Depression, which resulted in shortages of malted barley. Brewers had to use rice and cereal grains to make their beer, giving it a lighter, blander taste. Later, the massive advertising campaigns of the macrobreweries made it difficult for the small regional breweries to compete. By the mid-sixties, less than ten breweries remained in Pennsylvania, and that number gradually dwindled down to six by the early eighties.

Then in the mid-eighties, a new breed of Pennsylvanians, consisting of teachers, chefs, and entrepreneurs, rediscovered their brewing heritage and embarked on a mission to bring their state back to its brewing roots. Microbreweries began producing a variety of fresh ales and lagers, using the finest ingredients available and incorporating traditional brewing methods with new ones. Now many taverns, pubs, fine dining establishments, and retail beer outlets are promoting and selling beers from the nearly fifty brewpubs, microbreweries, and regional breweries now existing in the state.

I hope this book inspires you to visit and revisit all the brewing establishments in Pennsylvania as you enjoy the cultural, historical, and natural wonders the state has to offer. Read, visit, taste, and enjoy—and join us in preserving our state's great beer industry and heritage.

Carol A. Stoudt
President, Stoudt's Brewing Company

ACKNOWLEDGMENTS

There are some people I need to thank for their help in making this book happen. First, Chris Trogner of Tröegs Brewing Company, who said to an editor friend of his, "Hey, I know a beer writer from Pennsylvania!" My publishers, for putting me where Chris could see me: Tony Forder (*Ale Street News*) and John Hansell (*Malt Advocate*)—and special thanks to Bob and Connie Ryan (*Vat Talk*), who first paid me to write about beer. My editors at Stackpole Books, Kyle Weaver and Jane Devlin, for getting me through this first book, and Ann Harrison, for copyediting that made this a tighter, better book.

For teaching me about beer, my thanks to Dr. Paul Thibault, who first put a good beer in my hand, and the late Wilhelm Lauzus, who put that beer in Paul's hand and so many more in mine. Again to John Hansell, who opened my eyes to how very little I knew about beer after ten years of learning about it. To Tom Peters, Jim Anderson, and Ann Cebula, for strewing my path with excellent beers. To the people at Prodigy Online Services, who knew a good thing when they saw it and made me their Member Representative for Beer. To the people on Prodigy's Beer Talk bulletin board and the No Bull Inn chat room: you guys are *much* better than the New Mail.

My thanks to all the brewers of Pennsylvania, who have never let me down. To Ron Barchet and Bill Covaleski, whose freely given technical knowledge of brewing has helped me through many articles. To Carol Stoudt, who laughs damn near as loudly as I do and knows how to do a beer fest the right way. To Tom and Mary Beth Pastorius and their never-failing hospitality and cheerful honesty. To Mike Oehrlein, who *does* laugh as loudly as I do and never lets me out of arguments easily. To Bill Moore, who put up with a lot of stupid questions, and Henry Ortlieb, who restored my faith in brewpubs. To Trip Ruvane, who turned in the best questionnaire response, and Dan Weirback, who gave all of us a fruit beer no one can laugh at. To the master brewers of the six Old Guard breweries, whose stubborn determination makes me proud to be from Pennsylvania. To Eric Savage, a really cool guy, Jim Cancro, a man with a lot of patience, and Tom Kehoe and Jon Bovit, two good friends who always let me in on the straight skinny—as far as I know!

And special thanks to the people who have made me what I am. To my father, Lew, for the help with the maps and for driving on my

ix

big western Pennsylvania tour, and my mother, Ruth, for proofing the manuscript. To my children, Thomas and Nora, who went on a lot of brewery tours this year and got by on kisses and promises. And finally and always, to my wife, Catherine, I could not have done any of this without you. You do the greatest thing of all: You believe.

To all of you, *Cheers!*

HOW TO USE THIS BOOK

This book is a compendium of information about Pennsylvania's breweries. It also lists some of the interesting attractions and best bars in Pennsylvania. And it offers facts and opinions about brewing, brewing history in the United States and Pennsylvania, and beer-related subjects.

It does not present a comprehensive history of any brewery, nor is it one of the ubiquitous books that try to rate every single beer produced by every single brewery. It is not a conglomeration of beer jargon—Original Gravities, International Bittering Unit levels, Apparent Attenuations, and so on. And it's not about homebrewing. There are too many of these kinds of books anyway.

It is a travel guide about breweries and Pennsylvania, two subjects dear to my heart. Sharing information has been a central part of the success of the rise of microbreweries in the United States. Loyalty to local breweries has been key to the unique survival of older breweries in Pennsylvania. I have tried to keep to these traditions.

The book is organized in alternating parts. The meat of the book, the brewery information, is presented in seven sections. The first section begins with a general description of the large mainstream breweries that make up the Old Guard. Each of the six geographical sections—Philadelphia, Philadelphia suburbs, Pennsylvania Dutch Country, Capital region, Upstate Pennsylvania, and Pittsburgh—is prefaced with a description of the area for those unfamiliar with it. The "A word about..." sections are intended as instructional interludes on topics you may be curious about. There should be something there for almost everyone, whether novice, dabbler, or fanatic.

The breweries are profiled in the following manner.

The official name of the brewery
Address
Phone number
Website
History of the brewery, highlights, my observations, and other information about the company are presented in five to seven paragraphs.

Opened: Month and year listed for microbreweries; year given for regional breweries.

Type: *Brewpub, brewery, or regional brewery.* A brewpub sells beer to be enjoyed on location, whereas a brewery sells its beer primarily off premises. A regional brewery is one of the Old Guard.

Owner: Individual, partners, or corporation.

Brewer: Brewers are the most changeable element of small-scale brewing. Names were accurate as of early 1998; brewers may have moved on by the time you read this.

PA Microbrewers Guild: Membership status. See also page 166.

System: Size and manufacturer of the brewkettle. Potential annual capacity in barrels.

Annual production: 1996 or 1997 production in barrels.

Beers brewed: The brewery's regular year-round offerings, any seasonal or rotated beers, and where those beers are produced.

The Pick: A description of my favorite beer at each brewery, or what I feel is a notable beer there.

Take-out beer: Beer for sale at the brewery, if any, for off-premises consumption.

Tours: Schedule of brewery tours, if any. It is always best to call ahead to confirm. (Please remember to be polite on tours. Your opinions are welcome, but if they are negative it would be best to express them in a more private setting.)

Brewpub hours: Hours may change; call ahead if timing is crucial.

Food: Type of food available at a brewpub.

Extras: Whatever a brewpub may offer in addition to fresh beer: darts, pool, pinball, live music, cigar lounge, selections of single-malt whiskeys, small-batch bourbons, cognacs, or other liquors.

Special considerations: Are kids welcome? Is the building handicapped-accessible? Are cigars allowed? Are vegetarian meals available?

Parking: On- or off-street parking available.

Lodging: I've tried to list a nearby hotel, budget motel, and B&B or country inn wherever possible.

Nearby attractions: Parks, museums, scenery, events, amusement parks, and other fun stuff I may have heard about.

Other good beer sites in the area: These may be multitaps, historic bars, or restaurants with good beer selections. I have included brief descriptions, addresses, and phone numbers.

INTRODUCTION

Welcome to Pennsylvania and its breweries! You will find plenty of beer here these days, even though it's a far cry from the glory days of beer making 100 years ago. Almost every Pennsylvania town had a brewery then; some, like Philadelphia and Lancaster, had ten or more. You'll still find beautiful old bars in many small Pennsylvania towns, relics of the days when Pennsylvania's German and East European laborers crowded into taprooms in search of cool lager to relieve the heat of a day's hard work in forges and factories.

Pennsylvania is growing a new crop of breweries today. We're up to about 50 so far, with more on the way. This is reflected in the resurgence of different styles of beer in America and the rise of what have been called *microbreweries* or *craft breweries*. To understand where these new breweries came from, we need to take a look back at our country's history, during which American brewing went from a vibrant, broad industry to a fossilized oligopoly of brewers making one style of beer, take it or leave it. What happened?

The Rise and Fall of American Brewing

The most popular alcoholic drink in early America was cider, followed closely by rum. Americans drank a *lot* of these beverages and a lot of alcohol in general. Per capita annual consumption of alcohol was over ten gallons by the 1840s. That's gallons of pure alcohol, not gallons of rum at 40 percent alcohol or cider at 7 percent. Americans drank pretty much all the time.

When Americans did drink beer, they mostly drank imported British ales. And when Americans began brewing, they mimicked the English by producing similar unfiltered ales.

Cider was still the most popular drink through Andrew Jackson's presidency, but things changed rapidly in the 1840s. There were three complementing components to this change. German-style lager beers are believed to have been first brewed in America in Philadelphia, in 1840, by a brewer named John Wagner. This refreshing beer became very popular with laborers because it could be drunk quickly to quench a thirst.

Paradoxically, the temperance movements that swept the nation in the 1840s accelerated the rise of lager beer. Temperance had strong effects on many suppliers, retailers, and drinkers. One of its major "successes" was wiping out America's cider-producing orchards almost entirely. The 1840s saw fields of stumps on many farms. The demand for drink did not go away, of course, and lager brewers picked up the shifting market.

The third thing that drove lager's popularity was the rise in immigration to America after the squashed European rebellions of 1848. Germans and other beer-drinking Europeans came to America by the thousands, and they wanted their beer. America was happy to supply it.

There were over two thousand breweries in America at the turn of the century, mostly small, local breweries producing almost every style of beer, although lager was a clear favorite. The temperance movements, however, had not gone away. The Great Killer of breweries in America was the little social experiment called Prohibition (1920–1933). By 1939, when this fanaticism had run its course and the industry had settled down, only about 500 breweries remained.

Everyone knows that people didn't stop drinking during Prohibition, but the quality of the beer they drank was dramatically affected. Some drank "needle beer" (near beer injected with alcohol) or low-grade homebrew, made with anything they could get their hands on. They used cake yeast and the malt syrup that brewers were making to survive.

Other beer generally available during Prohibition was low-quality and relatively weak, made from cheap ingredients with large amounts of corn or rice for fermentation. Illicit brewers used the high-gravity system: Brew very strong beer, then water it down. This saved time and money, as did greatly shortened aging times. Federal enforcement agents knew that hops were a commodity really used only for brewing; brewers, therefore, lowered the amount of hops they used to avoid suspicion. For 14 years people drank literally anything that was called beer.

These changes brought on some long-term effects. The corn and rice and high-gravity brewing produced a distinctly lighter-bodied beer with an identifiable nonbarley taste. Low hopping rates made for a sweeter beer. Over Prohibition's fourteen years, people got used to light lager beer. The process continued over the next three decades as big brewers came to dominate the market.

The rise of big breweries and the decline of small breweries can be tracked to several important developments. World War II brought a need to get lots of beer to troops abroad. Huge contracts went to the brewers who were big enough to fill them. (Hops and malt for home-front brewing were considered nonessential.) Improvements in packaging made buying beer for home consumption easier, and refrigerated transportation enabled brewers to ship beer long distances to reach more customers. These improvements required large capital investment possible only for successful, growing breweries.

Mass market advertising during broadcast sporting events got the national breweries in front of everyone. The advertising further convinced Americans that light lagers were the only type of beer out there. Advertising was expensive, but effective. The big breweries got bigger, and small ones went out of business.

Why did the rise of big national brewers necessarily mean that American beer would become all the same type of light lager? Simple reasons, really: Making it all the same is cheaper and easier. Success breeds imitation. Image is easier to advertise than flavor. A large, national brand has to appeal to a broad audience of consumers.

This led to the situation in the 1970s in which one dominant style of beer was made by fewer than forty breweries. People who wanted something else had to seek out the increasingly rare exceptions made by smaller brewers (Stegmaier's and Yuengling's porters kept things going here in Pennsylvania) or buy pricey imports of unknown age and freshness. The varieties of beer styles were unknown to most Americans.

This is the real key to understanding the craft-brewing revolution. These beers are not better made than Budweiser; in fact, Budweiser is more consistent than many American craft-brewed beers. What craft-brewed beers offer is variety.

The American Brewing Revolution

How did microbreweries get started? Fritz Maytag bought the Anchor Brewery in San Francisco on a whim in the mid-1960s. He had heard they were going out of business and knew they brewed his favorite beer. Fritz was an heir to the Maytag appliance fortune and could afford to indulge his whims. But he got hooked on brewing, and Anchor led the return of beer variety in America. Fritz brewed Anchor's trademark "steam" beer, an ale and lager hybrid; he brewed the mightily hoppy Liberty Ale; and he brewed the strong, malty barley wine he called Old Foghorn. Things were off and running in the United States.

Next came the microbreweries. Ambitious homebrewers, maverick megabrewers, and military or businesspeople who had been to Europe and wanted to have the same kinds of beer they drank there started these small breweries, cobbling them together like Frankenstein's monster from whatever pieces of equipment they could find. The beer was anything but uniform—sometimes excellent, sometimes awful—but even so it found a receptive market.

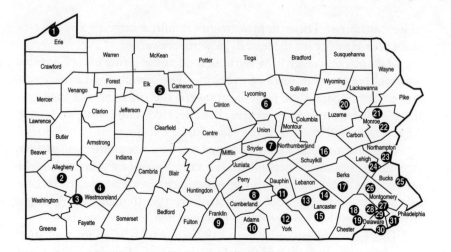

Appalachian Brewing Company, Harrisburg ⑪

Barley Creek Brewing Company, Tannersville ㉒

Buckingham Mountain Brewing Company, Lahaska ㉕

Bullfrog Brewery, Williamsport ⑥

Camelot Brewing Company, Reading ⑰

Church Brew Works, Pittsburgh ❷

Dirty Dawg Brewing Company, Limerick ㉖

Dock Street Brewing Company, Philadelphia ㉛

Foundry Ale Works, Pittsburgh ❷

The Franconia Brewing Company, Mt. Pocono ㉑

General Lafayette Inn, Lafayette Hill ㉗

Gettysbrew Pub and Brewery, Gettysburg ⑩

Gettysburg Brewing Company, Gettysburg ⑩

Hoppers Brewpub and Erie Brewing Company, Erie ❶

Independence Brewing Company, Philadelphia ㉛

John Harvard's Brew House, Springfield ㉚

John Harvard's Brew House, Wayne ㉙

John Harvard's Brew House, Wilkins Township ❷

Jones Brewing Company, Smithton ❸

Lancaster Malt Brewing Company, Lancaster ⑮

Latrobe Brewing Company, Latrobe ❹

The Lion Brewery, Wilkes-Barre ⑳

Manayunk Brewing Company, Philadelphia ㉛

Neversink Brewing Company, Reading ⑰

Old Lehigh Brewing Company, Allentown ㉔

Pennsylvania Brewing Company, Pittsburgh ❷

Pittsburgh Brewing Company, Pittsburgh ❷

Poor Henry's, Philadelphia ㉛

Pretzel City Brewing Company, Reading ⑰

Red Bell Brewing Company, Philadelphia ㉛

Rock Creek Brewing Company, Chambersburg ❾

Samuel Adams Brew House, Philadelphia ㉛

Selin's Grove Brewing Company, Selinsgrove ❼

Sly Fox Brewing Company, Phoenixville ㉘

Stoudt's Brewing Company, Adamstown ⑭

Straub Brewery, St. Marys ❺

The Strip Brewing Company, Pittsburgh ❷

Summy House and Prussian Street Brewing Company, Manheim ⑬

Tröegs Brewing Company, Harrisburg ⑪

Ugly Dog Brewing Company, West Chester ⑲

Valhalla, Pittsburgh ❷

Valley Forge Brewing Company, Wayne ㉙

Victory Brewing Company, Downingtown ⑱

Weyerbacher Brewing Company, Easton ㉓

Whitetail Brewing Company, Carlisle ❽

Yards Brewing Company, Philadelphia ㉛

York Brewing Company, York ⑫

D.G. Yuengling and Son, Pottsville ⑯

The revolution started in the West and grew very slowly. New Albion, the first new brewery in America since World War II, opened in 1976. Ten years later, Dock Street and Penn Brewing hired an existing brewery to brew their beers. The first new "brick and mortar" brewery in Pennsylvania, Stoudt's, opened in 1987. Progress was gradual in Pennsylvania until 1995.

By the end of 1994 there were twelve breweries in Pennsylvania, including the six "Old Guard" regional breweries. By the time the champagne popped again at the end of 1995, there were twice that many. In the next two years the number doubled again. I know of at least seven more breweries scheduled to open by the end of 1998. Microbrewing has taken hold in Pennsylvania.

Of course, there are signs and dire portents of the long-discussed shakeout of microbreweries. Most of the larger micros are having troubles, and some of the undercapitalized smaller ones are going under. There is already some consolidation and merging taking place. As we stand on the brink of this, the question is whether microbrewing will last or is just a passing fad.

In my opinion, the genie won't go back in the bottle. Brewpubs are established in their communities and people have discovered the many different ways beer can taste. No one thinks all wine comes in gallon jugs anymore, and everyone knows there are more types than red and white. Beer is on that same path.

How I Came to Love All Beer

A growing number of Pennsylvanians look for something a bit more stimulating than a mainstream mug o' suds these days. But even when it comes to those standbys, we have always been remarkably loyal to our local brewers. These were lessons I learned early, in a beer-drinking career reflective of America's beer revolution.

I had my first full beer as a freshman in college. When I was a kid, my father had often let me have sips of his beer with dinner. That was Duke Ale, from Duquesne Brewing of Pittsburgh, one of Pennsylvania's many defunct breweries. But I'd never had a beer of my own until Tim Turecek handed me a Genesee Cream Ale in that 16-ounce solidly brown and green returnable, dripping with condensation. I drank it, and it was good.

I drank a lot more of them over the next three years. "Genny" Cream, Prior's Double Dark, Stroh's, and Rolling Rock were my staples, along with Stegmaier, National Bohemian, and National Premium when the money was tight. Then one night in my senior year, I met my medieval history professor for drinks in Lancaster's Lauzus Hotel.

I grabbed my usual Stroh's. My professor laughed and slapped it out of my hand. He pulled an Altenmünster out of the cooler and popped the swingtop. "Try this," he said, and changed my life. It was big, full in the mouth, and touched by a strange bitterness that I'd never tasted before. That bitterness made another sip the most natural thing in the world, like pepper on potatoes.

I've been looking for beers outside the American mainstream ever since that night. It's increasingly easy to find that kind of beer right here in Pennsylvania. Our breweries are turning out everything from whopping Imperial stouts to crisp, bitter pilsners to rippingly hoppy India pale ales to bubbly, spicy hefe-weizens.

Is that all I drink, beers like that? Well, no. I mow my lawn in hot, humid, southeastern Pennsylvania summers, and sometimes I want a cold glass of something dashingly refreshing and fizzy. Then I keep it local and reach for one of Pennsylvania's regional brews, or an all-malt lager like Red Bell's Philadelphia Original Lager.

My family and I have enjoyed traveling to Pennsylvania's breweries and sampling these beers at the source. My son took his first tour of the Yuengling brewery on his first birthday. Beer traveling is a lot of fun, and this book will serve as a guide for your travels in Pennsylvania.

The Old Guard

Some call them fossils, some call them smokestack breweries, some call them beer factories. They are the regional breweries that somehow survived Prohibition, World War II, and three decades of brewery wars between 1950 and 1980. They are not national breweries that pump out oceans of beer supported by multi-million-dollar advertising campaigns. They are not hip, trendy micro-breweries that get tons of press coverage for their tiny beer output. They are gritty survivors, working with old plants, a fiercely loyal but aging customer base, and sheer guts.

Pennsylvania has six of these Old Guard brewers, more than any other state. They include Yuengling, America's oldest brewery, and Straub, the smallest pre-Prohibition brewery still operating in America. Two of them, Pittsburgh and Jones, are best known for brewing mainstream, blue-collar beers, but they also brew fine examples of the beers cherished by Pennsylvania's beer-aware. Latrobe is now owned by a Belgian brewing conglomerate. The Lion survived the last fifteen years mainly by brewing malt soda for the Hispanic market.

Some of them managed to keep alive elements of American brewing history. Yuengling and The Lion were the last pre-micro breweries in America to brew porter, a dark, rich brew with roots in London. Although porters are traditionally ales, these porters are lagers, which are easier to produce. Recently, the Lion took a traditionalist step by once again brewing their porter as an ale.

For the most part, these breweries produce mainstream American lager beers, brewed with adjuncts like corn and rice. The beers are not of great interest to a beer geek, but they are all well made and consistent in their high quality. When I'm in the mood for a sluicing, sloshing, "lawnmower" beer, I always buy local and support Pennsylvania brewers, and so should you!

You should also go visit them. Yuengling and Straub give two of the best industrial brewery tours in the country; they take you right down on the floor. Until recently you could actually climb the ladders and look into Straub's rare open lager fermenters, practically unheard of in these days of lawyerly precautions. Even if you don't go inside, simply viewing the architecture and the size of these buildings will give you a whole different angle on brewing.

There is a seventh large—very large—brewery in Pennsylvania, the Stroh brewery near Allentown. The brewery no longer gives tours, has closed the hospitality center, and is run entirely from the home offices in Detroit. Therefore, it is not included in this book.

Pittsburgh Brewing Company

3340 Liberty Avenue
Pittsburgh
412-682-7400
www.ironcity-beer.com

Pittsburgh Brewing Company (PBC) is proudly back on track. The big old brewery was bought by Swan Brewing of Australia in 1985 and then sold again in fairly short order to local Pittsburgh investors. This decade has seen the company rocked by fraudulent check-kiting scams and labor troubles that may have cost them some of their loyal customer base in this union town. There have been frequent shuffles at the top; the brewery is on its third president in as many years.

But Iron City beer keeps rolling out the doors by the pallet-load. The city of Pittsburgh loves pumping Iron, or "Arn," as the locals say. PBC holds most of Pittsburgh's beer-drinking loyalty, and sells most of its output within 100 miles of the brewery.

Much of this town's brewing heritage is reflected in PBC's brands and corporate lineage. The brewery stems from one started by Edward Frauenheim in 1861, which brewed Iron City Beer. In 1899 that brewery joined forces with the twenty-one other local brewers—including Eberhardt and Ober, whose old building now houses Penn Brewing—to form the consolidated Pittsburgh Brewing Company.

That made a big brewery, the largest in a state full of breweries. Until Latrobe's recent renovation and Labatt-financed rise in sales, PBC remained the biggest independent brewer in Pennsylvania, annual production hovering consistently around one million barrels. That has dropped off recently, perhaps because of all the bad press.

A strong bond exists between Pittsburgh's sports teams and Iron City. Sales shot up when the Steelers made it back to the Super Bowl in 1996. PBC has issued commemorative cans featuring local sports teams, along with other collectible cans. Among those are the infamous Olde Frothingslosh cans, featuring the huge Miss Frothingslosh in all her cellulitic glory. PBC did this as a spoof of beer beauty queens like Miss Rheingold and touted the beer as "the pale, stale ale with the foam on the bottom." People loved it, and you still hear of it in bars.

The brewery had great success with their I.C. Light beer, which was popular in Pittsburgh when I was there in 1982. That has dropped off as the original I.C. Light drinkers have aged, but the brewers and marketing mavens have spun off something new to attract the younger market: I.C. Light Twist, a line of fruit-flavored light beers. An innovative combination of megabrewer light beer and microbrewer experimentation, Twist has had a successful launch so far.

PBC also has done well brewing beer for Jim Koch's Boston Beer Company. Most of the Samuel Adams for the East Coast was brewed here for a time, although some found it incredible that the brewers of Iron City could produce Samuel Adams Boston Lager.

Why is that, and why does Iron City have such a bad reputation? It beats me. I've heard people say Iron City tastes salty, rusty, sour, or oily. Some say it's the worst beer made in America. After spending time in the 'Burgh drinking my share of Arn and tasting similar beers from regional and national brewers all over the country, I have to say that Iron City is no worse than most, and better than some.

I suspect that Pittsburgh will be pumping Iron for years to come. And the big old brewery on Liberty Avenue will be making it for them as it has for years. Stop in and take the tour, see the big twin brewkettles in their tiled setting, smoothly curving stacks reaching up through two stories of space. Hike the hill the brewery clings to and sense the size. Then go have some Iron.

Opened: 1861.

Type: Regional brewery.

Owner: Privately held partnership. Jim Gehrig, chief executive officer; Joe Piccirilli, vice chairman.

Brewers: Master Brewer Mike Carota, Assistant Brewer Greg King.

System: Two 600-barrel Enerfab brewkettles. Potential annual capacity 1 million barrels.

Annual production: 800,000 barrels in 1996.

Beers brewed: Iron City, I.C. Light (GABF silver, 1994), I.C. Light Twist (Lime and Cherry), Mustang Malt Liquor (Original and Melon), American, American Light, Sierra, Sierra Light, Keene's

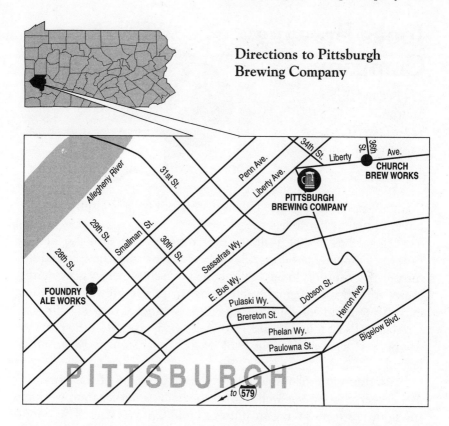

Directions to Pittsburgh Brewing Company

N.A. J. J. Wainwright brands: Evil Eye Ale, Evil Eye Amber Lager, Black Jack Black & Tan, Evil Eye Honey Brown. All beers brewed on premises.

The Pick: Gather round, children, and listen closely: The Pick is Iron City. That's right, the much-maligned Iron City. Maybe it's because of my time in the 'Burgh or maybe it's just because a survivor like this deserves it. The fact is, this is a mainstream American lager that's not bad for what it is, has no overt off-flavors, and is loved by the local market. How can you argue with that?

Take-out beer: None available.

Tours: Tuesday and Thursday at 11:00 A.M. and 2:00 P.M., and by appointment. Contact Missi Matta at 412-692-1191.

Events: PCB has an Oktoberfest. Call for dates and information.

Special considerations: Tours for adults and children over 12 only. Handicapped-accessible.

Parking: Small lot, on-street parking usually available.

Lodging, Nearby attractions, Other good beer sites: See pages 171–173.

Jones Brewing Company

254 Second Street
Smithton
724-872-6626
www.stoneysbeer.com

Man, myth, miner, brewer. This is a story of how a Welsh immigrant miner turned luck into lager.

Legend has it that William B. "Stoney" Jones won the Eureka Brewing Company of Sutersville in a card game sometime around the turn of the century. Jones, a big-boned Welsh miner, was evidently pretty shrewd for a gambler: He hung on to the brewery and then moved it to Smithton. Supposedly Stoney wanted to take advantage of artesian wells he found there. That seems odd, given that the present-day brewery sits on the right bank of the Youghiogheny River, but a legend is a legend.

Another more plausible tale explains the name of the brewery's major beer. Stoney was well known in the area, either from working the mines or from selling his Eureka Gold Crown Lager. The immigrant miners who bought his beer evidently found the name too tough to wrap their tongues around, so they just asked for "one of Stoney's beers." Stoney was smart enough to bow to the inevitable, and soon the beer was labeled "Stoney's."

In a twist that speaks volumes about today's image-conscious market, the brewery has resurrected the Eureka name for a new line of less mainstream beers, the Eureka 1881 line. It's something different for Jones, but the brewery has to evolve along with the rest of the industry to survive.

For decades, the brewery remained in the family, a family that includes actress Shirley Jones, Stoney's granddaughter. Sandy and Gabriel "Gabby" Podlucky bought the brewery in 1988, and Gabby has run it ever since. They continue to serve the loyal local market in traditional regional brewery ways, sponsoring a race car at the local dirt track, giving out calendars, and making banners for tavern accounts.

Recently it looked as if that might not be enough. The brewery hit some rough times in the 1990s and almost went out of business. A local bank stepped in to save the brewery at the last minute, and there

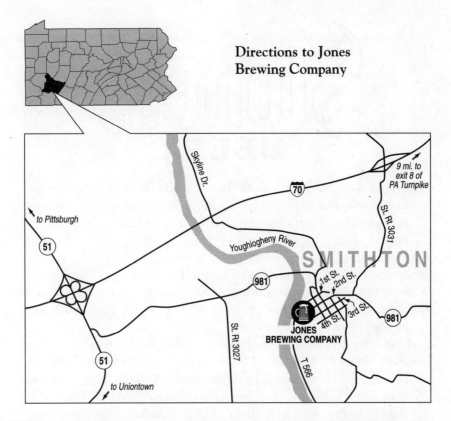

Directions to Jones Brewing Company

is now hope for the future. All they need is a little of old Stoney's legendary luck, and the beer will continue to flow from Smithton.

Opened: Original brewery, Eureka Brewing Company, opened in Sutersville in 1881. Renamed Jones Brewing Company, it moved to Smithton in 1907.

Type: Regional brewery.

Owner: Gabriel "Gabby" Podlucky.

Brewer: Head Brewer Dave Markle

System: 150-barrel Goetz & Flodin brewhouse. Potential annual capacity 130,000 barrels.

Annual production: 55,000 barrels in 1997.

Beers brewed: Stoney's (GABF silver, 1991; bronze, 1992), Stoney's Light (GABF silver, 1991), Stoney's Black & Tan, Stoney's Harvest Gold. *Eureka line:* Black and Tan, Gold Lager, Gold Light Lager, Red Irish Amber Ale. Penn Pilsner brewed here under contract. All beers brewed on premises.

The Pick: The Eureka Black & Tan is a nice little beer with some sweet malt character. You can sit down with some of this and happily while away an evening with friends, a deck of cards, and some cigars.

Take-out beer: Cases and kegs.

Tours: Call ahead, or just drop in. Gabby Podlucky says, "We try real hard to accomodate people for tours."

Special considerations: Visitors must be 21 or older. The tour is not handicapped-accessible.

Parking: Plenty of parking on the street and in the brewery lot.

Lodging: Holiday Inn, Route 51 and I-70, Belle Vernon (724-929-4600); Howard Johnson Inn, 112 West Byers Avenue, New Stanton (724-925-3511); Comfort Inn Greensburg, 1129 East Pittsburgh Street, Route 30, Greensburg (724-832-2600); Mountain View Inn, 1001 Village Drive, Greensburg (724-834-5300).

Nearby attractions: Driving down past Connellsville to see Frank Lloyd Wright's masterpiece Fallingwater (724-329-8501) is a worthwhile trip. In October, enjoy the foliage of the Laurel Highlands. If you stay in Greensburg, see nearby attractions on page 11.

Other good beer sites in the area: Gabby recommends the Longhorn Saloon (Pier Street, Smithton); the Holiday Inn in Belle Vernon (see above); and Cedarbrook Golf Course (right by the Holiday Inn).

Latrobe Brewing Company

119 Jefferson Street
Latrobe
724-537-5545
www.labatt.com

33. Think about that for a while, we'll come back to it.

Latrobe does not give regular tours. It is owned by Labatt, which in turn is owned by Interbrew, a giant Belgian brewing conglomerate. Over 95 percent of Latrobe's output is a beer best known for the advertising slogan, "Same as it ever was." So why should you visit?

Because it's so darned cool. Latrobe Brewing is better known in Pennsylvania (and everywhere else) as the brewer of Rolling Rock. Rolling Rock, with its mysterious "33" labeling, is a beer that inspires great loyalty. Same as it ever was? Thousands of Rock fans say, "It better be!" There is also a tremendous gift shop at the brewery, with some great-looking Rolling Rock stuff.

Latrobe Brewing was originally a cadet brewery of Pittsburgh Brewing. After Prohibition, Pittsburgh decided to drop some of its smaller breweries. Latrobe was sold to the Tito brothers, who ran it until the 1980s. One of the best moves they made was to create a new beer in 1939. It was Rolling Rock. On those very first silk-screened green bottles, the motto read as it does today, "Rolling Rock. From the glass-lined tanks of old Latrobe we tender this premium beer for your enjoyment, as a tribute to your good taste. It comes from the mountain springs to you." And at the end of the motto is the number 33.

What does it mean? Theories abound, although the owners of the brewery will admit that they don't actually know what it means. The number of words in the motto? Yes. The number of letters in the ingredients? Yes. The year Prohibition was repealed? Yes. Unfortunately, the Tito brothers sold only the brewery and the brands to Labatt, and not the corporate archives. The real meaning of 33 may be lost forever.

What has not been lost forever is the brewery. Labatt has spent a lot of money on this brewery, and has renovated it to a fare-thee-well. There's a new brewhouse, new fermentation hall, new valving system, fancy testing systems, and serious automation. Brewing is a one-person operation; fermentation is a *no*-person, remotely controlled operation.

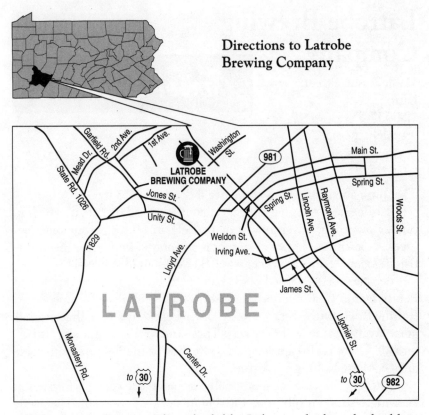

Directions to Latrobe Brewing Company

All the improvements make it look like Labatt jacked up the building and slid in a new brewery.

But "same as it ever was" still holds sway at Latrobe. For example, brewmaster Joe Gruss went to college right there in town, at St. Vincent's. Guess what Joe's dad did? Yup, he was brewmaster at Latrobe. "There are lots of second-generation guys here," Joe smiles, "even some third-generation guys." That's nice to think about.

Opened: 1939.
Type: Regional brewery.
Owner: Interbrew (of Belgium).
Brewers: Joseph Gruss, Mark Ecker.
System: 500-barrel Acme Brewing brewhouse. Potential annual capacity 1.2 million barrels.
Annual production: 1 million barrels in 1996.
Beers brewed: Year-round: Rolling Rock, Rolling Rock Light. All beers brewed on premises.

The Pick: Rolling Rock is one of the beers I grew up with and I still think it's one of the best mainstream American lagers.

Take-out beer: None available.

Tours: The brewery is no longer open for tours. The Rolling Rock Visitor's Center, however, has a twelve-minute video, a museum of collectibles, and a gift store. Tuesday through Friday, 9:30 A.M.–5:00 P.M.; Saturday, 9:30 A.M.–3:00 P.M.

Special considerations: Gift shop is handicapped-accessible.

Parking: Plenty of free off-street parking.

Lodging: Comfort Inn Greensburg, 1129 East Pittsburgh Street, Route 30, Greensburg (724-832-2600); Mountain View Inn, 1001 Village Drive, Greensburg (724-834-5300); Knights Inn, 1215 South Main Street, Greensburg (724-836-7100).

Nearby attractions: St. Vincent's College in Latrobe was the site of one of America's few monastic breweries, and some of the old brewery buildings still stand on the campus. Follow the signs to Strickler's Drug Store in Latrobe and stop in for a banana split; they were invented there about 100 years ago. Keystone State Park north of town offers camping, hiking, boating, fishing, swimming, skating, sledding, and cross-country ski trails. Idlewild Amusement Park in nearby Ligonier has rides, miniature golf, water rides, and Mister Rogers' Neighborhood with a trolley ride and life-size puppets (724-238-3666).

Other good beer sites in the area: Carbone's was the first account to serve Rolling Rock in 1939, and they've been serving it ever since. It's a decent Italian restaurant, in the center of Crabtree on Route 119.

Straub Brewery

303 Sorg Street
Saint Marys
814-834-2875

SINCE 1872

BREWERY, INC.

Straub has a few small claims to fame. It is, by Straub family reckoning, the highest brewery in the East, sitting at an elevation between 1,900 and 2,000 feet above sea level. This puts the brewery just below the Eastern Continental Divide, which means, as Dan Straub laughingly claims, "We get to use the water first!" It is the smallest regional brewery still in operation, with an annual capacity of 35,000 barrels. Most appealingly, it is the home of The Eternal Tap, which I'll explain later. First, let's see where Straub came from and where it's going.

Peter Straub came to the United States from Germany in 1869. He came to St. Marys and soon married Sabina Sorg, whose father owned the local brewery. Peter started his own brewery in 1872, then bought and merged with his father-in-law's brewery in 1876. The copper brewkettle from Sorg's brewery was in continuous use until 1995, when it was finally replaced with a new 160-barrel stainless kettle.

The fourth generation of the family is running the brewery now and the fifth is working there. Dan Straub runs the operation, Terry Straub handles the very low-key marketing operation, and Thomas Straub is the brewmaster. They're doing a good job, too. The main worry at Straub is how to control the brand's growth so they don't outgrow the brewery!

To hear the Straubs tell it, the real challenge is getting all their work in so they still have time left for fun, mainly hunting and fishing. Dan and Terry say that was the main reason behind the recent whirlwind of upgrades to improve the brewery's efficiency. The rare open lager fermenters were finally replaced with stainless tanks that better filled the available space. The bottling line was replaced with a new Krones filler and Krones labeler that does in four days what used to take the old line six. Terry told me that advertising costs have been pared to about two dollars a barrel, just about enough to pay for the brewery's fishing promotions and calendars.

Why does Straub face the happy problem of meeting high demand? Dan Straub gives beers like Samuel Adams some of the credit. "Up until about ten years ago, things were steady," he explains. "Then the micro craze started and drew people's attention to brands other than the nationals." At the same time, they saw that many small businesses had closed or been swallowed up by much larger concerns. "People noticed that all the local bakeries were gone. I guess they decided they didn't want to lose the breweries, too.

"We've got an excellent beer, and that helped too!" Dan hastens to add. Straub has always been free of additives, and the label proudly says that no syrup, sugar, or salt is added. It's all barley malt, shaved corn, and hops.

They've also been marking the beer with a bottling date since 1989. "Bud's born-on date is actually making people more aware that we've been doing it all along," Terry proudly pointed out.

The Straubs are content to stay small. "We're a brewery, not a beer factory," said Terry. It's the German ideal—sell the beer within the smell of the brewery. They sell 60 percent of their beer right in St. Marys, and 25 percent of their sales is draft, more than two times the national average.

Speaking of draft, I promised to tell you about the Eternal Tap. Anyone of age is welcome to walk into the brewery, up the stairs to the keg washing room, and over to the Eternal Tap to pour a beer. Free. All the brewery asks is that you limit yourself to two beers (for the ever-present legal reasons) and that you remember to wash your glass. Things like the Eternal Tap make Straub a rare and priceless gem, a brewery with one foot firmly in an older, simpler time.

Opened: 1872.

Type: Regional brewery.

Owners: The Straub family.

Brewer: Thomas Straub.

System: 160-barrel Vendome brewhouse. Potential annual capacity 35,000 barrels.

Annual production: 32,500 barrels in 1997.

Beers brewed: Straub, Straub Light. All beers brewed on premises.

The Pick: Straub is a good mainstream pilsner, and out here in Straub country, it turns over so fast that it's always fresh. If you're on the tour and they offer you a bottle right off the line, take it. This is the freshest beer you may ever get, fresher even than most beer from a brewpub. It's eye-opening.

Take-out beer: Straub has a brewery store in front of the brewery where you can get cases and kegs. They also do home delivery in the local area.

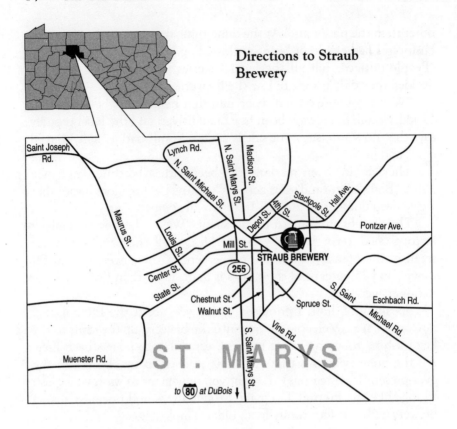

Directions to Straub Brewery

Tours: Monday through Friday, 9:00 a.m.–noon. (Gift shop and Eternal Tap open Monday through Friday, 9:00 A.M.–5:00 P.M., Saturday 9:00 A.M.–1:00 P.M.)

Special considerations: Children under 12 are not allowed on the tour, and the tour is not handicapped-accessible.

Parking: Off-street lot.

Lodging: Old Charm B&B, 444 Brussells Street, St. Marys (814-834-9429); Towne House Inn, (138 Center Street, St. Marys (814-781-1556); Comfort Inn, 976 South Street, St. Marys (814-834-2030); The Royal Inn, two miles south of Ridgway on Route 219 (814-773-3153).

Nearby attractions: The biggest attraction in Elk County outside of Straub is Pennsylvania's only elk herd. The free-ranging herd of 350 to 400 animals is most often seen near the St. Marys airport or in the Benezette area. Elk bugling can be heard in September. The other major attraction is the Allegheny National Forest (814-723-5150), where you can boat, canoe, camp, cross-country ski, snowmobile, hike, fish, hunt, and picnic. A very special part of the National Forest is Hearts Content Scenic Area, a rare stand of virgin Pennsylvania forest west of Sheffield. Visit The Winery at Wilcox (814-929-5598) if you need a change of pace from beer. Further north, but worth the trip, is the Knox-Kane Railroad, an excursion line that crosses the breathtaking Kinzua Railroad Viaduct. At 301 feet high and 2,053 feet long, it is the world's fourth highest railroad bridge. The railroad runs steam and diesel trains on two routes, a 96-mile route from Marienville and a 32-mile route from Kane. Reservations are required, call 814-927-6621. Bradford is the home of Zippo lighters and Case knives, two extremely sturdy and attractive pieces of American technology. Visit the museum and family store (814-368-2863).

Other good beer sites in the area: Dino's Place (233 Market Street, 814-834-6770) and Genevro's (901 South St. Mary's Street, 814-834-4968) in St. Marys are Dan Straub's recommendations. Who am I to argue? I spend all my time in St. Mary's hanging around the Eternal Tap!

The Lion Brewery

700 N. Pennsylvania Avenue
Wilkes-Barre
717-823-8801
www.lionbrewery.com

A relative newcomer among Pennsylvania regional brewers, The Lion Brewery of Wilkes-Barre was founded in 1901 as the Luzerne County Brewery. The Lion outlasted rival Stegmaier, swallowing up its labels and those of two other local brewers. By the early 1980's The Lion, with its 390-barrel brewhouse, was still brewing its own Liebotschaner Cream Ale and some American premium lagers, but was best known among beer geeks for the licorice-hinted, bottom-fermented Stegmaier Porter.

Lee Holland, who's been in American brewing for years and has done publicity work for The Lion, credits former owner Bill Smulowitz with the brewery's survival. "The brewery had to make money to survive, so whatever new idea came around, Bill gave it a try." Bill said yes to some weird stuff, like cherry-flavored Red Baron (named for the local minor league ball team) and an oat-bran lager for health-obsessed beer drinkers. The brewery pioneered malt-based coolers with the briefly popular Calvin Coolers. They also made the first clearmalt, the bizarre, gin-flavored Sting Ray. Such obscure and short-lived beers are the stuff of beer dinner lectures.

Oddest, yet most successful, was malta soda. Dark, sweet, and malt-based, malta is popular in Hispanic and Caribbean markets. It is not fermented, but must be made at a facility where it can be brewed, briefly aged, bottled, and pasteurized.

The Lion started contract brewing, too. Familiar names like Neuweiler's, Trupert, Hope Lager, Nude Beer, Tun Tavern, Red Bell, Commonwealth's Best Burton Bitter, and others came through The Lion, and the brewery continues to take new brands. Between contract brewing, malta and other sodas, and their own brands, The Lion squeaked by.

Smulowitz finally got tired and sold the business to an investment consortium, Quincy Partners. In 1993, they pumped new money and spirit into the brewery. Improvements to the plant were made, including the purchase of a new malt mill and a state-of-the-art lagering cellar from the old Val Blatz Brewery. Cellar B, as it is called, is the showpiece of the re-emerging Lion.

New emphasis on quality control and standard procedures paid off early: The Lion scored a double gold at the Great American Beer Fest in 1994 with Liebotschaner Cream Ale and Stegmaier 1857, an American Premium lager. Stegmaier Porter has become an honest, top-fermenting porter, with a resultant boost in character that is a pleasant surprise to beer snobs.

The brewery also started a new line, Brewery Hill, with a more craft-brewed approach. The line started with the smooth Black & Tan, full-bodied Honey Amber, and snappy Pocono Raspberry. With their success, other beers have been added: Saaz-hopped Centennial Lager, brightly aromatic Pale Ale, sweet Cherry Wheat, and the smooth, rich, Brewery Hill Caramel Porter. There is also a Brewery Hill root beer.

The Lion has seen its future, and it is diverse. The brewery is running at over 85 percent of capacity, still making malta and other sodas, and their own brands are growing. Bill Smulowitz would be proud. The Lion stands capable of doing whatever needs to be done, and doing it well.

Opened: 1901 (Stegmaier Brewery, later absorbed by The Lion, opened in 1857).

Type: Regional brewery.

Owner: Publicly owned, traded on the NASDAQ as MALT.

Brewers: Master Brewer Leo Orlandini, Bob Klinetob, Bob Seaman.

System: 390 barrel Pfaudler brewhouse. Potential annual capacity 400,000 barrels.

Annual production: 340,000 barrels in 1996.

Beers brewed: *Year-round:* Stegmaier Gold Medal Beer, Liebotschaner Cream Ale (GABF gold, 1994, 1995), Stegmaier Porter, Stegmaier 1857 Lager (GABF gold, 1994), Gibbons Beer, Lionshead Beer, Esslinger Beer, Bartels Beer. *Brewery Hill line:* Centennial Lager, Pale Ale, Pocono Raspberry, Honey Amber Ale, Black & Tan. *Seasonals:* Brewery Hill Cherry Wheat, Brewery Hill Caramel Porter. The Lion also makes a very good root beer. All beers brewed on premises.

The Pick: Because of the wide range of beers brewed at The Lion, I've got two picks. Brewery Hill Pale Ale is spankingly crisp and bitter, a great fridge filler beer, particularly for the price range. Liebotschaner

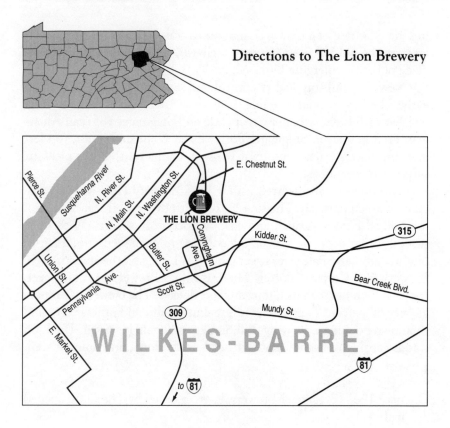

Directions to The Lion Brewery

Cream Ale took the Great American Beer Festival gold medal for cream ales in 1994 and 1995. It's authentic, one of the best examples you'll find of this mild yet distinctive American style.

Take-out beer: Kegs available Monday through Friday, 8:30 A.M.–4:00 P.M.

Tours: Every Saturday at 1:00 P.M. (please call ahead for reservations); not given in winter months.

Special considerations: The Lion tour is not handicapped-accessible.

Parking: Free on-site parking available.

Lodging: Best Western East Mountain Inn, 2400 East End Boulevard, Wilkes-Barre (717-822-1011); Red Roof Inn, Intersection of Routes 115 and 315, Wilkes-Barre (717-829-6422); Bischwind B&B in Bear Creek, on Route 115, three miles south of the Pennsylvania Turnpike (717-472-3820).

Nearby attractions: The River Commons is a park along the Susquehanna in the center of Wilkes-Barre. This was the site of numerous skirmishes during the all-but-forgotten Yankee-Pennamite Wars, a war over land rights that was fought by Pennsylvania and Con-

necticut between 1769 and 1785. Historic markers dot the Commons. The Japanese Double Blossom garden in the park is a colorful display of Japanese cherry trees, begonias, geraniums, and petunias (717-825-1701). Call the Luzerne County Tourist Promotion Agency (888-905-2872) or the Greater Wilkes-Barre Chamber of Commerce (717-823-2101).

Other good beer sites in the area: Elmer Sudds is Wilkes-Barre's original beer bar. It's nothing fancy, just a nice bar with good beer and people who dig it. 475 East Northampton Street (717-825-5286). Cooper's Seafood House is a nationally-ranked seafood restaurant with an outstanding beer selection. One of the first beer bars in the area. Washington Avenue and Pine Street, Scranton (717-346-6883). Cooper's on the Waterfront, son of Cooper's Seafood House, is a comfortably plush restaurant with a very good beer list. 304 Kennedy Boulevard, Pittston (717-654-6883).

D. G. Yuengling & Son

SINCE 1829

Yuengling™

★ *America's Oldest Brewery* ★™

Fifth and Mahantongo Streets
Pottsville
Brewery phone: 717-622-4141
Information: 717-628-4890
www.yuengling.com

Andrew Jackson was inviting all his friends to the White House when David Yuengling started brewing at his Eagle Brewery in Pottsville in 1829. The brewery burned later that year, and the new brewery opened up in 1830 on the slope of Sharps Mountain at Fifth and Mahantongo Streets. Brewing has been going on there ever since, making D. G. Yuengling and Son America's oldest brewery. The brewery is in its fifth generation of family ownership, and the sixth generation is settling nicely into the harness.

Those of you with an interest in American history may be thinking, "Did they brew during Prohibition?" Under the leadership of Frank Yuengling, who ran the brewery from 1899 through 1961, Yuengling made it through the Noble Experiment in pretty good shape. They started a dairy (Yuengling ice cream was made until 1986), opened large dance halls in Philadelphia and New York, and yes, they brewed. Yuengling invested in an expensive vacuum distillation process that made it possible to brew Juvo, the best-tasting near beer in Schuylkill County. Juvo outsold competitors by a large margin.

When Prohibition was repealed, Yuengling was sitting pretty. The dairy business provided a fleet of refrigerated trucks and a steady cash flow, the successful near beer business meant they had retained almost all their trained workers, and the dance halls had made them a lot of friends in big markets. On the day of Repeal, Frank sent a truckload of Yuengling's new Winner beer to FDR at the White House. Happy days were here again.

They didn't last forever. By the 1970s the brewery was in trouble, operating from payroll to payroll some months as national megabrewers pushed hard to level all markets. In the end, two things saved the brewery. The dogged loyalty of Schuylkill County beer drinkers made for a steady demand that sustained the brewery on a week-to-week basis. The American Bicentennial in 1976 raised interest in American history and made the brewery's status as America's oldest a bankable quality. There was a slow rise in sales from 1976 through the 1980s.

In 1985, when Dick Yuengling Jr. bought the brewery from his father—the traditional Yuengling family way of gaining control of the business—he felt continued pressure from the national breweries threatening to throttle his business. He also saw the rising interest in nonmainstream beer and thought there might be a way to tap that market. "I was not going to be the last Yuengling to own the brewery!" he told me once.

Dick already had one of the most varied lineups of any regional brewer. Besides the mainstream Yuengling Premium there was the dark, roasty Celebrated Pottsville Porter and the hoppy Lord Chesterfield Ale. Dick and brewmaster Ray Norbert added Yuengling Light—"because we had to," Dick explained, "and it's a good light beer"—and Yuengling Traditional, an amber-colored, somewhat more robust lager. He also pushed the brewery's history and nonnational underdog appeal. Yuengling started to appear in Philadelphia markets.

Another important boost for the brewery had actually been around for years. People in Schuylkill and Berks counties had been mixing Yuengling Porter with Premium or Lord Chesterfield for years, to create a custom-made black and tan. But then Pete Cammarano from the NorthEast Taproom in Reading asked the brewery for a pre-mixed barrel of half Porter, half Lord Chesterfield. Yuengling made it up, and Pete sold it as Molesterfield. He sold a lot of it, and the brewers saw they had a winner. They switched the mix to Porter and Premium, put it in a snazzy 16-ounce can, and released it on the market. It was very successful. "Got any Black & Tan?" became the question every beer distributor in eastern Pennsylvania hated to hear. Even after the first major expansion to the brewery in decades, they're still trying to catch up to the demand. The brewery churns along seven days a week, two shifts a day to keep up.

After years of soul-searching, Dick recently made the decision to build a second brewery to meet the unending demand for Yuengling. The new brewery is sited about a mile away and is scheduled to come on line in 2000, with an initial capacity of 1 million barrels. Fear not, loyal fans. Yuengling is committed to being a regional brewery and has no national aspirations, nor do they intend to close the original historic brewery.

I recently took my twenty-third Yuengling tour on the day after Christmas (I took my first one in 1986). The brewery staff had a rare weekday off, but the gift shop was busy and workers were taking advantage of the quiet to put in a new tile floor in the brewhouse. Success looks good on the oldest brewery in America. It appears Dick won't be the last of the Yuenglings after all.

Opened: 1829.
Type: Regional brewery.
Owner: Richard L. Yuengling Jr.
Brewers: Brewmaster N. Ray Norbert (since 1961), James Helmke (vice president for production and operations).
System: 450-barrel Enerfab brewhouse. Potential annual capacity 600,000 barrels.
Annual production: 525,000 barrels in 1997.
Beers brewed: Yuengling Premium, Lord Chesterfield Ale, Dark Brewed Porter (GABF bronze, 1987), Yuengling Traditional Lager, Yuengling Light, Yuengling Black & Tan (packaged blend of Porter and Premium). All beers brewed on premises except for some Black & Tan brewed at the Stroh Brewery near Allentown.
The Pick: I prefer a do-it-yourself black and tan mixed from Porter and Lord Chesterfield Ale. The Chet is Yuengling's hoppiest beer and cuts through the Porter more sharply than the Premium. Get a big mug and a few bottles of each beer and find the ratio you prefer.
Take-out beer: None available.
Tours: Monday through Friday at 10:00 A.M. and 1:30 P.M. This is without a doubt one of the best brewery tours in the country. Others may be more polished or more intimate, but few take you right down onto the floor of a hard-working sizeable brewery. Tours include two complimentary beers in the uniquely handsome brewery taproom. Gift shop open 9:00 A.M.–4:00 P.M. Monday through Friday.
Events: The only special event at Yuengling is an unofficial one: the First Day of Beer Season. In rural Pennsylvania, deer hunting is almost a religion, and most public schools have declared the Monday after Thanksgiving—the opening of deer season—a day off, since most of the male students and teachers (and a few females) didn't show up anyway. Some non-hunting teachers from Reading began coming out for a brewery tour on that Monday, and it's grown—but not too much. After all, it *is* deer season!
Special considerations: Kids will enjoy Posty's Birch Beer in the taproom. It's a locally made soda that's traditional and delicious, a good choice for designated drivers, too. The tour is not handicapped-accessible.

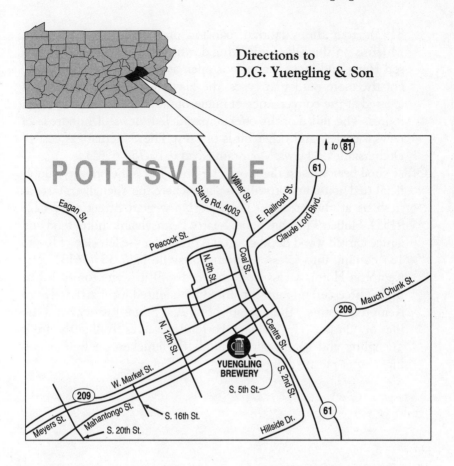

Directions to D.G. Yuengling & Son

Parking: On-street parking. Don't use the church lot on the far side of the street or you will be ticketed or towed.

Lodging: Quality Hotel, 100 South Center Street, Pottsville (717-622-4600); River Inn, Route 61, south of Pottsville (717-385-2407); The Stone House B&B, 16 Dock Street, Schuylkill Haven (717-385-2115).

Nearby attractions: Go on up Mahantongo Steet from the Yuengling brewery to the Yuengling Mansion, the family's restored Victorian-era home, for the short but interesting self-guided tour (717-622-2788). Then hit the road for other attractions. Jim Thorpe, Pennsylvania, named for the famous American Indian athlete, has a restored Victorian-era downtown, with shops and taverns, that's great for an afternoon stroll. You'll also find an extensive model train layout (41 Susquehanna Street, 717-325-2248) and whitewater rafting expeditions (Pocono Whitewater Rafting, 800-944-

8392). Tour the Victorian mansion of coal baron Asa Parker, which is on the hill overlooking downtown (717-325-3229). His son Harry's adjacent mansion is open as a B&B (717-325-8566). For the more outdoorsy types, the Hawk Mountain Sanctuary is located at the convergence of numerous raptor autumn migration routes. The fall months offer unparalleled views of hundreds of hawks, eagles, and other birds of prey. The Sanctuary is east of Drehersville on Hawk Mountain Road (610-756-6961).

Other good beer sites in the area: The Brass Tap is the brewery's unofficial tied house in Pottsville, a place where the Yuenglings taste as fresh as at the brewery. 112 East Norwegian Street (717-622-9155). Hubert's Inn has good, hearty Pennsylvania hotel food and a nice carved wood backbar. You'll find it on the left side of Route 183 coming into Cressona from Pottsville (717-385-3613). The Kempton Hotel, across from the feed mill in Kempton, is a real find. Three ceiling murals painted by talented local artists depict Kempton history, "the pageant of United States history," and the life of Christ. The snappy bartender serves brilliantly fresh Yuengling and good regional food (the chicken on waffles and hickorynut pie are delicious).

A word about . . .

The Pennsylvania Liquor Code & Regulations

The Pennsylvania Liquor Code and Pennsylvania Liquor Control Board (PLCB) Regulations govern the manufacture, purchase, sale, and taxation of alcohol in the Commonwealth. The PLCB, a three-person administrative board, controls the state retail liquor and wine system and the licensing of taverns, hotels, restaurants, clubs, stadiums, and beer retailers (known as distributors in Pennsylvania). It also regulates the licensing of alcohol importers and wineries and breweries in the state.

Paradoxically, this huge booze monopoly—the Pennsylvania State Store system is the largest purchaser of wine and spirits in the world—is also responsible for the enforcement of the liquor code's sometimes odd and often anticonsumer laws on beer sales.

The biggest of these anticonsumer laws is known as the case law. Pennsylvania beer distributors can sell beer only by the keg or case. If you want a single bottle or six-pack, you have to go to a tavern, where you'll pay their justifiably marked-up price and usually find a smaller selection.

The PLCB has also interpreted this law to mean that distributors may not open cases to mix them for a customer's convenience. Whole cases only in Pennsylvania, please. Many microbrewers and some regional brewers have developed "variety cases" to circumvent this aspect of the law.

Some people think it's a disadvantage that we have to buy our beer from distributors instead of in supermarkets and convenience stores, as other states allow. I've lived all over the United States and I've found that grocery store beer sales are at best a mixed blessing. Sure, you can get beer everywhere, but the selection is often limited, the care of the product is spotty, and buying a keg of anything but the national brands is all but impossible. Besides, do you really want to buy beer from people who sell pork chops and oven cleaner? Pennsylvania beer distributors know beer, not cold cuts, and they are quickly getting educated about micro-type beers.

We have these distributors thanks to a legacy of Repeal, the three-tier system. The three tiers are brewer, wholesaler, and retailer (distributor), and state law requires that the three be separate businesses. Brewpubs are conspicuous exceptions, and other exceptions have been made for small brewers to distribute their own beer. Pennsylvania's regional brewers credit the state's strong enforcement of the three-tier system for their survival. The law ensures everyone a fair shot at selling beer.

Another law seems to be in our favor, but isn't. It's about prices. Any price reduction from the manufacturer or importer must remain in place for at least 120 days. Sounds good, right? Now look at it from the retailer's side. Any price reduced for four months will be the price customers come to expect. They won't want to buy it at the regular, higher price after the sale. Consequently, prices are never lowered at all.

It may seem like this price law keeps the playing fields level; after all, if it is a burden for one distributor, it's a burden for all of them. But Pennsylvania borders states with relatively loose laws on beer sales: New York, New Jersey, Delaware, and Maryland. Philadelphians can easily cross the Delaware to buy beer at short-term sale prices that would be illegal in Pennsylvania. The sales are advertised in Philadelphia newspapers! Plenty of beer geeks cross state lines to buy singles or six-packs of new or expensive beers.

Who pays the price of these screwy laws? You do. You shell out more for beer and you have limited options. Guess who's responsible? It's not neo-Prohibitionists or the religious right or the safety-obsessed left or any of the anti-alcohol factions. Surprisingly it's beer wholesalers and tavern owners.

Wholesalers wrote the case law back at the time of Repeal to make the business run the way they wanted. The tavern owners lobby to keep it that way because it protects their six-pack business. The wholesalers want the price law in effect to keep their job easy and profitable. These groups are well bankrolled and well organized. Things are not going to change any time soon.

PLCB inspectors also check tap-cleaning records and health codes when they're not running sting operations to fight underage drinking or raiding bars suspected of selling beer not registered for sale in Pennsylvania.

If any of Pennsylvania's beer laws bother you, do what I do. Write to state legislators and write to the Governor. Nothing will happen unless you ask. That's how we got the right to buy case beer with a credit card a couple years ago. Someone happened to ask his legislator why he couldn't. Four months later it was law.

Philadelphia:
The City of
Brotherly Brewers

W. C. Fields wrote his own tongue-in-cheek epitaph: "On the whole, I'd rather be in Philadelphia." Well, me too, W. C. The city has come out of the dark days of the MOVE disaster quite well. The vibrancy that was missing for years here is back, thanks largely to Mayor Ed Rendell. When he took office in 1992, former District Attorney Rendell began a whirlwind of action reminiscent of FDR's 100 Days. His landslide reelection gave the city's seal of approval to his work.

Rendell is well known as an avid fan of Philly's major contribution to American fare, the cheesesteak. Local papers have printed plenty of photos showing "Fast Eddie" with his big happy mouth wrapped around these hot, greasy beauties. Check out some classics at Pat's Steaks (1237 East Passayunk Avenue) or Tony Luke's (Front and Oregon Streets). The city's other staple, the soft pretzel, is available all over and should be eaten with a good squirt of yellow mustard.

Philadelphia is one of the great unknown restaurant centers of the United States. Proprietor-chef Georges Perrier's Le Bec Fin (1523 Walnut Street) is one of the best French restaurants anywhere, and the prix fixe lunch is a major bargain. You'll find all kinds of food in the city. There's imaginative Oriental cooking at Susanna Foo's (1512 Walnut Street), authentically *ausgezeichnet*—excellent—German cooking at the Blüe Ox Brauhaus (7980 Oxford Avenue in Northeast Philly), *tapas* at Pamplona (225 South Twelfth Street). You can sample the French bistro menu at Dock Street Brewing Company (see brewery entry), or American colonial fare at City Tavern, a restored historic site with a good restaurant and costumed waitstaff (138 South Second Street).

But for the beer lover, Philadelphia has three treasures: restaurants devoted to Belgian beer. Bridgid's (726 North Twenty-fourth Street, near the art museum) is a small, warmly welcoming bistro. It has an impressive cellar of vintage beers, cask-conditioned beers, and a very reasonably priced menu of delicious entrees and desserts. Cuvée Notredame (1701 Green Street) has an extensive Belgian menu including the "Belgian national dish," *waterzooi*, and the omnipresent *frites* (fries). Finally, Monk's (264 South Sixteenth Street) is one of the very best beer bars in America, with a number of Belgian taps and plenty of bottled Belgian beers aging in the cellar. The must-have dishes are mussels steamed in Belgian beers such as Rodenbach or *gueuze lambic*, served with *frites* and delicious French rolls.

But you didn't come to Philadelphia just to eat! This is the heart of American independence, home of the Liberty Bell and Benjamin Franklin and the birthplace of the Declaration of Independence and the Constitution. At Independence National Historical Park (215-597-8974), visit Carpenter's Hall, Congress Hall, Independence Hall, Franklin Court, and the Liberty Bell Pavilion. The Betsy Ross House at 239 Arch Street has been restored as a working-class house of the colonial period. Christ Church (Second and Church Streets) contains William Penn's baptismal font and was the church of fifteen Declaration signers. Benjamin Franklin and four other signers are buried in the Christ Church burial ground at Fifth and Arch Streets.

Other famous people lived in Philadelphia. The peripatetic Edgar Allen Poe lived at 532 N. Seventh Street for a year. There is a tour of the house, and a library and audiovisual program are next door. Louisa May Alcott was born in Germantown; the Germantown Historical Society's museum is at 5501 Germantown Avenue. The National Shrine of St. John Neumann is at Fifth and Girard Streets, where the saint's remains can be viewed in a glass casket under the main altar.

Philadelphia has a number of fine museums. The Philadelphia Museum of Art (215-763-8100), at the end of the Benjamin Franklin Parkway, houses one of the world's best collections. And yes, that's where Sylvester Stallone did his dance in *Rocky*. Just down the parkway is the Franklin Institute Science Museum, an extensive display of hands-on science exhibits. You could easily spend a day in these two museums, but I would also send you down to the river to see the Independence Seaport Museum at Penn's Landing. You can visit this museum of Philadelphia's maritime heritage and crawl around the USS *Becuna*, a World War II-era submarine, and the USS *Olympia*, Admiral Dewey's flagship from the Spanish-American War.

Philadelphia hosts a number of annual events, starting on January 1 with the Mummers Parade, a unique folk-art festival of music, dance, and elaborate feathered outfits. The Philadelphia Flower Show draws flower-fanciers to the Convention Center in early March. Later in the month, the Book and the Cook Festival brings chefs and cookbook authors from around the world for a week of fantastic food events, including a mass tutored tasting by beer writer Michael Jackson. May brings the Dad Vail Regatta on the Schuylkill, a happy, exciting mob scene. In December, international attention focuses on Veterans Stadium for the Army-Navy Game.

There's so much more. Call the Philadelphia Convention and Visitor Center (800-537-7676) and tell them you want the full package of travel information. You'll have a great time. And don't forget the cheesesteaks!

Independence Brewing Company

1000 East Comly Street
Philadelphia
215-537-2337
www.independencebrew.com

You can't judge a book by its cover,
and the same is true for Independence Brewing. The brewery is in an older industrial building. When it was first bought, there was a lot of cleaning up to do, particularly of the surrounding grounds. Brewer Bill Moore tells how, before the brewery came along, the popular weekend entertainment was to torch one of the abandoned cars on the lot and watch it burn. Independence has changed the neighborhood. Successful businesses have a way of doing that.

Inside that old exterior is some pretty slick equipment. A successful financial campaign raised sufficient money to allow construction of a large brew house. An initial public offering (IPO) raised enough money to buy an automated kegging line, a high-speed and even higher-tech bottling line, and some decidedly non-micro tankage to support their growing sales. They also launched a high-visibility, award-winning series of billboards and print ads. This is a secret of a successful brewery: capitalization sufficient to the needs of the business.

Another reason for that success has been big Bill Moore himself. After working at Stoudt's—I remember seeing Bill delivering kegs to retailers—he moved on to be a true brewmaster at Independence. He has already won two GABF medals for the clean, crisp Golden Ale and the malty, flawless Franklinfest. Bill's also had a hand in the start-up of a number of the area's new breweries. He has unselfishly helped new brewers master their equipment and get the routine down. He's the Johnny Appleseed of the Delaware Valley's brewing scene.

The Pennsylvania/Philadelphia tradition is strong at Independence: They brew lagers as well as ales. You don't find that in most areas of the country. Franklinfest hits the lager market right in the sweet spot and is Independence's biggest seller. It takes a masterful and meticulous brewer and a technically tight brewery to brew lager beers this consistent and clean. Independence has it down.

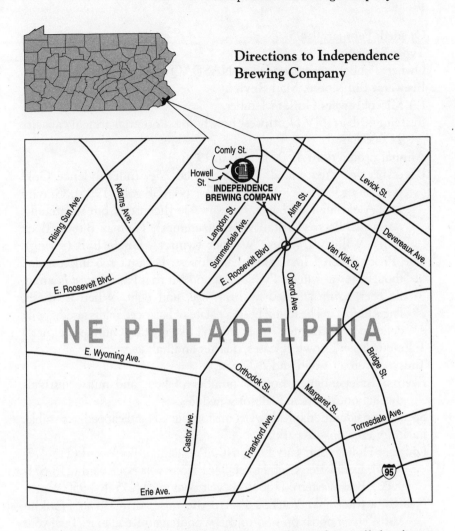

Directions to Independence Brewing Company

If you want to tour Independence, you'll need to call for directions. Once you reach the brewery you'll find a warm Philly welcome. There's a cozy little tasting room where you'll experience wonderfully fresh, right-at-the-brewery beer while you look out at the big-iron Independence brewhouse. You'll be impressed by the size of this place. Independence is one microbrewery that's not cramped for space.

There's no mistaking that this is a brewery. There is no kitchen, no waiters, not even any lines painted in the parking lot. The floors are concrete, and the sheetmetal ceiling is forty feet away. This is a production facility, and the business is beer. Such single-minded determination deserves recognition.

Opened: February 1995.

Type: Brewery.

Owner: Publicly owned, traded on NASDAQ small-cap market as IBCO.

Brewers: Bill Moore, Matt Revier.

PA Microbrewers Guild: Member.

System: 40-barrel JV Northwest brewhouse. Potential annual capacity 25,000 barrels.

Annual production: 4,500 barrels in 1996.

Beers brewed: *Year-round:* Independence Ale, Independence Gold (GABF bronze, 1996), Franklinfest (GABF gold, 1996), Gravity Pale Ale, Blue Hen Lager, Nittany Ale (licensed from Whitetail). *Seasonals:* Betsy's Kristall Wheat (summer), Thomas' Blonde Bock (fall), William's Winter Warmer (winter), Uncle E$B (spring).

The Pick: When I first tasted Franklinfest, I wasn't too impressed. I thought it was wimpy. I've since found out that Franklinfest is a fragile beer, easily affected by heat, age, and light. When it's fresh, Franklinfest is a beautiful beer, a palate of balanced malts and happily delicate hop bitterness. (Hey, I didn't like my first Guinness, either!)

Take-out beer: Growlers, cases, quarter and half kegs.

Tours: Saturday, noon and 2:00 p.m.

Events: Independence hosts a number of beer and music festivals throughout the year. Call for schedules.

Special considerations: Kids welcome for tours. Handicapped-accessible.

Parking: Free on-site parking.

Lodging: Holiday Inn City Line, 4100 Presidential Boulevard (215-477-0200); Doubletree Club Hotel, 9461 Roosevelt Boulevard (215-671-9600); Best Western, 1150 Roosevelt Boulevard (215-464-9500).

Nearby attractions: You're close to the miles of malls at Franklin Mills. Head north on I-95 to the Woodhaven Road exit. Take your golf clubs and play a round at the Melrose Country Club (215-379-5300); greens fees are required.

Other good beer sites in the area: The Grey Lodge is the only real beer bar in northeast Philly. Its pleasantly eccentric owner, Scoats, has a pretty good sense of what beer he can get away with at this reluctantly evolving neighborhood bar. Want ferns, tablecloths, perky waitresses? Don't come to the G-Lodge. Want good beer and no BS? You're gonna like it here. 6235 Frankford Avenue (215-624-2969). The Blüe Ox Brauhaus serves seriously authentic and delicious German and Swiss food. They match it with great German tap beers and a nice assortment of bottles. 7980 Oxford Avenue (215-728-9440).

Poor Henry's

829-51 North American Street
Philadelphia
888-886-HOPS
www.poorhenrys.com

Here's a comeback story to make your heart swell. Ortlieb's was one of Philadelphia's last breweries. The brewery on American Street had brewed beer for over one hundred years, then closed in 1981, with the onslaught of the national breweries, who apparently couldn't stand the thought of anyone else having a share of the market, no matter how small. The Ortlieb brand was sold, and several mergers later, wound up at Stroh in 1996. There has not been a beer named Ortlieb brewed since then.

Henry Ortlieb had gotten out of the family business when it was sold to his cousin Joe in 1977, but beer was always in his blood. When Joe closed the brewery in 1981, Henry decided he wanted to open his own brewery. Sixteen years later, after a number of false starts and a successful career in commercial real estate, he wound up buying the old Ortlieb brewery's bottling house and began a new brewery there.

The problem was that Stroh owned the Ortlieb name. That's one reason the brewery is called Poor *Henry's* instead of Ortlieb's. (It's *Poor Henry's* because Henry has sunk $800,000 into it.)

Particularly for a beer geek, Poor Henry's is a trip. The brewpub and brewery are actually inside the old Ortlieb brewery, in a neat juxtaposition of old and new. Poor Henry's sports two brewing systems. A 7-barrel system allows the flexibility that a brewpub and pilot brewery require, while a 60-barrel system offers economies of scale and labor for the packaging brewery.

I once described Poor Henry's pub as looking as if a cafeteria and a brewery had collided at sixty miles per hour. That's a bit harsh, perhaps, but fairly accurate. Take away the jumble such a collision would cause, and you've got the pub: a lot of tile, metal, blond wood, and very high ceilings. Behind a glass wall, metal tanks gleam in the large open space of the brewery.

That's not to say the pub isn't a nice place to be. When the lights are turned down a bit, the ceiling seems not so high, the tile not quite so shiny. And the food is good, served by a cheerful and knowledgeable staff.

Drinking beer at Poor Henry's is like going back to the exciting first days of brewpubs in America. Drinking in a brewpub in the early 1980s was like hearing jazz for the first time: surprising, electric, enlarging. Many great beers later, I cannot decide if it was astounding because it was so good, or simply because it was so new. I do know that the latest tweak on Poor Henry's IPA made it shockingly fresh and packed with a hoppy verve that most IPAs only dream of. The Porter was similarly sprightly, like the first brewpub porter I remember tasting, charged with roasty energy.

How do they do it? Maybe it's the yeast they use, but that seems too basic. Maybe brewer John Ruhl's a genius, but there are plenty of bright brewers. Maybe it's just being in that old brewery with barrels of beer karma. Whatever it is, Poor Henry's is rich with it.

Opened: June 1997.
Type: Brewpub and brewery.
Owner: Henry A. Ortlieb.
Brewers: John Ruhl, Larry Kennedy.
PA Microbrewers Guild: Not a member.
System: 7-barrel Pub Brewing System brewhouse with potential annual capacity of 1,700 barrels, and a 60-barrel Pub Brewing System brewhouse with potential annual capacity of 50,000 barrels.
Annual production: No figures available.
Beers brewed: *Year-round:* Old Stock Lager, Awesome (Pale) Ale, Poor Henry's Porter, Stout, Creame Ale, Märzen (Fest). Dock Street brands: Amber, Bohemian Pils, Illuminator Bock, Extra Best Pale Ale. *Seasonals:* Hefe-Weizen, Summer Wheat, Winter Brew, October Fest, IPA, ESB, Helles, Pilsner, Imperial Chocolate Cherry Stout, Bock, Doppelbock.
The Pick: Just to be ornery, I'll say my favorite drink at Poor Henry's is a half-and-half mix of Porter and IPA. Either beer is good on its own, but the mix is a lip-smacking eye-opener. The Porter has a touch of sweet roastiness, the IPA has the lip-stripping hoppiness (65 IBU) you'd expect, but the mix is synergistically more than the sum of the parts. If you're not a regular mixer of beers beyond the classic Guinness-Bass black and tan, introduce yourself to the notion with my custom-made potion at Poor Henry's.
Take-out beer: Six-packs of Awesome Ale, Porter, and Old Stock Lager are currently available; other beers will follow.
Tours: On request, seven days a week, noon–8:00 P.M.

**Directions to Poor Henry's,
Samuel Adams Brew House,
Dock Street Brewing Company,
and Red Bell Brewing Company**

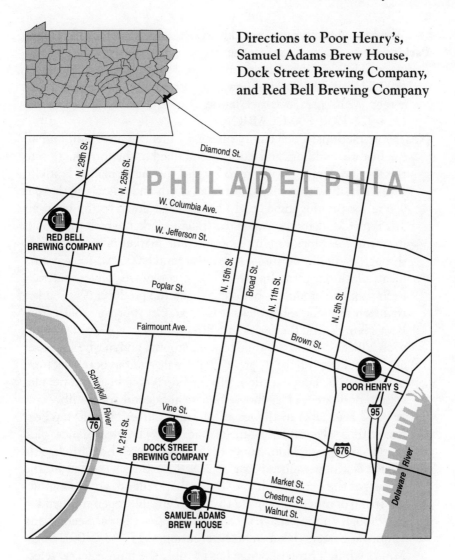

Brewpub hours: Seven days a week, noon–1:00 A.M.

Food: The menu is upscale, innovative, and not unreasonably priced. It includes appetizers, salads, soups (the brewery white bean soup is made with Bavarian hops), pizzas, pasta, burgers, sandwiches, delicious steaks, wiener schnitzel, seafood, and chicken. The dessert list includes Chocolate Bourbon Bock Pecan Pie. Your driver might want to try some of the house-brewed birch or root beers.

Extras: Full liquor license, a fine selection of single malts, small-batch bourbons, and wine. Mega-martinis a house specialty.

Special considerations: Kids welcome. Handicapped-accessible. Cigars allowed, and Henry's own brand is on sale. Vegetarian meals available.

Parking: Free, secure lot across the street.

Lodging: Holiday Inn Independence Mall, 400 Arch Street (800-THE-BELL); Penn's View Inn, historic hotel, 14 North Front Street (215-922-7600); Clarion Suites, 1010 Race Street (215-922-1730, 800-CLARION).

Nearby attractions: Poor Henry's is near Independence Mall and all the historic buildings and exhibits described in the introduction to this section. You're also close to I-95, so the outlet mall at Franklin Mills is easily within reach; just head north and follow the signs. If you're looking for some "real Philly," head down to the open-air 9th Street Market, also called the Italian Market, which runs south from the 700 block of Ninth Street. The market is open Monday through Saturday mornings, starting around 8:00 A.M. You can find meat, clothing, great Italian cheeses, cookware, olives, pastries, fresh fish, and produce—but don't touch the produce; it's a market tradition that the seller picks it for you. On your way south from Poor Henry's, you'll cross South Street, Philly's answer to Greenwich Village. Take some time to walk around, and maybe stop over at the Dickens Inn for its great single malt and tap beer selection, or Bridget Foy's, an excellent place to sip a cool beer and people-watch. Both are on Headhouse Square at Second and South.

Other good beer sites in the area: Jake and Oliver's is a 60-tap beer bar with a beautiful new-make backbar. There's a dance club upstairs, 22 South Third Street (215-627-4825). John Patrick's Ale House is a new multitap bar at 208 Race Street opened by the owners of the excellent J. P. O'Malley's in Allentown and a growing string of other mulitaps (215-574-0296). Nitrogen runs wild at the Plough and the Stars, an all-nitro-tap beer bar at Second and Chestnut Streets. It's a smooth sensation (215-733-0300). Sugar Mom's Church Street Lounge has possibly the most eclectic selection of taps in town and great music. This subterranean saloon is at 225 Church Street, well back from the alley and downstairs (215-925-8219).

Samuel Adams
Brew House

1516 Sansom Street
Philadelphia
215-563-2326

Did you know there is a Samuel
Adams Amber? It's a good trick question for micro-beer trivia. The
Boston Beer Company, brewer of the Samuel Adams line of beers, does
not brew an Amber beer. But the Samuel Adams Brew House in
Philadelphia does brew an Amber—Poor Richard's Amber—and the
brewery is part-owned by Jim Koch, the man behind Samuel Adams.

That's pretty much where the similarity ends. For one thing, the
Samuel Adams Brew House is a one-shop show. Everything you see as
you walk up the steps is it. Another, bigger difference is that the Brew
House uses malt extract and specialty ingredients to brew its beer.

Is extract brewing that big a deal? A lot of homebrewers think so.
Those who do "all-grain" brewing claim that there is a definite difference between beers brewed with extracts and beers brewed from an all-
grain mash. A lot of extract beers I've had display a characteristic
thinness and vegetal aroma, but I've never detected anything like that
in beers from the Brew House. They're good beers; some of them are
excellent beers. You can make good beers with extract, but brewing
beers like these is impressive.

The pub itself is a nice little place. In the main pub area there are
stools around the stairwell and two large, upholstered, wraparound
booths—very comfortable for relaxing with a friend and a pint. The bar
is small and busy, with a handpump for serving cask-conditioned treats
like the ripsaw Infamous Pale Ale, a real mind-opener of a hoppy beer.
Behind the bar is a small bandstand, a pool table, and three dartboards.

The food was not great when the Brew House opened, but it has
improved markedly. The smoked fish platter is very good, especially
with a glass of Smartass Stout. Follow that with a cigar and a bit more
Stout, and it's not a bad way to spend an hour or so.

If you should happen to see a little cask perched up on the bar, be
sure to ask for a nip of what's inside. That's how they serve the
renowned Samuel Adams Triple Bock at the Brew House, and you do
want to try some of the gold-medal-winning potion. The beer that

won was actually brewed here at the Brew House, and local aficionados swear they can tell the difference.

The Triple Bock, a high-alcohol beer (17.5 percent ABV), is called Triple Bock just for whimsey. It is actually an ale, made with malt and maple syrup and fermented with a tag team of different yeasts, including champagne yeast. The champagne yeast is used because of its resistance to higher alcohol levels, not for its effervescence; Triple Bock is essentially still. But it is a gripping beer, one that must be sipped like sherry. It is rich, winelike, and usually suitably aged and ready to drink there at the Brew House.

The Brew House is a kind of place where you can get a beer, grab the paper, and relax. You don't have to do anything here but enjoy life.

Opened: February 1989.
Type: Brewpub.
Owners: Judi Mink, Jim Koch.
Brewer: William Reed.
PA Microbrewers Guild: Not a member.
System: 7-barrel Pub Brewing System extract and specialty grain brewhouse (one of their first). Potential annual capacity 800 barrels.
Annual production: 700 barrels in 1997.
Beers brewed: *Year-round:* Ben Franklin Gold, Poor Richard's Amber, George Washington Porter (GABF silver, 1989), Infamous Pale Ale (available "more often than not"). *Seasonals:* Triple Bock (GABF gold, 1997), Smart Ass Stout, Eleven Pound Ale, Tart Ale. All beers brewed on premises.
The Pick: The Triple Bock seems like an easy choice. This beer, dispensed from a cask sitting right on the bar, is unlike any other: Rich, heavy, vinous, and powerful, it's more like a potion than a beer. But my true pick would be the Eleven Pound Ale, brewed as a differing "single hop" beer, a variable varietal. That means William Reed takes a different hop each time and throws eleven pounds of it into this showcase beer. The result is sometimes surprising and sometimes spectacular, but it's always interesting.
Take-out beer: 2-liter German-style growlers.
Tours: Informal tours are available anytime during normal hours, brewery is entirely visible from bar with informational signs.
Brewpub hours: Monday through Saturday, 11:00 A.M.–2:00 A.M. Closed Sunday.
Food: Pub fare like fish and chips and burgers, and comfort food like

meatloaf make up most of the menu, but the Brew House has a delicious smoked fish plate that I find hard to pass up.

Extras: Three dart boards (league play on Tuesdays), good jukebox, pool table, full liquor license.

Special considerations: Kids welcome. The Brew House is on the second floor and is not wheelchair accessible. Cigars allowed. Vegetarian meals available.

Directions: See map on page 35.

Parking: Parking garage across street (Fifteenth & Sansom Streets); ticket validated with $15 purchase after 5:00 P.M.

Lodging: Abigail Adams Bed & Breakfast, 1208 Walnut Street (215-546-7336); The Bellevue (If you want to shoot the works, this is the place to do it.) Broad Street between Walnut and Locust Streets (215-893-1776); Holiday Inn Express Midtown, 1305 Walnut Street (800-HOLIDAY or 215-735-9300).

Nearby attractions: City Hall is a gorgeous piece of architecture, with a huge statue of William Penn on the roof. There are free, one-hour tours at 12:30 on weekdays, and tower tours every 15 minutes (215-686-2840). But the big ticket attractions of the city—the art museum, Franklin Institute, and Independence Mall—are more than a walk from here. The thing to do around the Brew House is eat, drink, and shop. Just stroll around, you're bound to find something. By the way, Holt's, over on 1522 Walnut Street, is the place to go for cigars in Philadelphia. And right downstairs from the pub is the Sansom Street Oyster House, one of the best places for raw shellfish in the city. You can't go wrong unless you get caught up in keeping to a schedule. This isn't that kind of an area!

Other good beer sites in the area: McGillin's Old Ale House, Philly's oldest bar, is a great place to have a beer with a buddy, and they have some really good stuff on tap. 1310 Drury Lane (215-735-4515). Copa, Too! has a good selection of taps and bottles, a very comfortable streetside bar. 263 South Fifteenth Street (215-735-0848). Don't miss Fergie's, where Fergie himself runs a square house and pulls one of the finest jars of Guinness in the city. 1214 Sansom Street (215-928-8118). Fergie is also a partner in Monk's Cafe with the beer genius and Burgundian *bon vivant* Tom Peters, a man who has brought much incredibly good beer to Philadelphia. Go see what Monk's has on tap today, and eat some mussels! It's one of America's foremost beer bars. 264 South Sixteenth Street (215-545-7005). See also other good beer sites on page 42.

Dock Street Brewing Company

2 Logan Square
Eighteenth and Cherry Streets
Philadelphia
215-496-0413

Dock Street stands out as one of the first brewpubs in Pennsylvania. The menu has always been adventurous, and the waitstaff and bartenders are particularly beer-savvy, thanks to a tradition of involvement on the part of the brewmaster. There are original murals behind the bar, a madly eclectic sequence of styles and deliberately unfinished subjects, that I must confess I've always found a bit disconcerting, although good conversation pieces.

The best thing, of course, is the beer! Dock Street has one of the most varied selections of any American brewpub. In fact, it brews a greater variety of beers than almost any brewery in the world. And these beers are good; there are not many clinkers at Dock Street. If you go often enough, chances are you'll be able to try good examples of almost every beer style—lagers, ales, heavyweight barley wines and spritzy wheats, oak-aged Grand Cru, and "live" real ale.

This is a power-lunch kind of place during the day. Suits and dresses dominate the dining room and talk of depositions and deals fills the air. The bar itself is usually a bit more informal. In the evenings there may be a theater crowd, gradually replaced by a relaxed bunch of talkers and chalkers hanging around the pool tables.

After years of confusion, you can finally get Dock Street's bottled beers at the brewpub. Pennsylvania law originally allowed brewpubs to sell only beer brewed on premises. Dock Street's bottled beers (Amber, Pale Ale, Bohemian Pilsner, and Illuminator Bock) were brewed under contract at Matt's, in Utica, New York, and now at Poor Henry's in Philadelphia. The brewpub has never had the capacity to brew them or the room to bottle them. Now the law has changed and the bottles can be served at Dock Street, but why would you want to pass up the great draft beers, some of which you can get only at these taps?

You may occasionally find the brewpub's beers on tap at other bars in the area. Some of the exceptional beers are sold by the keg to bars whose clientele can appreciate them. That says a lot about the quality of Dock Street's beer.

People compliment Dock Street's food as well. The hearty French-Alsatian food inspired by chef Olivier de St. Martin's mother's kitchen has gained excited reviews and loyal patrons. This is a brasserie in the classic sense, a house-brewery with food to match the beer.

Dock Street has developed a solid reputation in Philadelphia. This is not surprising, since owner Jeffery Ware has been in the restaurant business here for over twenty years. Dock Street is consistent, interesting, classy, and handsome. If you're looking for a brewpub that has a sense of style and isn't aggressively informal, where a coat and tie won't stick out, this is it. It's a comfortable, relaxed place to have a beer in surroundings that give the beer a little respect.

Opened: October 1990.
Type: Brewpub.
Owner: Jeffery Ware.
Brewer: Eric Savage.
PA Microbrewers Guild: Not a member.
System: 8-barrel JV Northwest brewhouse. Potential annual capacity 1,600 barrels.
Annual production: 1,500 barrels in 1996.
Beers brewed: One of the most eclectic breweries in America, Dock Street has brewed at least sixty-eight different styles since opening. The following styles are on tap most often: hellesbier, dunkel, Dortmunder, American Pale Ale, India Pale Ale, and 90 Shilling Scotch Ale. These are some of Eric's favorites: Thomas Jefferson Ale, a tasty strong ale at a surprisingly quaffable 9 percent alcohol by volume (ABV); Belgian Grand Cru, aged in oaken wine barrels; and the vaunted Barleywine, which last year came out around 13 percent ABV. Dock Street Cream Ale won GABF silver in 1992. All beers brewed on premises.
The Pick: Make mine a Dortmunder! I've had a lot of different beers at Dock Street, made by three different brewmasters. But the Dortmunder, balanced between the soft maltiness of a hellesbier and the sharp hoppiness of a pilsner, is a sit-down-and-keep-drinking beer, and sometimes I really like those.
Take-out beer: Half, quarter, and mini (5 liter) kegs, six-packs of the contract-brewed Dock Street beers.
Tours: Saturday at 3:30 P.M., Wednesday at 6:00 P.M., or by appointment.

Brewpub hours: Monday through Friday, 11:30 A.M.–midnight; Saturday, noon–2:00 A.M.; Sunday noon–11:00 P.M.

Food: Dock Street has a good French brasserie menu with a heavy Alsatian influence. Expect hearty but not weighty dishes and a waiter or waitress who knows something about beer pairings.

Extras: Darts and free regulation-size pool tables.

Special considerations: Kids welcome. Handicapped-accessible. Cigars allowed. Vegetarian meals available.

Directions: See map on page 35.

Parking: Two parking garages on the block.

Lodging: Embassy Suites, next door at 1776 Benjamin Franklin Parkway (215-963-1500); Korman Suites Hotel, 2001 Hamilton Street (215-569-7000); Holiday Inn Select Centre City, 1800 Market Street (215-561-7500).

Nearby attractions: It's only a ten minute walk to the Philadelphia Museum of Art (215-763-8100), the Franklin Institute Science Museum (215-448-1200), the Please Touch Museum (215-963-0667), and the Rodin Museum, with the largest collection of Rodin originals outside of Paris (215-763-8100). Following the Benjamin Franklin Parkway toward the art museum will lead you into Fairmount Park, Philly's immense greenway. There you'll find Boathouse Row, the Victorian boathouses of the city's sculling teams, decorated with strung lights that sparkle across the Schuykill. Also in the park are the restored Fairmount homes, including Strawberry Mansion the largest of the homes, and Cedar Grove, an eighteenth-century Quaker farmhouse (215-684-7922). In the other direction stands City Hall, unmistakable with its 37-foot statue of William Penn on the top. You can tour this impressive "hollow square" building Monday through Friday at 12:30. You could also walk down to the Reading Terminal Market, one of two great Philadelphia markets, studded with great little restaurants, cooking with the fresh food from the market. (See page 36 for the 9th Street Market.) If you want something a bit more exotic, Philly's Chinatown wraps around the Convention Center north of the market.

Other good beer sites in the area: Bridgid's (726 North Twenty-fourth Street) and Cuvée Notredame (1701 Green Street) are described in the introduction to this section (page 28). Two others, the Irish Bards and the Irish Pub, are practically side-by-side at Twentieth and Walnut Streets. Take your pick: The Bards probably has a better jar of Guinness, but the Pub's food seems better to me. See also other good beer sites on page 39.

Red Bell Brewing Company

Brewery: 3101 Jefferson Street
  Philadelphia
Brewpub: 1 CoreStates Center
  Broad and Pattison Streets
  Philadelphia
215-235-2460

A hundred years ago this massive brick building throbbed with energy and purpose. Inside its mammoth walls, men toiled and horses snorted and stamped their hooves. Clouds of steam rose from the chimneys, and the sweet, heavy odor of the mash cloaked the surrounding area like a blanket. This was the F. A. Poth Brewery, one of the big pre-Prohibition breweries that gave this area the name "Brewerytown."

Today the thick walls enclose the Red Bell Brewing Company. With a new name, new beer, and new people, the building lives again. Beer lovers with a sense of history can be proud that this brick behemoth has been restored to the purpose for which it was built.

Red Bell has had a tempestuous history. At the beginning in 1993, Red Bell splashed I-95 with billboards to jump-start its brand. The beer, however, contract-brewed at The Lion, was a little too much for the mainstream beer drinker, yet way too little for the beer geek. There were also some small production problems with the beer. As a result, Red Bell lost a lot of the free good will that a new brewery usually gets from the local market.

The big brick building at Thirty-first and Jefferson saved the day. From 1995 to 1996, the building was renovated, although it was a labor even Hercules might have shirked. The brewhouse was dropped in through the three-foot-thick ceiling, new recipes were developed, and soon Red Bell was making its own beer. The days of the wimpy beer were gone. But could the brewery recapture the market's interest?

So far, reports look good. Director of brewing operations Jim Cancro says the brewery is on track to brew 10,000 barrels in 1998, a sizable increase over 1997's production. More importantly to a beer geek, the lineup of beers has changed dramatically.

Gone are the Blonde and Amber that came first. In their place are heartier brews like the all-malt, mainstreamish Philadelphia Original Lager, the big, malty Vienna Lager, a fine, aggressive IPA, an impressive American Pale Ale, and a couple of fruit beers. The heavy hitters are at the bottom of the lineup. The strangely popular, strangely delicious Black Cherry Stout combines a good solid stout with ripe fruit flavors. The star of the show, however, is the vaunted Wee Heavy, a Scottish-style ale with heaps of malt character and dark depths of power and sophistication.

Red Bell has branched out with its high-profile brewpub at the CoreStates Center. The brewpub is open for business during sports events and it packs in the beer fans. Another Red Bell brewpub is scheduled to open in October of 1998 in the Reading Terminal Headhouse building at Twelfth and Filbert Streets, by the Convention Center.

You should tour the main brewery, if only to see how a huge old brewery looked. The walls are over two feet thick, the floors about three feet. This was insulation for the lagering process—good old Victorian-era over-engineering. The new, state-of-the-art brewery has plenty of bells and whistles. The heart of the tour is the tank farm, where you are often given a taste of beer right from the tanks.

Red Bell seems to be on the right track. Maybe the brewery will fill the big shoes of the old F. A. Poth building yet.

Opened: November 1993, contract brewing; June 1996, main brewery; August 1996, brewpub at CoreStates Center.

Type: Brewery and brewpub.

Owner: Corporation. Jim Bell, president.

Brewers: Jim Cancro (vice-president and director of brewing operations), Bob Barrar.

PA Microbrewers Guild: Member.

System: Main brewery: 40-barrel Century brewhouse. Potential annual capacity 20,000 barrels. Brewpub: 10-barrel Newlands brewhouse. Potential annual capacity 800 barrels.

Annual production: Main brewery, 6,000 barrels; brewpub, 800 barrels in 1997.

Beers brewed: *Year-round:* American Pale Ale, Philadelphia Original Lager, Vienna Lager, IPA, Lemon Hill Wheat, Irish Amber. *Seasonals:* Wee Heavy, Strawberry Mansion Wheat, Black Cherry Stout, Hefe-Weizen. All beers brewed on premises.

The Pick: I'll pick two here to save my marriage. My wife loves Red Bell's Black Cherry Stout. It's a rare combination of a good stout and a tasty fruit beer. My own pick is the seasonal Wee Heavy, a silky surface of sophisticated malt hiding a deep reservoir of complexity and power. Wee Heavy is the kind of beer that makes me wish summer never came so I could drink it all year round.

Take-out beer: Cases, kegs at the main brewery.

Tours: By appointment, at the main brewery only.

Brewery and Brewpub hours: Main brewery is open Monday through Friday. Brewpub at the CoreStates Center is open only during appropriate events, so don't expect to get a beer during Disney on Ice.

Food: The brewpub has a very limited menu: really good roast beef sandwiches and chili.

Special considerations: Kids are welcome on main brewery tours. This is also an excellent opportunity for wheelchair users; the brewery has a large elevator that goes directly to the brewhouse on the fourth floor.

Directions: See map on page 35.

Parking: There's plenty of pay parking at the CoreStates Center, and off-street parking at the big brewery. It needs to be said: The brewery is not in a great neighborhood, but if you take reasonable precautions, you should be fine.

Lodging: There is none close to the brewery. Check the listings for Dock Street or Yards, instead.

Nearby attractions: Although you'd never know it looking out the brewery's front door, you're actually very close to three of Philadelphia's best attractions. All you have to do is go down Thirty-first Street to Girard and turn right. If you go to the first light and turn left you enter Fairmount Park. Boathouse Row is right in front of you when you turn onto Kelly Drive; turn left and you'll come out at the Philadelphia Museum of Art (Twenty-Sixth Street and Benjamin Franklin Parkway, 215-763-8100), one of the world's foremost collections. Renoir, Monet, Cezanne, Van Gogh, Rubens—they're right here in Philadelphia. If you go straight across the Schuylkill on Girard Avenue you will see the signs for the Philadelphia Zoo (3400 Girard Avenue), which features a children's zoo and a newly rebuilt primate house. Another great attraction—and it's really close—is the view from the roof of the brewery; try to get them to take you out there!

Other good beer sites in the area: The North Star Bar is a neat place to hang out: a good bar with good beer and cool musical acts. 2639 Poplar Street (215-235-7827). London Grill is a beer-oriented bar with one handpump and a menu of delicious appetizers. 2301 Fairmount Avenue (215-978-4545). See the descriptions of Bridgid's and Cuvée Notredame on page 28.

Yards Brewing Company

5050 Umbria Street
Philadelphia
215-482-9109

Yards Brewing Company is a classic microbrewery story. Two friends, Jon Bovit and Tom Kehoe, started homebrewing together at Western Maryland University and discovered a knack and a love for it. They thought about brewing, then they considered what they were in college for . . . and the next thing you know they were doing an apprenticeship at a microbrewery—Oxford, in Linthicum, Maryland.

Then it was time to hit up every source of capital they could think of: family, friends, VISA. Meanwhile, they were carefully designing a tiny brewhouse and devising ways to cut costs. Sure enough, they found a local steel fabricator who did the job for thousands less than any brewing equipment outfit would. They set the brewhouse up in a tiny, back-alley space, and started going to beer festivals to get their name out there.

That is when I met Jon and Tom, back in 1995, when I was starting out as a beer writer. I was wandering through a fest, writing notes, when a cloud of East Kent Goldings hop aroma enveloped my head and drew me into the Yards booth. WOW! How did they do that? Turns out, they put a little cloth bag full of Goldings—a hop pocket—into each keg. This extra little step (which is a pain in the neck when it comes to cleaning kegs) keeps the beer dry-hopped right up to the moment each pint is dispensed. It's traditional, but labor intensive.

That respect for tradition, regardless of the effort required, characterizes Yards brewing. When they decided to make a porter, they did it in the time-honored way, by brewing a strong ale and a mild ale, then blending the two together to age. Their first non-British beer was a saison, a Belgian farmhouse ale with odd fermentation requirements. Yards is also one of the foremost Pennsylvania brewers of "real ale," cask-conditioned ales which must be racked into special kegs and cellared at the serving tavern until it is ready to serve. It's hard work, but it's paying off.

Beer geeks caught on to Yards first, and spread the word. Customers found the ESA surprisingly approachable, and many had their first beer from a handpump because of it. The Saison became a very popular local summer beer. Even though all the beer was sold in draft form, Yards quickly maxed out the brewing capacity of its 3.5-barrel brewhouse and the space available for fermenters at the old site.

Jon and Tim moved Yards into new digs on Umbria Street, in the back of a Pennsylvania Liquor Control Board warehouse. (Brewing sometimes makes for strange bedfellows.) They now have a 25-barrel brewkettle and, for the first time, temperature-controlled tanks. In the old small brewery, temperature control means an air-conditioner and a space heater. They now have a bottling line for their bottle-conditioned ESA. And since they have hefty payments on a big space now, they've created a "mass-market" beer. Mass-market for Yards, that is: Brawler is a well-hopped bitter meant to be dispensed under pressure from beer gas, a 75/25 carbon dioxide/nitrogen mix like that used by Guinness Stout to give the beer a creamy feel in the mouth.

The seat-of-the-pants days may be a receding memory, but Yards is not a big brewery by any means. Jon and Tom still hold the hand of tavern-keepers who serve their cask-conditioned beer. Every year they make up a batch of Love Stout, a stout brewed for Valentine's Day with a very traditional addition of oysters, shells and all. Best of all, Tom and Jon get out to the bars where their beer is served, making sure it's properly served and that people understand what they're drinking.

Opened: March 1995.
Type: Brewery.
Owners: Jon Bovit, Tom Kehoe.
Brewers: Joe Diaz, Mike Martinovich.
PA Microbrewers Guild: Member.
System: 25-barrel brewhouse (designed by Bovit and Kehoe, locally fabricated). Potential annual capacity 6,000 barrels.
Annual production: 1,500 barrels in 1996.
Beers brewed: *Year-round:* Yards ESA (Extra Special Ale—the only Yards beer currently available in bottles), Entire Porter, Brawler Ale. *Seasonals:* Old Bartholomew, Saison, Love Stout. All beers brewed on premises.
The Pick: I love all these beers. The ESA has been one of my favorites from the first day I tasted it. It is a beautiful example of how a beer can be very hoppy without being overwhelmingly bitter. The hop aroma is outstanding and Brit to the core. The slippery fullness of the malt body is sensually delighting, and the

unabashed fruitiness of the yeast is enough to make you laugh out loud with pleasure. A day spent with friends eating good food and drinking this beer will be one you remember for years. And if you're there on one of the rare occasions that the Mild, which makes up half of the Entire Porter, is available on its own, be sure to try it. It's my alternate Pick.

Take-out beer: Kegs (call for availability), cases (ESA only).

Tours: By appointment.

Special considerations: Kids welcome. Handicapped-accessible.

Parking: Plenty of off-street parking.

Lodging: Days Inn, 4200 Roosevelt Boulevard (215-289-9200); Chestnut Hill Hotel, 8229 Germantown Avenue (215-242-5905); Holiday Inn City Line, 4100 Presidential Boulevard (1-800-HOLIDAY or 215-477-0200).

Nearby attractions: See nearby attractions on page 52.

Other good beer sites in the area: Dawson Street Pub is Yards's unofficial house pub and you'll always find at least two Yards beers on tap here. 100 Dawson Street (215-482-5677). McMenamin's Tavern at 7170 Germantown Avenue in Mt. Airy is a great neighborhood bar (215-247-9920). Bridgid's is a favorite of Philly's beer cognoscenti for its small but superb selection of draft beers and great bottled beers. You may find Yards here; you may also find Tom Kehoe or Jon Bovit themselves. 726 North Twenty-fourth Street (215-232-3232). See also other good beer sites on page 52.

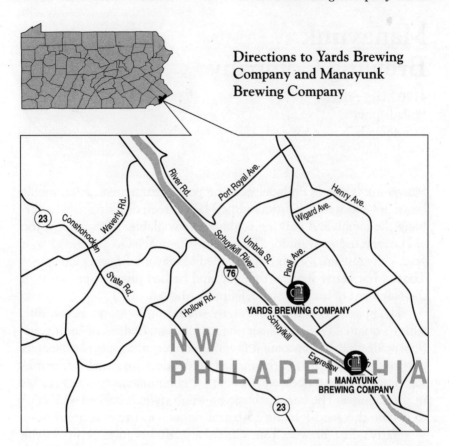

Directions to Yards Brewing
Company and Manayunk
Brewing Company

Manayunk
Brewing Company

4120 Main Street
Philadelphia
215-482-8220

Manayunk is one of Philadelphia's hippest, hottest areas. Fashionable beaneries and trendy boutiques line Main Street, drinking decks over-hang the canal, and parking is almost unavailable. Manayunk is the old Lenape Indian word for "The Place Where We Go To Drink," so it practically screams for a brewpub called Manayunk Brewing Company. That's what Harry Renner thought, and he had just the spot for it in the basement of his Manayunk Farmer's Market.

The space—originally a water-powered mill—works beautifully, with its original brick walls, seating for four hundred, an operating, in-floor scale that has become a favorite conversation spot, an upstairs pub for the lunch area of the market, and a deck for canal-side drink-ing. There's even a dock with a boat for complimentary canal cruises in the summer. The bar, in classic brewpub style, is backed with glass to expose the good-looking 15-barrel Bohemian Brewing brewhouse.

Harry's first brewer, Tom Cizauskas, left his fingerprint on the place. He had the idea that a brewpub is more than just beer and food; it is beer *with* food. Tom felt that the waitstaff should know as much about the beer as they did about the food: everything. Now, more than a year after Tom moved to a larger microbrewery in Ohio, his philoso-phy lives on at Manayunk.

Tom's replacement, Jim Brennan, is a native Philadelphian. He's my hero because he designed the Liebert & Obert Lager, Manayunk's highly drinkable session lager. The number of styles brewed at Man-ayunk has exploded since Jim and his assistant Ted Briggs took over the brewhouse. They've brewed over twenty-five different beers in less than a year. It's a lot of fun to watch the taps rotate and to try all those beers.

The two standbys are Schuylkill Punch, a happily tart raspberry wheat ale, sometimes added to orange juice for a surprisingly good mimosa-like drink, and Krook's Mill American Pale Ale, a Sierra Nevada Pale Ale tribute beer with a zippy blast of Cascade hop aroma and flavor.

The menu changes regularly as the months go by. My favorites have been the mahogany wings, a sweet and hot variation on Buffalo wings, grilled meatloaf that combines comfort food with the intensity of the grill, and the tender, flavor-drenched smoked brisket. You can be sure that whatever is on the menu is up to the caliber of these past offerings.

This is a good place to spend an evening, to end an evening, or to while away a weekend afternoon. Come on down—it's The Place Where We Go To Drink!

Opened: October 1996.
Type: Brewpub.
Owner: Harry Renner IV.
Brewers: Jim Brennan, Ted Briggs.
PA Microbrewers Guild: Membership pending.
System: 15-barrel Bohemian Breweries brewhouse. Potential annual capacity 2,800 barrels.
Annual production: 1,365 barrels in first full year of operation.
Beers brewed: *Year-round:* Schuylkill Punch, Krook's Mill American Pale Ale. *Seasonals:* Robert Hare Oatmeal Porter, Hidden River India Ale, Grand Cru, Blueberry Ale, "A Winter's Tale" Scotch Ale, Colonial Ale, Burrow of Rocks Barleywine, Renner's Red Best Bitter, Sorrel Horse Scottish Ale, Flat Rock SPA, Chequer'd Shade Brown Ale, Wissahickon Gold, Bohemian Blonde, Blue Mountain Sparkling Ale, Grinning Cow Milk Stout, Mule Bridge XXXX Stout, Blanche de Manayunk, Engine #12 Smoked Porter, Polish Alps Porter, Platt Brothers' Pumpkin Ale, Celtic Ale, Main Street Wheat, Chock Full O' Hops, Hog & Grog Ordinary, Kelpius Cave Brown Ale, 1,000 Steps Special Bitter, Golden Session Ale, Moon Dahg Imperial Stout, Liebert & Obert Dortmund Export, Vienna Waltz, Cervesa Rosa, Prohibition Pils, Dutch Hollow Munich Dunkel, ManayunkFest, Devil's Pool Black Bier. So far. All beers brewed on premises.
The Pick: It's an intimidating list of beers, but my choice is clear: Liebert & Obert Dortmund Export. This is a smoothly malty beer with a low snarl of hops in the back of the mouth. It is usually my second beer at Manayunk after I've tried whatever's new. It's session lager. A session beer should be good enough to savor but not so outrageous that it breaks up conversations with a "Whoa, this beer is something else!" L & O is perfectly adapted for that: not too hoppy, not too sweet, not too strong. It's simply good, drinkable beer.

Take-out beer: 2-liter growlers, kegs.

Tours: By appointment for groups of two or more.

Brewpub hours: Monday through Thursday and Sunday, 11:00 A.M. – midnight; Friday and Saturday, 11:00 A.M.–2:00 A.M.

Food: The menu at Manayunk varies somewhat as months pass, but it maintains a high level of quality and innovation. The mahogany wings appetizer is sopping and sweet and robust, the grilled meatloaf is real man-food, the beer floats are a dessert made by Gambrinus. Your server will suggest some thoughtful food and beer pairings, a pleasant addition to brewpub service.

Extras: Live music (call for schedule), darts, pool table, pinball. In summertime, there are free boat rides on the canal for brewpub patrons.

Special considerations: Kids welcome. Handicapped-asccessible. Cigars are allowed (also for sale at the bar). Vegetarian meals available.

Directions: See map on page 48.

Parking: Parking on the street and at some small lots is available, but can be a bear on weekends. The brewpub has a valet parking service during evening hours, Wednesday through Sunday.

Lodging: Days Inn, 4200 Roosevelt Boulevard (215-289-9200); Chestnut Hill Hotel, 8229 Germantown Avenue (215-242-5905); Holiday Inn City Line, 4100 Presidential Boulevard (800-HOLIDAY or 215-477-0200).

Nearby attractions: Main Street, Manayunk, is a very happening strip of shops, bars, and restaurants, pleasant to stop in or stroll along, and the brewpub is right on it. In fact, you can start with the Manayunk Farmer's Market right in the same building. It's more like a yuppie's dream of a farm market, but it's fun and the food's great. Then wander on down Main Street, shopping, eating, and drinking as you go. It's also very easy to get to Boathouse Row, the Franklin Institute, the Please Touch Museum (an outstanding children's science museum), or the Philadelphia Museum of Art by simply driving down Main Street toward the city and sticking close to the river until you come out at the art museum.

Other good beer sites in the area: The Dawson Street Pub's three handpumps, outstanding selection of tap and bottled beer, and really good vegetarian chili are within a ten minutes' walk. (100 Dawson Street, 215-482-5677, ask for directions). Brewmaster Jim Brennan recommends the Flat Rock Saloon (4301 Main Street, 215-483-3722) and T. Hogan's Pub (5109 Rochelle Avenue, 215-482-8583), both within walking distance.

A word about . . .

Micros, Brewpubs, and Craft Brewers

My young son Thomas sometimes accompanies me on brewery tours. Much to my delight, he's fascinated by words and what they mean and how people use them. I've explained to him that much of what people say is said because they don't want to say something more blunt or honest. Code words, euphemisms, and evasions are part of our everyday speech. Here's a little secret of the beer world: "Microbrewery" is just another code word.

When the new brewing movement started in America in the 1970s, no one knew what to call these little breweries. "Brewery pub," "boutique brewery," and "microbrewery" were all used. By the early 1980s two words had settled into general use: microbrewery and brewpub. At the time, the industry's pundits defined a brewpub as a brewery that sold most of its beer in an in-house taproom. They defined a microbrewery as a brewery that produced under 15,000 barrels a year.

These terms gained legal recognition in some states, as deals were struck to allow the new businesses to start up and as tax rates were determined. The federal government acknowledged the special nature of small breweries in the early 1990s, granting a substantial tax break to those with an annual production under 50,000 barrels.

Eventually the industry itself came up with a whole set of labels. "Brewpub" continued to be used for breweries that sold the large majority of their beer on premises by the glass. "Microbrewery" was for packaging breweries whose production was less than 50,000 barrels. "Regional" brewery applied to smaller breweries established before 1970 that did not distribute to all of America, and nationally distributing giants like Anheuser-Busch, Miller, Coors, and Stroh were dubbed "national brewers" or "megabrewer."

But the growth of some successful microbreweries has made even 50,000 barrels an uncomfortable fit. Boston Beer Company, the contract brewery responsible for the Samuel Adams line of beers, sold more than one million barrels in 1996, and Sierra Nevada Brewing Company, an early microbrewery that produces all its own beer, is pushing 300,000 barrels. Clearly these are no longer microbreweries, yet their beer is exactly the same as it was. To be called a microbrewery has a cachet to it that most microbrewers don't want to surrender. What to call them?

Some propose the blanket term "craft brewery." This implies that the beer is somehow crafted rather than produced in a factory. Craft breweries are different, the brewers explain, because the beer is made in single batches, not in several that are then combined in one huge tank or blended after fermentation to ensure consistency.

Putting a label on a brewery these days is not as easy as putting a label on a bottle. For example, what do you call a place like The Lion, a regional brewery that brews mainstream lagers but also brews the small, all-malt line of Brewery Hill beers? Penn Brewing has a beautiful brewery pub and bottles beer brewed in-house, but it also has its Penn Pilsner brewed on contract. Then there's Poor Henry's in the old Ortlieb Brewery bottling house, with two side-by-side brewhouses, a 7-barrel for the welcoming on-premises pub, and a 50-barrel for the wholesale trade. These breweries aren't readily pigeonholed.

The fact is, microbrewery has *always* been a code word, and so has craft brewery. They both mean the same thing. They describe a brewery that makes beer in an authentic manner—using ingredients and techniques appropriate to a given style of beer or brewing—and that brews beers other than mainstream American-style lager. What do I think such places should be called? How about *breweries?*

The distinctions are really all nonsense. Brewery size has nothing to do with the quality of a beer. Guinness Stout, the beer to which most microbrewers hopefully compare their own dry stouts, is brewed by a globe-girdling gargantuan of a brewer. Blending is likewise a non-issue. It goes on at microbreweries across the country.

In this book I have bowed to convention and called Pennsylvania's Old Guard breweries regionals, and used the words brewpub, microbrewery, and craft brewery. Brewpub is the best of these terms. A brewery where beer is taken directly from the conditioning tanks to serving tanks and sold from a tap on premises truly deserves a unique name. But if I had my way, the others would all be called simply breweries. To differentiate a brewery based on the kind of beer it makes seems to be missing the point. Categorizing them by size penalizes the ones that succeed and outgrow the class. Call them breweries, and then let the beer do the talking.

Beer from Horse Country to the Delaware

Southeastern Pennsylvania is often called "the five-county area." This includes Philadelphia, Bucks, Montgomery, Chester, and Delaware Counties. If you take out Philadelphia County, the remaining counties are considered the suburbs of Philadelphia, even though they reach almost to Bethlehem in the north and well into Amish farm country in the west.

Of course, there are suburbs and there are suburbs. Bucks County has cookie-cuttered Levittown and Montgomery County has the gritty streets of Norristown. The tightly-packed streets of Upper Darby blend Delaware County right into Philadelphia, and Chester County's Coatesville is like a little bit of Rust Belt. These are border counties, where farmers and financiers coexist in the gently rolling countryside.

The well-known Main Line area stretches out through Montgomery, Delaware, and Chester Counties. This is a wealthy strip of beautiful old homes, boutiques, and Mercedes-Benz dealerships along what used to be the Main Line of the Pennsylvania Railroad, now the SEPTA commuter rail line. Out here, tucked away among the big homes, you'll find the controversial Barnes Foundation, where one of the world's great art collections is trying to work out its future.

There is a substantial presence of the arts in the suburbs. Chadds Ford on Brandywine Creek is home to the Wyeths and the Brandywine River Museum. On the northeast edge of the five-county area is New Hope, a well-known artist's colony and haven for alternative lifestyles on the Delaware River. Both Chadds Ford and New Hope are worth a visit, but here's a word to the wise beer traveler: BYOB. Wine from the Chaddsford Winery is the drink of choice on the Brandywine, and the only place to get a good beer around New Hope is across the river in Lambertville, New Jersey. There you'll find the River Horse Brewery and the Inn of the Hawk, an excellent little beer bar.

Not far from New Hope is Doylestown, where James Michener lived and endowed an excellent art museum. You'll also find the Mercer Museum and the Moravian Pottery and Tile Works, the lifework of Dr. Henry Mercer, an enthusiast of American folk art and craftsmanship. His mansion, Fonthill—a concrete castle—is a unique example of free-form architecture filled with artwork and memorabilia that Mercer collected.

Valley Forge National Historical Park is here in the suburbs, with miles of trails and reconstructions of the cramped huts where the Continental Army spent the harsh winter of 1777.

In Bucks County, at Washington Crossing Historic Park, they do an annual re-enactment of General Washington's famous Christmas crossing of the Delaware. You can get a dramatic overview of the area from Bowman's Hill Tower, a 110-foot tower atop the hill used by Continental Army lookouts.

The area is dotted with Revolutionary War battle sites. Brandywine Battlefield near Chadds Ford is where Washington was defeated by the British in 1777. Historical markers note little skirmishes like the battle of the Crooked Billet Inn in Warminster and a set-to that supposedly occurred in the alleys of my own little town of Newtown.

Chester County is horse country. The area's biggest equestrian event, the annual Devon Horse Show, is where the cream of the county show off their horses—and themselves!

If all this sounds a bit upper-crust, it can be. Although the suburbs have plenty of working stiffs and average joes and janes, you can't help noticing that this is a very wealthy area. Big $350,000 homes are commonplace, luxury cars clog the narrow roads, and you can't throw a rock without clocking a doctor or lawyer. So don't throw any rocks around. Just relax, see the sights, and stop someplace nice for a beer.

Victory Brewing Company

420 Acorn Lane
Downingtown
610-873-0881
www.victorybeer.com

Victory is aptly named. It is a victory of beer geek over marketer. The two principals, Ron Barchet and Bill Covaleski, are childhood friends who homebrewed together for years. Then through an odd set of circumstances they wound up brewing at the same microbrewery. One thing led to another, and they decided to open their own. Years of plans, salesmanship, and sweat later, Victory was born.

Now that they are running their own show, they have decided to give their beer a fair chance. Victory doesn't compromise for the market, because Ron and Bill believe that there is a market for uncompromising beer. "Everyone else is brewing what they think the market wants," says Ron. "We're brewing what we want, and we're beer geeks."

They're uncommon beer geeks, at that. Victory brews lager as well as ales, bucking the national trend in microbrewing. Pennsylvania has the greatest concentration of lager microbrewers in the country. Brandywine Valley Lager and its big brother St. Victorious Hellerbock are examples of two styles which, though uncommon in America, have been successful for Victory. Another winner is the unabashed Prima Pils, a beer that blows away any lame ideas about being "just another pilsner."

Victory's beers are winning critical acclaim across the country even though they're only available within about 100 miles of the brewery. Locals mail samples to their friends in other states. The Internet beer newsgroups continually buzz with the praises of Victory beers.

The pub in Downingtown does represent some compromises. The brewery was built in part of an old Pepperidge Farm complex, so it's very much an industrial space. When I was there, the concrete floor and cinder block walls were exposed. High, echoing ceilings had been hung with empty malt bags in an attempt to deaden the sound. Since then Victory has put in carpet and acoustic tile. The industrial feel is easily overlooked, however, because the service is friendly and the food is as fresh and carefully made as the beer.

The big, wood-fired brick oven in the pub goes through about a cord of wood each week. From its flaming maw comes crisp-crusted pizzas with imaginative ingredients and piping hot calzones. This is definitely a place for families. My kids love Victory's size, the brewed root beer, and the kids' menu. Don't take this the wrong way, but I love the bathrooms at Victory. They are spacious, bright, and spotlessly clean.

You can plant yourself at the bar, which is made from the wooden crates in which the brewhouse was shipped. Get a glass of cask-conditioned HopDevil from the handpump and get an eyeful of the fermentation tanks behind the bar. When you're done, pick up some six-packs to take home. After all, don't your friends deserve some of this beer?

Opened: February 1996.
Type: Brewery and brewpub.
Owners: Ron Barchet, Bill Covaleski, and private investors.
Brewers: Ron Barchet, Bill Covaleski.
PA Microbrewers Guild: Not a member.
System: 25-barrel Century Manufacturing brewhouse. Potential annual capacity 22,500 barrels.
Annual production: 3,200 barrels in 1997.
Beers brewed: *Year-round:* Brandywine Valley Lager, Victory Festbier, Prima Pils, HopDevil India Pale Ale. *Seasonals:* Old Horizontal Barleywine, St. Victorious Doppelbock, St. Boisterous Hellerbock, Sunrise Weissbier, Moonglow Weizenbock, Storm King Imperial Stout, Munich Dunkel. All beers brewed on premises.
The Pick: I'll have to go with the big guy, the HopDevil IPA. HopDevil is the East's answer to the western hop-monster beers, but with the East's trademark balance. HopDevil has a bedrock foundation of malt that makes its wildly aromatic hoppiness even more appealing. Outstanding, galactic-class beer.
Take-out beer: Growlers, six-packs, cases, kegs.
Tours: Saturday at noon and 3:00 P.M.; Sunday at 2:00 P.M.
Brewpub hours: Tuesday through Saturday, 11:30 A.M.–midnight, Sunday, 1:00 P.M.–10:00 P.M.
Food: Victory's wood-fired oven bakes great pizzas (the four-mushroom topping is my favorite) and calzones. You can get fresh salads and sandwiches and some of the best fries around. Victory also brews a great root beer.
Extras: Victory has darts and regulation-size pool tables. There's also

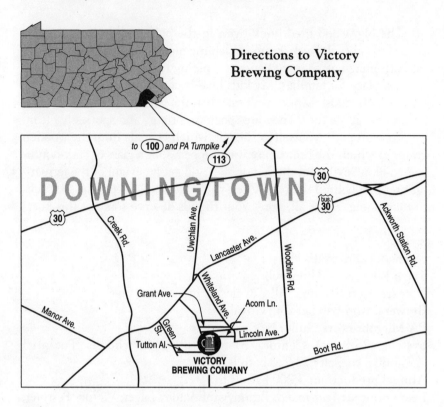

Directions to Victory Brewing Company

live music every Saturday night and often on Fridays.

Special considerations: Kids welcome. Handicapped-accessible. Cigars allowed. Vegetarian meals available.

Parking: Free off-street parking.

Lodging: Desmond Great Valley Hotel, 1 Liberty Boulevard, Malvern (610-269-9800); Duling Kurtz House and Country Inn, 146 South Whitford Road, Exton (610-524-1830); Holiday Inn Express, 120 North Pottstown Pike, Exton (610-524-9000); Marsh Creek Campground, Route 282, Lyndell (610-942-2282).

Nearby attractions: Vertical Extremes has indoor rock climbing; they're right behind Victory (610-873-9620). If it's apple-picking time, go to Highland Orchards to pick your own. They do have apples for sale too (610-269-3494). If you have younger kids you'll want to visit Springton Manor Farm, a demonstration farm with pigs and poultry in a petting area. Admission is free. Five miles west on Route 322., on Springton Road (610-942-2450).

Other good beer sites in the area: See other good beer sites on page 69.

Ugly Dog Brewing Company

Unit #7, 520 East Bernard Street
West Chester
610-430-8060
www.uglydog.com

A beer named Ugly Dog? Sounds like a marketing nightmare, right? Not so. Mutts are evidently highly salable when it comes to micro-brewed beer. In Ugly Dog's case, even the "beeraphenalia" sells like hotcakes. I thought for almost a year that Ugly Dog was a "stealth" brewery—just a name to sell T-shirts. I saw those dogs everywhere! Turns out, owner Kathryn Hanzsek sold T-shirts and hats to raise cash to operate the brewery.

Ugly Dog is an extract brewery, and a small one. When I visited the "garage-front" brewery, there were drums of malt extract stacked everywhere, and the little 3-barrel brewkettle was steaming away. I was apprehensive. Extract beers are often thin and vegetal in flavor, and I have had some bad ones. But there was a keg on tap and I had to try it. Whoosh! It was good! Some brewers manage to wring good beer out of extract breweries, and Kathryn Hanzsek is one. This beer was like a fresh, well-muscled and maltier Bass Ale. I had another.

Ugly Dog is contract-brewed in bottles. Like the T-shirts, the con-tracted bottles are helping to raise the cash needed for Ugly Dog's next venture. The Dog Haus, an Ugly Dog brewpub, should be opening in West Chester in 1998. A 10-barrel Specific Mechanical brewhouse has been ordered. Kathryn has plans for "a highly canine theme for the brewpub. There will be pictures of dogs on the walls, pawprints on the floor, and our paw tap handles." Not surprisingly, there will also be a gift shop to sell Ugly Dog stuff.

Kathryn's inspiration is easy to trace. She has numerous dogs (though, sadly, the Ugly Dog himself has died), and she is an avid supporter of ani-mal welfare. Ugly Dog donates a portion of its still-brisk T-shirt sales and hosts beer tasting events to benefit the Chester County SPCA.

It seems that Ugly Dog is doing well for his misstress. Soon he'll have a place to call his own.

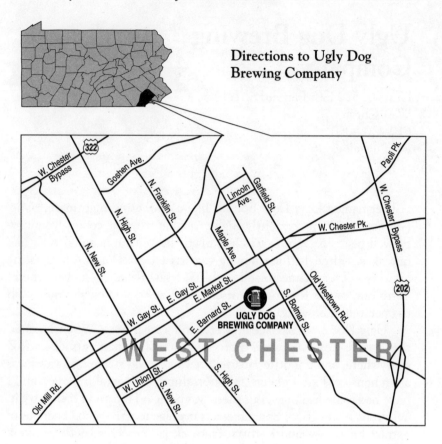

Directions to Ugly Dog
Brewing Company

Opened: December 1995.

Type: Brewery.

Owner: Kathryn Hanzsek.

Brewer: Kathryn Hanzsek.

PA Microbrewers Guild: Not a member.

System: 3-barrel locally fabricated extract brewhouse. Potential annual capacity 500 barrels, plus contract-brewed beer.

Annual production: 1,500 barrels in 1996.

Beers brewed: *Year-round:* Ugly Dog Ale, Ugly Dog Gold. Draft Ugly Dog Ale brewed on premises. All bottled beer brewed on contract at Frederick Brewing Company, Frederick, Maryland.

The Pick: Draft Ugly Dog is one of the best extract beers I've ever had. It's strong, muscular, malty stuff that tastes like a half-and-half mix of a good Scottish ale and fresh Bass Ale.

Take-out beer: None available.

Tours: Upon request.
Special considerations: Handicapped-accessible.
Parking: On street.
Lodging: Abbey Green Motor Lodge, 1036 Wilmington Pike (610-692-3310); Beechwood Motel, 1310 Wilmington Pike (610-399-0970); Holiday Inn West Chester, 943 South High Street (610-692-1900).
Nearby attractions: West Chester boasts a number of Victorian-era homes and is undergoing a restaurant renaissance. It has been bruited as "the next Manayunk." Nearby is Longwood Gardens, the former country estate of Pierre du Pont and one of the most impressive horticultural displays in the United States. The Conservatory building and 3.5 acres of greenhouses allow year-round displays of bounteous flowering plants. There are three sets of impressive fountains in the gardens as well. Reservations are suggested for seasonal shows. Call 800-737-5500 or 610-388-1000 for tickets and information. This is also mushroom country; growers in Kennett Square and Avondale supply most of the country's mushrooms. The Phillips Mushroom Place provides an interesting look at this edible fungus. 909 East Baltimore Pike, Kennett Square (610-388-6082). Not far away are the Brandywine area attractions, including Brandywine Battlefield Park (Routes 1 and 100) and the Brandywine River Museum, which houses artworks by the Wyeths (610-388-2700). The Brandywine River offers a beautiful, serene canoe trip; paddle your own or check into the canoe rental services in the area.
Other good beer sites in the area: Kathryn recommends that visitors to West Chester try their beer luck at The Bar and Restaurant at 18 West Gay Street (610-431-0770) and Clemente's, an Italian restaurant at 116 East Gay Street (610-344-7644). See also other good beer sites on page 69.

Dirty Dawg
Brewing Company

Limerick Airport Business Center
211 Commerce Court, Suite 101
Limerick
610-495-6801
www.dirtydawg.com

Dirty Dawg came trotting in just under the line—my deadline, that is. As I was finishing the manuscript, beer-stained notes and hoagie wrappers littering my desk, there was a whining and scratching at my door. I opened the door, and there they were: four Dirty Dawgs! I took them in, chilled them, and gave them a new home in my beer-drinking belly!

Dirty Dawg is Pennsylvania's newest brewery. There will surely be others by the time you read this book, but every dawg has its day.

The brewery is the pet project of Sue Jarrell and Chuck Faust, two former Lockheed Martin employees who found that they had interlocking abilities and interests. Sue is an experienced, top-gun marketer who has learned how to do the grunt work required to run a brewery. Chuck is an experienced homebrewer who is learning to make sales calls.

Why Dirty Dawg? The two had originally intended to call the brewery Salty Dog. They registered the name, then started raising money and spreading the word about the brewery. One day they got a letter from a lawyer representing Sea Dog Brewing of Maine. Sea Dog's lawyers thought that Salty Dog was too close to Sea Dog and told Sue and Chuck to cease and desist. "Those dirty dawgs!" the two exclaimed, and the new name was born. "It's in honor of those lawyers," says Sue with a sweet smile.

The brewery is in a business park near the Limerick Airport, about three miles from the Limerick nuclear plant. When I visited, the interior was still a shell, with the brewery equipment installed along one wall. There were plans for a small tasting area and a brewery store to sell gift items emblazoned with the brewery's dog illustrations. The brewery will also sell beer, fresh as can be, direct to consumers in the store. They expect to do a fair business with the growing number of employees in the business park.

Sue and Chuck sounded like typical start-up brewers when I phoned them shortly before their brewery opened. They were harried, anxious, and excited to be finally making beer after years of raising money and negotiating prices, and after months of backbreaking labor and foot-wearying advance sales calls. There was breathless, rapid-fire chatter, muffled yells, and finally an abrupt but cheerful "I've got to go now. Thanks, good-bye!" That start-up adrenaline rush strikes again!

Dirty Dawg is now off and running. The rest of the pack is out ahead, but time will tell how much fight is in this pup.

Opened: January 1998.
Type: Brewery.
Owners: Sue Jarrell, Chuck Faust.
Brewer: Chuck Faust.
PA Microbrewers Guild: Not a member.
System: 7-barrel John Cross brewhouse. Potential annual capacity 2,500 barrels.
Annual production: No figures available yet.
Beers brewed: *Year-round:* City Slicker Lager, Sir George's Vienna-style Lager, Horny Dog Pale Ale, Wolfhound Stout, Murky Perky Porter, Houndstooth Black & Tan, Great Dane Bohemian Pilsner, Buster's Dirt Bag Brown Ale. *Seasonals:* Rock-n-Rodney Pumpkin Ale. All beers brewed on premises.
The Pick: I tried the City Slicker Lager, Sir George's Vienna, Horny Dog Pale Ale, and the Wolfhound Stout. Taste, taste, sip, sip. . . . It's Wolfhound, romping home to win in a big finish! This is big beer, folks. There's anise, a touch of wintergreen, coffee, and chocolate around the edges of a huge pool of roasted barley and black malt dryness. There's enough flavor for *three* beers in this one.
Take-out beer: Six-packs, cases, quarter and half kegs.
Tours: Three Saturdays a month, 10:00 A.M. and 3:00 P.M. (call ahead for schedule). During the week, tours by special appointment only.
Special considerations: Kids welcome. Handicapped-accessible.
Parking: Plenty of off-street parking.
Lodging: Shearer Elegance B&B, 154 Main Street, Linfield (610-495-7429); Days Inn Pottstown, 29 High Street (610-970-1101).
Nearby attractions: You're close to Valley Forge National Historical Park (described in the introduction to this section) down Route 422. You could also take a tour of the Limerick nuclear plant on Longview Road (610-495-6767). Two state parks are close by. Marsh Creek State Park, to the south off Route 100 near Downingtown, has boating, fishing, swimming, and skating and ice fish-

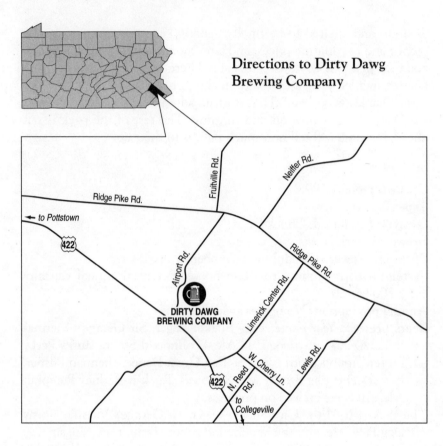

Directions to Dirty Dawg Brewing Company

ing in the winter. There are six miles of hiking trails. The more extensive French Creek State Park, which is west on Route 23, then north on Route 345, has camping, swimming, boating, fishing, thirty-two miles of hiking trails and fifteen miles of cross-country skiing trails. The park is also the location of the Hopewell Furnace National Historic Site, a reconstructed anthracite iron furnace and ironmaking village (215-582-8773).

Other good beer sites in the area: Trappe Inn, a friendly bar with a Guinness tap, is easy to find on Main Street in Trappe (610-489-8686). See also other good beer sites on page 69.

Sly Fox Brewing Company

Route 113, Pikeland Village
Phoenixville
610-935-4540
www.slyfoxbrew.com

Yoicks! Tally ho! And all that foxhunting talk. Officially known to the Pennsylvania Liquor Control Board as Chester County Brewing Company, the Giannopoulos family's brewpub is known to its adoring fans as the Sly Fox. The grinning fox that is the emblem of the brewpub comes from Chester County's horse-country tradition of riding to the hounds, or foxhunting.

You start to get out in the country when you hit Phoenixville. Route 23 runs through some pretty open territory west of there, and if you go south past Downingtown it gets downright empty. That's where the horses leap, the dogs bay, and the foxes laugh their bushy, bushy tails off. If you're getting the idea that the Sly Fox doesn't take itself all that seriously, you're on the right trail.

The beer, however, is taken quite seriously. This is some of the cleanest brewpub beer I've ever had, free of any off-flavors. I regret that I've never been out to the Sly Fox in winter. Their bigger beers are reputed to be fat and jolly, the kind you want to curl up with in a corner of the brewpub and not stir until Groundhog Day. But I have had the pleasure of an Amber Fox with a rare cheeseburger; the cut of the hops and the rich juices of the burger seemed made for each other.

Though the brewpub sits in a shopping center, it does not lack character or charm. The central staircase gives it a homey feel, as if Grandma decided to build a brewery in her home (we should all be so lucky). Take a seat upstairs, or sit downstairs at the bar and eye those tanks. It's a comfortable place, not harshly lit or nightclub dark.

The Sly Fox is part of a nice little tour I've thought up. You and your designated driver can start in Phoenixville at the Royal Scot with a jar of something tasty, then come out Route 113 to the Epicurean, a somewhat upscale beer bar and restaurant just north of the Sly Fox. Have one of their uncommon tap selections, then come down to the Sly Fox for a "tap dance" of the house specials. After that you can

Directions to Sly Fox Brewing Company

either go back to the Scot and start over, or tool on down Route 113 to Downingtown and visit the boys at Victory Brewing Company.

Be sure to slip back to the Fox for a beer at the end of the day. It's just like a fox to double back, and you may throw the dog-eat-dog world off your trail while you hole up in this cozy den.

Opened: December 1995.
Type: Brewpub.
Owners: The Giannopoulos family.
Brewer: Brady Van Druff.
PA Microbrewers Guild: Member.
System: 15-barrel Pub Brewing Systems brewhouse. Potential annual capacity 1,500 barrels.
Annual production: 1,000 barrels in 1996.
Beers brewed: *Year-round:* Amber Fox, Olde English Nut Brown, Honey Wheat, Raspberry Wheat, Light Ale, Dr. Lager, Stout Fox,

Golden Fox. *Seasonals:* Fat Fox Winter Warmer, Fox Fest, Black Cherry Stout. All draft beers sold are brewed on premises; bottled Amber Fox is contract-brewed.

The Pick: The Amber Fox is an IPA with a pleasantly subtle fruitiness and slightly restrained but sure hop bitterness. This is a category of beer that often represents a brewer's best attempt to rip your head off. Sly Fox makes it a beer you'll come back to again and again. Now *that's* sly!

Take-out beer: Half-gallon growlers.

Tours: Tours given upon request.

Brewpub hours: Monday through Thursday, 11:30 A.M.–midnight; Friday and Saturday, 11:30 A.M.–2:00 A.M.; Sunday noon–midnight.

Food: There's a full menu with appetizers, American Colonial and continental fare, and a kids' menu for the "Fox Pups."

Extras: Sly Fox has no liquor license, but you're allowed to bring your own wine.

Special considerations: Kids welcome. Handicapped-accessible. Cigars allowed. Vegetarian meals available.

Parking: Plenty of free parking in off-street lot.

Lodging: Comfort Inn, 99 Robinson Street, Pottstown (610-326-5000); Exton Comfort Inn, Routes 113 and 100, Lionville (610-524-8811); Holiday Inn, Routes 113 and 100, Lionville (610-363-1100).

Nearby attractions: See nearby attractions on page 65.

Other good beer sites in the area: The Epicurean, a very nice restaurant with six good taps and a wide bottle selection, also has a six-pack store that sells bottles to go. Route 113 and Township Line Road, Phoenixville (610-933-1336). The Royal Scot is a comfortable older beer bar, a good place to relax with a pint. 400 Bridge Street, Phoenixville (610-983-3070). See and be seen with a glass of great beer at the Drafting Room, a neon-lit, designer-friendly bar. 635 North Route 113, Exton (610-363-0521). See also other good beer sites on page 66.

Valley Forge Brewing Company

267 East Swedesford Road
Wayne
610-687-8700
www.vfbc.com

It took a long time for Valley Forge Brewing Company to get any respect around Philadelphia. I can think of several reasons. It was one of the first brewpubs to open in the Philadelphia suburbs, and there's a very strong city prejudice. It is located in an old movie theater in a shopping center, not in an old historic building or fancily designed urban space. The brewpub has always been popular with a young crowd who seem mostly interested in pounding down the pints on the weekend. But I think the big reason was the covered bridge.

There is a covered bridge inside the restaurant, a visual *non sequitur* in a brewpub where darts, pool, and big-screen ESPN are taken quite seriously. The bridge was made out of heavy oak timbers by an Amish carpenter from Morgantown. The covered bridge doesn't actually bridge anything. It's just a semiprivate dining space with a somewhat more romantic air to it due to the electric candle lighting and lower ceiling.

Owners David and Greg Biles wanted a covered bridge after they saw one in Valley Forge National Historic Park. "We knew we couldn't actually put *that* bridge in the pub," laughs David, "But it was a good-looking bridge and it would be another tie to Valley Forge." There are also historical murals on the walls, and the exterior of the restroom inset has been painted to quite convincingly resemble a colonial-era cottage. After all, the pub's in an old movie theater; it needs every possible distraction to help you forget that.

Whatever the reason for the lack of respect, it all ended in fall of 1996. Vindication came in the form of a GABF gold medal for Valley Forge Brewing Company's Imperial Stout. That kind of confirmation is hard to ignore, particularly in such a showcase category. The Biles brothers were walking tall after that, and rightly so.

They can be proud of the food at the pub too. They have a professionally-trained chef serving a variety of pub fare as well as a number

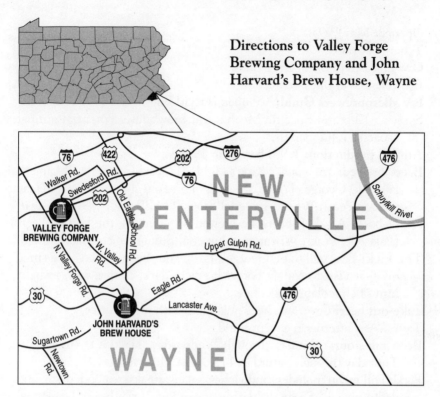

Directions to Valley Forge Brewing Company and John Harvard's Brew House, Wayne

of dishes prepared with beer. Among these are some seafood dishes steamed in beer, a specialty of the brewpub since its opening. Valley Forge was a fairly regular stop for me when I worked out in Great Valley, and the menu was almost as tempting as the beer.

I've always liked Valley Forge, the l-o-n-g bar, the brewing history timeline in the men's room done by local beer historian Rich Wagner, and the beer, of course. Valley Forge makes some beers that drink well by the pint, real session beers like the King's Gold Ale and Red Coat Ale. Either of those would work for an afternoon of watching sports, playing darts, and checking out the other people along the bar.

That's the kind of brewpub this is. There are no pretensions to some higher worshipful purpose of beer. This is a place for fun, where the emphasis is on the people drinking the beer, not the beer itself. Once you've visited, it makes a lot of sense.

Opened: May 1995.

Type: Brewpub.

Owners: David Biles, Greg Biles.

Brewer: David Biles.

PA Microbrewers Guild: Member. (David Biles is the 1998 president)

System: 10-barrel Specific Mechanical brewhouse. Potential annual capacity 1,400 barrels.

Annual production: 1,100 barrels in 1996

Beers brewed: *Year-round:* King's Gold Ale, Red Coat Ale, Regiment Pale Ale, George's Porter. *Seasonals:* Three are always on tap and may include Peach Wheat, Imperial Stout (GABF gold, 1996), or Doublebock. All draft beers are brewed on premises; the bottled beers (Pale Ale, Peach Wheat, and Imperial Stout) are contract-brewed.

The Pick: Easy call. The George's Porter has been my favorite since my first visit to Valley Forge. It's rich, dark, chewy, with a slight hint of chocolate and coffee.

Take-out beer: Growlers; kegs (available with prior notice).

Tours: Any afternoon except Sunday.

Brewpub hours: Sunday through Wednesday, 11:00 A.M.–midnight; Thursday through Saturday, 11:00 A.M.–1:00 A.M.

Food: Full menu includes sandwiches, salads, steaks, seafood, pasta, and daily specials. Some dishes are cooked with the house beers, and some pairing suggestions are made. There is also a children's menu. The root beer's pretty good too.

Extras: VFBC has one of the longest bars in Pennsylvania, pool tables, English dartboards, a game room, and large TVs.

Special considerations: Kids welcome. Handicapped-accessible. Vegetarian meals available.

Parking: Free off-street parking in shopping center lot.

Lodging: Courtyard by Marriott, 1100 Drummers Lane, Wayne (610-687-6700); Comfort Inn, 550 West DeKalb Road, King of Prussia (610-962-0700); The Inn at King of Prussia, 127 Gulph Road, King of Prussia (800-528-1234).

Nearby attractions: See the introduction to this section for a description of nearby Valley Forge National Historical Park. If you want to work off your lunch, try indoor rock climbing at Philadelphia Rock Gym, 422 Business Center (610-666-7673).

Other good beer sites in the area: The multitap Boat House has good food, but drink at the bar. Located in the Great Valley Corporate Center. Take Route 29 North off Route 202, go about a mile to the Center, turn left. See also other good beer sites on page 69.

John Harvard's Brew House, Wayne

629 W. Lancaster Avenue
Wayne
610-687-6565
www.johnharvards.com

John Harvard's Brew Houses have invaded Pennsylvania! The time must have seemed right, because we got three in less than a year. We're not alone. There are fifteen in nine East Coast states so far, and more are on the way. Grenville Byford and Gary Gut started the first Brew House on Harvard Square in Cambridge, Massachusetts in 1992, and the idea has proven to have some serious legs.

The idea is embodied in the company slogan: "Honest food, real beer." The corporate history tells the tale of the young John Harvard watching William Shakespeare brew beer in Southwark, England. We are told that Shakespeare wrote, in addition to his plays and sonnets, a book of brewing recipes that John Harvard brought with him to America in 1637. The book was found in 1992 and is claimed as inspiration for the brewpub's beers. Decide for yourself how "honest and real" the story is.

Don't doubt the sincerity of the slogan, though. The menu is innovative and eclectic, with a number of regional influences. The desserts are excessive, just the way you want them. A few local specialties may show up, but the food varies little from pub to pub.

The pubs have very similar brewing equipment with which they brew the same core beers. Right now, every Brew House is running the very tasty Manchester Alt that won a GABF Gold medal in 1997. Each location has a handpump for serving cask-conditioned versions of the beers.

The Brew Houses exchange recipes and information, a practice the brewers find very helpful. If a brewer runs into a problem, chances are someone else has had the same problem and can offer a solution, or at least some ideas. Brewers can also make some of their own beers, and they are encouraged to tweak the core beers towards local tastes. Brewer Todd Marcus finds his Springfield customers tend to like their beers on the malty side. Chris Rafferty keeps the Wayne brewpub's beers in a hoppy tune.

Even the decor is similar. The three Pennsylvania pubs all have dark wood paneling. The brewhouse is visible from the dining area. There are backlit "stained glass" portraits of Jerry Garcia and JFK in saintly garb and poses. It's not obtrusive, just similar enough to be familiar.

Hardly anyone outside the world of beer geeks seems to be bothered by this "McBrewpub" phenomenon. In fact, these two John Harvard's Brew Houses were named Best of Philadelphia, Best Brewpubs, by *Philadelphia Magazine* in 1997. The Brew Houses I've been to always seem to be at least half full of happy customers who often come up to the brewmaster and compliment him on the beer.

I must confess that when I try to work up a good head of righteous beer geek indignation over this chain brewpub idea, it never lasts longer than half a pint of whatever beer is best at the local Brew House. Would restaurant critics hate McDonald's so much if they served exciting, healthier fare with more flavors than just fat, sugar, and salt? It's a deep philosophical problem, and I intend to ponder it the next time I'm at one of the Brew Houses. Maybe over a pint of that medal-winning Alt.

The Wayne Brew House is in a big comfortably rambling place with a great location right on the Main Line. Brewer Chris Rafferty is a John Harvard's veteran and a Pennsylvania native who runs the brewery side of the pub with a relaxed yet precise hand. His local signature beers tend to be the Belgian styles he's most fond of.

Opened: February 1997.
Type: Brewpub.
Owner: John Harvard's Brew House, Boston.
Brewer: Chris Rafferty.
PA Microbrewers Guild: Not a member.
System: 15-barrel Pub Brewing System brewhouse. Potential annual capacity 3,000 barrels.
Annual production: 2,000+ barrels in 11 months of 1997.
Beers brewed: *Year-round:* All-American Light Lager, John Harvard's Pale Ale, Nut Brown Ale, a rotating fruit-wheat beer, and either a porter or stout. Manchester Alt and Loch Lanier Scottish Ale took gold and silver medals, respectively, for their recipes (GABF 1997), although the winning beers were actually brewed at other John Harvard's locations. *Seasonals:* Mid-Winter Strong Ale, Pres-

idential Ale, Celtic Strong Ale, Big Bad Bock, Crystal Pilsner, Harvard Hefe-Weizen, Summer Ale, Oktoberfest, Harvest Spiced Ale, Christmas Ale. All beers brewed on premises.

The Pick: Choosing John Harvard's Pale Ale is the right thing to do. It may be a standard, a staple, but Chris does it right. The hops and malt are in balance—a distinctively East Coast concept. This is the beer I'd send to brewers in the Pacific Northwest and say to them, "When you get tired of overhopping your beer, try making something like this."

Take-out beer: Half-gallon growlers.

Tours: Tours available during lunch through dinner hours.

Brewpub hours: Seven days a week, 11:30 A.M.–1:30 A.M.

Food: The John Harvard's menu features upscale pub fare including a mixed grill, chicken pot pie, salmon salad, and calamari, plus a few local specials.

Extras: The Brew House has a full liquor license.

Special considerations: Kids welcome. Handicapped-accessible. Cigars allowed. Vegetarian meals available.

Directions: See map on page 71.

Parking: Large on-premises lot, free valet service in the evenings.

Lodging: Radnor Hotel, 591 East Lancaster Avenue, Radnor (610-688-5800); Courtyard by Marriott, 762 West Lancaster Avenue, Wayne (610-687-6633); Wayne Hotel, 139 East Lancaster Avenue, Wayne (610-687-5000).

Nearby attractions: King of Prussia has some massive shopping malls where you'll find the only Nordstrom's in the area and the excellent Gene's Books. There is also plenty of shopping in the sometimes pricey stores along Route 30 through Wayne and Radnor. In May, the Devon Horse Show is the place to rub elbows with the horsey set. See the introduction to this section for a description of nearby Valley Forge National Historical Park.

Other good beer sites in the area: Jake & Oliver's, Bala Cynwyd, is a new branch office of the Philadelphia multitap beer bar. Same idea, different locale. 261 Montgomery Avenue, Bala Cynwyd (610-644-3000). See also other good beer sites on pages 72 and 78.

John Harvard's Brew House, Springfield

1001 Baltimore Pike
Springfield
610-544-4440
www.johnharvards.com

For the John Harvard's story, see the entry for John Harvard's Brew House, Wayne.

The Springfield Brew House is in a strip mall, but it's a nice one, anchored by a Borders bookstore and located right across the street from Springfield Mall. That's perfect positioning for holing up while friends or significant others go shopping!

Brewer Todd Marcus comes to John Harvard's from several years brewing at Long Trail, in Vermont, an excellent, adventurous brewery. He has a penchant for big beers but also has a deft hand with lighter styles like kölsch.

Opened: June 1997.
Type: Brewpub.
Owner: John Harvard's Brew House, Boston.
Brewer: Todd Marcus.
PA Microbrewers Guild: Not a member.
System: 15-barrel Pub Brewing Systems brewhouse. Potential annual capacity 2,000 barrels.
Annual production: No figures available yet.
Beers brewed: *Year-round:* All-American Light Lager, John Harvard's Pale Ale, Nut Brown Ale, a rotating fruit-wheat beer, and either a porter or stout (Pilgrim's Porter was on when I visited). The recipes for Manchester Alt and Loch Lanier Scottish Ale took GABF gold and silver medals in 1997. *Seasonals:* Mid-Winter Strong Ale, Presidential Ale, Celtic Strong Ale, Big Bad Bock, Crystal Pilsner, Harvard Hefe-Weizen, Summer Ale, Oktoberfest, Harvest Spiced Ale, Christmas Ale. All beers brewed on premises.
The Pick: Pilgrim's Porter, as Todd brews it, is a deep, dark secret, a

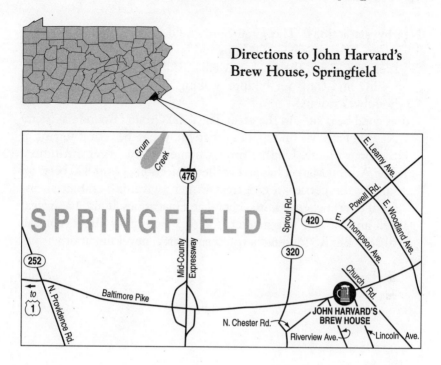

Directions to John Harvard's
Brew House, Springfield

beer that slowly yields more and more to a thoughtful drinker. The process accelerates as the beer warms a bit in the glass. I'd like just a bit more fruitiness in this beer to make it perfect, but it's pretty much excellent as it is.

Take-out beer: Pending.

Tours: Tours available during restaurant hours.

Brewpub hours: Seven days a week, 11:30 A.M.–1:00 A.M.

Food: The John Harvard's menu features upscale pub fare including mixed grill, chicken pot pie, salmon salad, calamari, and a few local specials.

Extras: The Brew House has a full liquor license. There is live music occasionally; call for schedule. They also do a nice Sunday brunch, and have a regular happy hour Monday through Friday, 4:00 P.M.– 8:00 P.M.

Special considerations: Kids welcome. Handicapped-accessible. Cigars allowed (and sold at the bar). Vegetarian meals available.

Parking: Plenty of parking in off-street lot.

Lodging: McIntosh Inn of Media, Routes 1 and 352, Media (610-565-5800).

Nearby attractions: The large Springfield Mall is right across the street. If you prefer small shops and boutiques, there are plenty of them just down the road in Media. Ridley Creek State Park has fishing and trails for biking, walking, cross-country skiing, and horseback riding.

Other good beer sites in the area: The local Ground Round has Sierra Nevada Pale Ale on tap, but otherwise you're better off staying at the Brew House. Upper Darby is home to a real beer institution: The Ashton Market has an excellent selection of over 800 beers for sale by the bottle—a rare treat in Pennsylvania—and an assortment of beer glasses, shirts, books, and magazines. It also has a great deli and bakery. The market is at 121 Springton Street, but call 610-53-BEERS for directions because you'll never find it otherwise.

General Lafayette Inn

646 Germantown Pike
Lafayette Hill
610-941-0600
www.lafayettebrewery.com

Brittingham's Irish Pub on Germantown Pike is a favorite of Owen Hutchins, the brewer at the General Lafayette Inn, and not just because it's only two doors away. "They have a great jar of Guinness!" Owen says happily. Brittingham's is in a building that pre-dates the American Revolution, built in 1744.

Big deal, 1744. Owen says the staff at the General Lafayette call the Brittingham "the new kid on the block." The General Lafayette was built in 1732 and has been a tavern, hotel, or restaurant nearly the whole time. The age of the building is evident in the small rooms and low doorways in the older parts.

This is apparently the building's first incarnation as a brewpub. The front porch has been enclosed in glass to hold the brewhouse and ranked vertical fermenters. It makes quite an arresting display sitting right on the big curve of Germantown Pike. "The staff has a pool on how long it's going to be before someone loses control and plows into the brewery," laughs Owen. He's betting it'll be a long time. "No one's hit this building in a century of automobiles, so I don't think it's going to happen next week."

Informed wagering is one of the benefits of having a long history. A more valuable benefit is obviously the attraction of a truly historic building. At the Inn, that appeal has been enhanced with careful restoration and period decoration. Even the menu reflects in part the eighteenth century origins of the Inn, featuring seafood and shellfish, game, and grains. It sounds like a menu recorded by a diarist in the Continental Congress or on General Washington's staff, perhaps even the young Lafayette himself. When the meals are presented in the older, smaller rooms of the Inn (the Franklin Room seats at most four diners) you get the sense of time rolling back. You're dining in another era.

Your beer, however, you'll want as fresh as last week. Owen was the Delaware Valley Homebrewer of the Year in 1995, and he runs the General Lafayette like a big homebrewery. What does that mean? It means that the place serves pretty much whatever Owen feels like making. Only four of the seven to ten beers on tap at all times are regulars. The rest might include a mad mix of multigrains ("I laugh at four-grain beers," Owen brags, "We make multigrain beer with *fifteen* grains!"). Or you might luck into a small, long-aged batch of Russian Imperial Stout served on the Inn's handpump under natural carbonation. That stout, when I sampled it, was a treat, a rich dessert in a glass.

The only problem the Inn has right now is success. The beer is doing so well that they need to expand the brewery. The plan is to extend the glassed-in porch further around the building. That will make plenty of room for more tanks.

The General Lafayette offers the pleasures of an earlier time combined with the best amenities of the modern age. Stop and savor. Who knows? Perhaps your ancestors did the same 200 years ago.

Opened: January 1997.

Type: Brewpub.

Owners: Mike McGlynn (principal partner), Ken Kaufmann (chef), Jackie O'Neil Cook, Jeff Bill, Owen Hutchins.

Brewer: Owen Hutchins.

PA Microbrewers Guild: Membership pending.

System: 7-barrel DME brewhouse. Potential annual capacity currently 900 barrels; expansion is in progress.

Annual production: 600 barrels in 1997.

Beers brewed: *Year-round:* Germantown Blonde, Barren Hill Bitter, Lafayette's Porter, Innkeeper's Pale Ale. *Seasonals:* Belgian Grand Cru, American Wheat, Multi-grain, English Mild, Belgian Dubbel, Winter Warmer, cask-conditioned Barleywine, Raspberry Mead Ale, Imperial Stout, and others. All beers brewed on premises. Seven to ten beers on tap at all times.

The Pick: Owen's Imperial Stout is a deep, dark treasure of a beer. Owen has nailed this baby. It's like eating dessert. A very adult dessert.

Take-out beer: Half-gallon growlers, half kegs.

Tours: By appointment or by request as possible.

Brewpub hours: Monday through Friday, 11:00 A.M.–2:00 A.M., Saturday and Sunday, 10:00 A.M. (for brunch)–2:00 A.M.

Food: American colonial and regional, with a strong emphasis on game, seafood, and grains. This is an interesting menu with a lot of influences from early Delaware Valley dishes.

Extras: The Inn has a pool table and darts (league play starting in

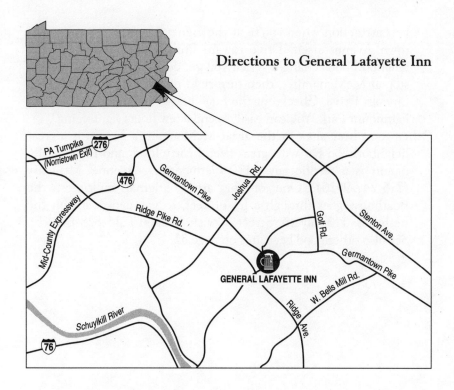

Directions to General Lafayette Inn

1998). There's live music Wednesday and Thursday nights, occasional cigar dinners, and a homebrewers dinner twice a year, with a competition to win the honor of doing a full-scale brew at the Inn. Every other Monday—Tuesdays during football season—the Inn has a Grateful Dead evening.

Special considerations: Kids welcome (special menu). Handicapped access to first floor. Cigars permitted in upstairs cigar lounge and sold at the bar. Vegetarian meals available.

Parking: Large off-street lot.

Lodging: Doubletree Guest Suites, 640 West Germantown Pike (610-834-8300); Chestnut Hill Hotel, 8229 Germantown Pike (215-242-5905); The Inn at King of Prussia, 127 Gulph Road, King of Prussia (800-528-1234).

Nearby attractions: You're not far from Valley Forge National Historical Park, described in the introduction to this section. At Plymouth Meeting Mall, right off Germantown Pike, on the other side of the turnpike, you'll find plenty of good shopping. But the best attraction when you're at the General Lafayette is Germantown Avenue itself. Drive toward Philadelphia and watch the neighborhoods change. When you get down to Mt. Airy, make a stop at McMenamin's, then turn right down the hill and pick up Lincoln Drive. Check out the huge houses before you drive into Fairmount Park. You can easily spend a few hours sightseeing.

Other good beer sites in the area: McMenamin's Tavern is a great neighborhood bar with great beer, hearty food, and P. J. McMenamin is a terrific guy. 7170 Germantown Avenue, Mt. Airy (215-247-9920). One of the area's original multitaps, the Boathouse goes through a lot of beer, so you can count on the freshness. 113 Fayette Street, Conshohocken (215-828-BOAT). See also other good beer sites on page 52.

Buckingham Mountain Brewing Company

5775 Route 202
Lahaska
215-794-7302

Don't expect to bring your pitons and carabiners along for a little rock climbing on Buckingham Mountain before having some beers at the brewpub. The mountain is a gentle fold of ground in this rolling countryside, just high enough to afford a good view of the surrounding farmlands. The most attractive aspect of the site for a brewpub, however, wasn't topographical; it was demographical.

Buckingham Mountain Brewing Company sits at the west end of Peddler's Village, forty-two acres of shops, restaurants, and other ways to separate shoppers from their shekels. Big Ed McGowan and his family figured that the constant stream of people through the shops would be good for some brewpub business, and it looks like they were right. I suspect that many couples make a deal when they visit: shopping now for me, fresh-brewed beer later for you. It might be the best deal in Peddler's Village.

Business was good for a while. But about a year and a half after it opened, Buckingham Mountain had an almost terminal fire. The kitchen was destroyed along with the brewpub's large back deck, which overlooked the long slope of the ridge. Happily, the stainless steel brewing equipment was untouched except for hoses and gaskets.

After a lot of sweat and strained muscles and wallets, the brewpub reopened almost exactly two years after its first opening. Buckingham Mountain rose from the ashes with a larger upstairs dining room, expanded into what used to be the deck. Appropriately, Ed has recently done some beers with names like Phoenix and Backdraft.

The beer at Buckingham is a moving target. Ed brews something new at the drop of a brewer's boot. The seasonals listed in this book are just the ones he's done lately. Some are one-shots, some make return appearances by popular demand. It boils down to this: Ed has fun. That's obvious with names like Tannen Bomb, one of my favorite brewpub beer names ever.

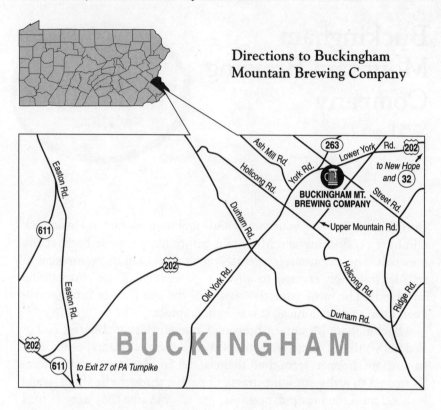

Directions to Buckingham Mountain Brewing Company

You pass the fermenters as you enter Buckingham Mountain, and the brewhouse is tucked in off to your left. The serving tanks sit behind the high-ceilinged bar. There is a striking neon shamrock on the high wall back of the barstools. The McGowans are proud of their Irish roots.

Be sure to get something to eat. The food is fresh and delicious, with a number of innovatively spiced dishes and traditional area favorites. If you get a burger, get some of the locally packaged horse-radish to go with it. You may also want to try the soft pretzels if you're sitting at the bar; they're the best beer-drinking food around.

Buckingham Mountain is all about relaxed good times and conversations with friends. It truly is a good place to hole up after a hard day of shopping, to refresh your palate and revive your spirit.

Opened: September 1995 (closed due to fire February 12, 1997, reopened September 1997).
Type: Brewpub.

Owners: The McGowan family.

Brewer: Ed McGowan.

PA Microbrewers Guild: Not a member.

System: 10-barrel Pub Brewing Systems brewhouse. Potential annual capacity 1,500 barrels.

Annual production: 850 barrels in 1996.

Beers brewed: *Year-round:* Hermit Albert's Pale Ale, Wolf Rocks Amber, Liam's Lager, Ed's Red, Pighouse Porter, GannaSee Ale, Slaughter House Stout. *Seasonals:* Falldown Fest, Tannen Bomb, Jingle Your Bells Desperation Ale, Holiday Honey Brown, Winter Wheat, Jonathan Sebastian Bock. All beers brewed on premises.

The Pick: Ed's Pighouse Porter is the winner here. It's dark and full with a toffeelike sweetness that has a nice little undercurl of molasses to it. Good cold-weather beer for long nights . . . particularly if you're staying at the Inn out front!

Take-out beer: Half kegs and half-gallon growlers.

Tours: On request.

Brewpub hours: Monday through Thursday, 11:30 A.M.–midnight; Friday and Saturday, noon–1:00 A.M.; Sunday, noon–10:00 P.M.

Food: Buckingham Mountain presents an upscale, well-crafted bar menu. Tuesdays are Burger Special Days featuring, for $2.50, large, juicy burgers with your choice of six cheeses on a big fresh kaiser roll. Get the horseradish to go with it; it's local and fiery delicious.

Extras: Full liquor license. Darts.

Special considerations: Kids welcome. Handicapped-accessible.

Parking: Plenty of off-street parking available.

Lodging: The Inn at Lahaska, a country inn right in front of the brewpub, offers "brews and snooze" packages (215-794-0440); Golden Plough Inn, Route 202 and Street Road (215-794-4004); Red Roof Oxford Valley, I-95 and Oxford Valley Road (215-750-6200).

Nearby attractions: Next-door Peddler's Village is a 42-acre complex of shops and boutiques, a favorite shopping destination for the area. Another favorite, about two miles from the brewery, is Rice's Market, a long-running (since the 1920s) flea market open every Tuesday, rain, snow, or shine. Lahaska also has the Carousel World, a carousel museum with a working carousel available for rides. Buckingham Valley Vineyards is just three miles south of Buckingham on Route 413 (the intersection is west of the brewpub on Route 202) and has an interesting self-guided tour and a tasting room (215-794-7188). East of Lahaska on Route 202 is New Hope on the Delaware River, home of the Bucks County

Playhouse (215-862-2041) and an amazing plethora of shops and restaurants. New Hope is a favorite strolling spot; parking can be tough. Washington Crossing Historic Park is just downstream from New Hope by way of a pleasant drive along the river. In warm weather, Sesame Place is very attractive for young children. Big Bird's theme park (which is owned by Anheuser-Busch, by the way) is only fifteen minutes south of Lahaska in Oxford Valley.

Other good beer sites in the area: Mugs is a good multitap, at 211 South Main Street in Doylestown. The upscale but comfortable Inn of the Hawk in Lambertville, New Jersey, has a number of good taps. Take the first right across the bridge from New Hope then go left at the end of the street. Take a tour of the River Horse Brewery at 80 Lambert Lane in Lambertville. It's just a walk across the bridge from New Hope. Isaac Newton's, my local bar, has seventeen outstanding taps including a handpump, two Belgian taps, and two nitro taps, and good selection of Belgian bottles. Find it off the town parking lot in the middle of Newtown (215-860-5100).

A word about . . .

Ales and Lagers

If you're going to go to the breweries in this book, you'll have to know how to talk shop with the bartenders and tourguides and not embarrass yourself on the tour. First off, *beer* is any fermented beverage made from malted barley, usually with an addition of hops. The two main types of beer are *ales* and *lagers*.

What's the difference between the two? It's quite simple: two different yeasts. These have a number of small differences, the most important of which is that the optimum temperature for fermentation and aging is higher for ale yeasts (in the 60s F) than for lager yeasts (in the 40s F).

That's more than just a thermostat setting. The warmer operating temperature of ale yeast encourages a faster, more vigorous fermentation that creates aromatic compounds known as *phenols* and *esters*. These can give ale-fermented beers aromas such as melon, banana, raisin, clove, and vanilla. (I call these aromas "alefruit.")

On the other hand, the cooler lager fermentation produces a very clean aroma and flavor palette. Lagers generally have purer malt and hop characteristics. A lager brewer will tell you that there's nowhere to hide when you make lager beer; the unadorned nature of the beer makes flaws stand out immediately.

I like to think of the two yeasts in terms of jungles and pine forests. Warm ale fermentations are like lush jungles—exotic arrays of flavors, splendid in their diversity. By comparison, cold lager fermentations are more like northern pine forests—intense, focused, and pure.

Among small brewers in America, ale brewers outnumber lager brewers by over ten to one. Given that lagers are by far the most popular beers in the world, how did this come to be? Tom Pastorius of Penn Brewing puts it quite simply: "More ale is being made because it's cheaper, easier, and more flexible." Hard words, perhaps, but the facts bear them out.

After lagers are fermented, they undergo an extended aging period of at least three weeks at low temperatures. The cooling and the tank-time required add energy costs and decrease turnover. In the same amount of time, it would be possible to put twice as much ale through those tanks. Add the energy and labor costs of the more complicated decoction brewing process used for lagers, and you wind up with a product that costs substantially more to brew than ales but has to be priced the same. No wonder there are more ale brewers!

When it comes to lager, Pennsylvania has been blessed. Five craft breweries—Franconia, Penn, Red Bell, Stoudt's, and Victory—make excellent lagers, as do our six surviving regional lager brewers. A number of brewpubs produce at least some lagers. By any measure, these breweries include some of the very best lager brewers in the country. How did we get so lucky?

In a word, ethnicity. It's no coincidence that the areas of the United States where old brewers survived and new lager brewers sprang up are those that welcomed vast numbers of German, Scandinavian, and Eastern European immigrants. Where those lager-lovers settled—Pennsylvania, upstate New York, Wisconsin, and Minnesota—is where lager brewing thrives today.

American beer enthusiasts are slowly coming around to microbrewed lagers. Carol Stoudt attributes their hesitation to a megabrew backlash: "People who have had nothing but bland lagers for years want the extremes: heavy-handed hops, fruit beers, even smoked beers. As their palates become more sophisticated, they'll come around to appreciate the subtleties of a good lager beer." If you haven't had some of Pennsylvania's fine fresh lager beers, be sure to put one or more of these brewers on your list. Put a little sophistication on your palate!

Pennsylvania Dutch (Beer) Country

Most people think of Lancaster County alone as Pennsylvania Dutch country, thanks to the county's busy tourist bureau! There are indeed a lot of Amish farms and "Dutchie" accents in Lancaster, but you'll find them up through Lebanon and Berks Counties as well, and on into the Lehigh Valley. This is my home territory. I was born and raised in Lancaster County, like all my family since 1741, so I'm a bit nuts about the place.

The small cities of the area—Lancaster, Reading, Allentown, Bethlehem, and Easton—were at first market towns. They became industrial towns, and now they are finding their own ways in the shifting economy of the late twentieth century. All of them have come to realize that their heritage is bankable, so you will find them eager to please tourists. Lancaster, of course, has been this way for years, but Reading and the towns of the Lehigh Valley also have learned the art of promotion and the value of tourism.

This is Pennsylvania's breadbasket. Watered by rivers like the Schuylkill, Conestoga, and Lehigh, small farms cover the landscape, producing milk, fruit, vegetables, soybeans, and even cigar tobacco.

There are some fine restaurants here, serving everything from nouvelle cuisine to massive, multicourse "Pennsylvania hotel" dinners. The regional fare is hearty and simple with farmboy's delights such as chicken pot pie, dripping with gravy and freighted with great raftlike noodles, and molasses and cake-filled shoofly pies.

You'll also find good beer here, thanks to some great little breweries. Carol and Ed Stoudt started things in northern Lancaster County back in 1987 with Pennsylvania's first microbrewery in modern times. They have since been joined by a bevy of brewers, all making fine products. True to their heritage, some of them brew German-style lager beers and the local population laps it up.

Visiting these breweries will give you an opportunity to take a leisurely drive through gently rolling hills and past beautifully kept farms. One of my favorite drives is to head east from New Holland on Route 23, along the ridge through the Twin Valley area to Morgantown. You can also take a shopping trip from the factory outlets along Route 30 in Lancaster up Route 222 to the factory outlets in Reading. (Camelot Brewing is very conveniently located near Reading's VF Outlet Village, and Stoudt's is just off Route 222!)

Of course, there is also the attraction of the Amish themselves. They live among us "English," as the Amish call all people outside the faith, but they strive to keep themselves separate. Please respect their privacy. While the Amish of Lancaster County are more worldly than some of their brethren in upstate New York or Indiana, they still try to live in accordance with their beliefs. There are plenty of Amish attractions; some are better than others. The Amish Farm and House is one of the more accurate ones, on Route 30 east of Lancaster (717-394-6185).

There are two other areas in Pennsylvania Dutch country that you should visit. The high bluffs on the lower Susquehanna near Holtwood Dam are breathtakingly beautiful in spring and fall. Trails there range from easy strolls by Pequea Creek along old trolley beds to soaring climbs that challenge the experienced day hiker.

Far to the east is the Delaware River, curving quietly with gentle splendor through some of the prettiest countryside in Pennsylvania. Taking a drive along the Delaware is a wonderful way to spend the afternoon.

Wherever you go in Pennsylvania Dutch country, take your time; the pace is wonderfully slow here. You'll find plenty to see, lots of shops to visit, and countless back roads to explore. You may come for the Amish, but be sure to take a look around. You'll be back for the beauty.

Lancaster Malt
Brewing Company

Plum and Walnut Streets
Lancaster
717-391-MALT

Lancaster Malt Brewing Company is
a brewpub with a seasoned brewer
and a top-notch brewing system. It's a microbrewery with some beautifully packaged, hot-selling products. It's a restaurant with delicious,
fresh food prepared by an innovative chef. It is all these things, which
makes it a delightful place to stop and enjoy a few hours of beer-sip-
ping while you're touring Lancaster's Amish country.

Lancaster Malt Brewing (LMB) is the brainchild of Mike
Oehrlein, an energetic, buoyant, live wire of a guy, who has built up a
very attractive and successful brewpub. LMB opened in April of 1995
in a renovated tobacco warehouse. The historic brick building has dark
wood floors, massive wooden beams, high, intricate brick ceilings, and
copper accents. The warehouse works well as a showcase for LMB
beers. The bar and the casual dining area wrap around an open drop to
the attractive 15-barrel JV Northwest brewhouse below, an interesting
change from the usual behind-the-bar setup.

The brewer down there is Christian Heim, a graduate of America's
premier brewing school, the Siebel Institute of Chicago. Christian
worked as an assistant brewer at the now-closed Happy Valley brewpub
in State College, then moved on to work in quality control at Pittsburgh
Brewing. He's a self-effacing, open person with a deft and subtle hand for
brewing. The beers at LMB never overwhelm, and rarely disappoint.

Brewing in Lancaster is a natural. The county once had fourteen
breweries and was known nationwide as a brewing center. H. L.
Mencken favored beer from the city's Rieker Star Brewery. Lancaster
beers sold for $10 a keg in Boston in the 1940s, a princely sum for beer.
But the last brewery went silent in 1956, and local folks drank other
people's beer for thirty-nine years.

Locally made beer has made a comeback with LMB, but is this a
microbrewery or a brewpub? "The brewpub is a marketing tool for the
microbrewery," explains Oehrlein. "It will always be secondary to the
microbrewery. We get a lot of tourists through here because of the

draw of Lancaster County. They try the beer, and when they get home, they see it, or they ask for it."

Of course, one thing they won't find at home is the food. LMB's chef, Mike's son Fred, builds innovative and delicious fare on a rock-solid foundation of kitchen competence. The menu features a raw bar, burgers, deli sandwiches, salads, and full-blown entrees. At least a quarter of the menu has been developed with the help of Lancaster's Mid-Atlantic Heart Institute to be heart-healthy, which is possibly a first for a brewpub. It's certainly healthy for LMB. "We're doing as well as any restaurant in the city," says Mike.

LMB has revived Lancaster's old tradition of brewing. With Oehrlein's drive and enthusiastic cheer, the local beer should be around for a long time.

Opened: April 1995.
Type: Brewery and brewpub.
Owner: Mike Oehrlein.
Brewer: Christian Heim.
PA Microbrewers Guild: Member.
System: 15-barrel JV Northwest brewhouse. Potential annual capacity 8,000 barrels.
Annual production: 3,000 barrels in 1996.
Beers brewed: *Year-round:* Golden Ale, Red Rose Amber, Plum Street Porter, Milk Stout. *Seasonals:* Strawberry Wheat, Spring Bock, Hefe' Wheat, Pilsner, Harvest Ale, Oktoberfest, Maple Cranberry Ale, Winter Warmer. All beers brewed on premises.
The Pick: The Milk Stout is a sweet stout that is still somewhat roasty, a drink refreshing yet rich. It's a prime example of Christian Heim's mastery of the subtleties of brewing. My wife would walk over my back to get this beer. The new Winter Warmer, a malty powerpack, is worth a look, too.
Take-out beer: Six-packs, cases.
Tours: Daily 10:00 A.M.–5:00 P.M.
Brewpub hours: Open Monday through Thursday 11:30 A.M.–11:00 P.M.; Friday and Saturday, 11:30 A.M.–midnight; Sunday 11:00 A.M.–10:30 P.M.
Food: LMB is one of the busiest restaurants in Lancaster, and a popular spot for private parties. It features a full menu with plentiful seasonal specials. There are a number of heart-healthy items developed with the assistance of Lancaster's Mid-Atlantic Heart

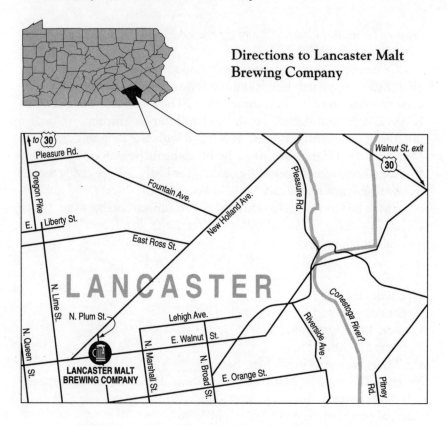

Institute. Consider indulging in the Porter Float, a delicious scoop of vanilla ice cream in a glass of Plum Street Porter. Don't make that face; it's good! A bit more challenging is LMB's Oyster Shooter: a small glass containing Porter, a dash of hot sauce, and a whole raw oyster. Screw up your courage and try it. It's delicious.

Extras: There is a dart board, and backgammon and chess-checkers boards are built into the bar tables. Live music (acoustic and electric) on Fridays.

Events: There are special menus and entertainment for Mardi Gras and Oktoberfest, and also quarterly cigar dinners. Call for information.

Special considerations: Kids welcome (special menu). Restaurant is handicapped-accessible, but access to the brewery is limited. Cigars are allowed in the bar area, and LMB has a selection of fine cigars for sale. Vegetarian and specially prepared meals are available.

Parking: LMB has a small lot on Plum Street. Street parking can get tight at times.

Lodging: Holiday Inn Host Resort, 2300 Lincoln Highway East

(717-299-5500); Travelodge, 2101 Columbia Avenue (717-397-4201 or 800-578-7878); Gardens of Eden B&B, 1894 Eden Road (717-393-5179); The King's Cottage B&B, 1049 East King Street (717-397-1017 or 800-747-8717).

Nearby attractions: Call the Pennsylvania Dutch Visitor's Bureau (717-299-8901) to get a large package of literature about their many attractions. Lancaster's selection of factory outlets rivals Reading's these days. You'll find most of them on Route 30 east of Lancaster. Reading China and Glass in Rockvale Center has cheap pint glasses and sometimes sells "yards of ale" glasses. Wheatland, the home of James Buchanan, Pennsylvania's admittedly not-very-notable contribution to the Presidency, is a beautifully restored Federal-era mansion with original furniture. 1120 Marietta Avenue (717-392-8721). For tubers, a float down the Pequea Creek is a great way to cool off in the sticky heat of a Lancaster summer. You can rent tubes at Sickman's Mill (717-872-5951) in Marticville. Take old sneakers and don't wear a white suit; the river's muddy sometimes! Just north of Ephrata, the Green Dragon Farmers Market and Auction is open every Friday, with a livestock auction, food stands, and more interesting people than you can shake a shoofly pie at. Don't forget to stop by the Julius Sturgis Pretzel House in Lititz for their tour. 219 East Main Street (717-626-4354). Then walk over to the Wilbur Chocolate Company. 48 North Broad Street (717-626-3249).

Other good beer sites in the area: McFly's is a sprawling multitap, where most of Lancaster's beer geeks who aren't at LMB tend to show up. 10 South Prince Street (717-299-3456). The Reading beer sites described in this section are less than an hour away. See also other good beer sites on page 102.

Summy House and Prussian Street Brewing Company

31-35 South Main Street
Manheim
717-664-3333

Scott Bowser is the owner and chef at the Summy House restaurant in Manheim. When I asked him why he stuffed a 3.5-barrel brewery into a tiny space in the Summy House, he laughed and said "I needed an excuse to get out of the kitchen for a while!"

Scott has been cooking since he was sixteen, so his desire is understandable, but there's more to it than that. He's been homebrewing since he was in college. "When I bought this place, I wanted to put a brewery in," Scott recalls. "But it's not to make money. It's not about money at all. I just wanted to brew and to give the restaurant a little something special."

The Summy House has been a restaurant or hotel since it was built in 1876. Scott claims that at one time it was a house of ill repute. My mother, a lifelong Lancaster County resident, confirms that she has heard stories to that effect. Whatever it may have been in the past, when Scott bought it in May of 1995, it was closed. "Defunct," says Scott.

Building business strictly on word of mouth and Scott's good cooking, sales in 1996 were double those of 1995. The Summy House still doesn't advertise, but it has benefited from a number of local awards, including one for "best-kept secret."

With the small system he has, Scott is limited to producing enough beer for the restaurant to sell. That's his only customer. The restaurant and the brewery are separate businesses (as was required by an old Pennsylvania law, which has since been changed). Scott brews the beer, then runs over to the restaurant, puts on his restaurant manager hat, and buys it from the brewery. Neat and tidy, a legal business transaction. "I get paid right away as the brewer, too!" laughs Scott.

Although Scott has years of experience as a homebrewer, the "brewing big leagues"—even at this modest production level—are a different story. "I went into this blind," he admits, "but I've only had to dump one batch. I use a lot of Old World brewing techniques that are a bit more labor-intensive, but they work."

The beer has won local acceptance. Scott says it is now thought of as "Manheim's beer." He hopes to spread that identity to another town: "I'm thinking about opening a place in Lancaster, someplace where you can get fresh-brewed beer at a cheaper price. That's the kind of market we have around here."

It sounds like Scott Bowser has his finger on the pulse of Manheim, and maybe Lancaster too. If he can buck the trend and expand his operations, that should keep him out of the kitchen altogether.

Opened: January 1997.

Type: Brewpub.

Owners: Scott Bowser, Thomas Drennen.

Brewers: Scott Bowser, Thomas Drennen.

PA Microbrewers Guild: Not a member.

System: 3.5-barrel REC Industries brewhouse. Potential annual capacity 600 barrels.

Annual production: 262 barrels in 1997.

Beers brewed: *Year-round:* Grant Street Golden, Susquehanna Amber Ale, Stiegel Street Stout, Back Street ESB. *Seasonals:* Pumpkin Ale, IPA, Spice Holiday Ale, Hefe-weizen, Raspberry Brown Ale. All beers brewed on premises.

The Pick: The ESB was the pick of the litter: round in the mouth, malty, and possessed of a good firm hop bitterness.

Take-out beer: Growlers (glass or plastic half gallons), 22-ounce swingtop bottles.

Tours: Upon request, when possible. It's a short tour; the entire brewery is in 265 square feet of space.

Brewpub hours: Monday, 4:00 P.M.–11:00 P.M.; Tuesday through Saturday, 11:00 A.M.–1:00 A.M.; closed Sunday.

Food: Brewer Scott Bowser is also the chef. The food ranges from club sandwiches to steak and lobster, an innovative New American cuisine menu.

Extras: Live acoustic music every other week; call for schedule.

Special considerations: Kids welcome. Vegetarians meals available. Handicapped-accessible.

Parking: Two lots out back. On-street parking a block away on the Square.

Lodging: Quality Inn and Suites, 2363 Oregon Pike, Lancaster (717-569-6479); Manheim Manor, 140 South Charlotte Street, Man-

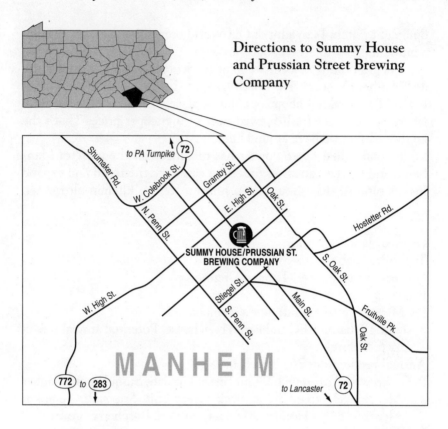

Directions to Summy House
and Prussian Street Brewing
Company

heim (717-664-4168); Rose Manor English B&B, 124 South Linden Street, Manheim (717-664-4932).

Nearby attractions: Manheim has several antique shops and the Manheim Historical Society Museum at 210 South Charlotte Street (717-664-3486). Go east to Lititz to learn how to make a pretzel at the Julius Sturgis Pretzel House. 219 East Main Street (717-626-4354). The Wilbur Chocolate Company is just a short walk from there at 48 North Broad Street (717-626-3249). Route 501 North from Lititz to Shaefferstown is one of the prettiest drives in Lancaster County. You might want to stop at Big Jake's in Shaefferstown for an exceptional breakfast. Leave the diet at home and get a grilled sticky bun and the Big Jake's Special.

Other good beer sites in the area: See other good beer sites on page 95.

Stoudt's Brewing Company

Route 272
Adamstown
717-484-4386

Carol Stoudt is a pioneer. When she founded Pennsylvania's first microbrewery in 1987, she was one of the country's few female brewers. She followed her own course, brewing the German-style lagers she and her husband, Ed, adored. She set high standards and met them. Stoudt's is one of the winningest breweries in the history of the Great American Beer Festival (GABF), with a total of twenty medals and an unbroken streak of at least one medal at each festival since 1988.

I remember being at a tasting of Belgian beers with Carol and Ed just before they left for a long tour of Belgium a few years back. They didn't know a lot of technical information about Belgian beers, but they knew they liked what they tasted. Carol came back from Belgium ("With a full beer notebook!" she says) and started the wheels turning. Now Stoudt's Abbey Triple is one of the best American Abbey-style brews around.

Stoudt's doesn't brew a huge amount of beer; it is definitely still a micro. The effect that Carol and her brewery have always had on the industry, however, is macro. She makes good beer. The Stoudts don't hold with average; they want the best.

The Great Eastern Invitational Microbrewery Festival lives up to this standard. Carol and Ed host the event, which has grown to three festivals each summer. They are not the biggest; each session is limited to 1,200 people. However, most people consider them the best beer fests on the East Coast. The brewers are well taken care of, and they are easily accessible to visitors. Carol and Ed try to make it fun for everyone.

The brewery hall at Stoudt's is a spacious roofed area with a small open courtyard. When you enter it, two things are clear. First, signs of the Stoudts' German heritage are proudly displayed. Coats of arms from German cities and provinces adorn the walls. Trestle tables enhance the "permanent tent" beer hall aura of the place. Second, the Stoudts have willingly embraced the idea that the beer hall can be a place for the whole family. Children are welcome at the Bavarian Beer Festivals that fill the hall on weekends in July, August, and October.

These are not sloppy, beat-the-clock swill fests, but rather a time for people to enjoy good company in the warm glow of a few mugs of festbier and the comfort of a plate of wurst and potato salad. As the accordion plays and feet stamp the dance floor, you can forget the world outside in the happy whirl of skirts, a beer, and a cigar.

It's not your average beer fest, but Carol Stoudt's not your average brewer. She makes whatever suits her fancy. "We keep experimenting. I guess we're one step above some crazy homebrewer," she laughs. "At our size, our beers need to be assertive. They need to stand out. If you aren't making aggressive beers, then you're trying to compete with the bigger, broader-market breweries. People keep talking about a shakeout in the microbrewery section. It's coming, and the survivors will be the ones making assertive beers."

Pioneer spirit—that's what's kept Carol going since 1987. Her microbrewery was Pennsylvania's first, and she's making sure it remains one of Pennsylvania's best.

Established: May 1987.
Type: Brewery.
Owner: Carol Stoudt.
Brewers: Marc Worona, Jonathan Matson, Brett Kintzer.
PA Microbrewers Guild: Member.
System: 30 barrel Century/Criveller brewhouse. Potential annual capacity 8,000 barrels.
Annual production: 4,600 barrels in 1996, plus additional contracted at The Lion.
Beers brewed: *Year-Round:* American Pale Ale, Abbey Double, Abbey Triple, Scarlet Lady ESB, Fat Dog Stout, Pilsner (four GABF medals), Gold (five GABF medals), Fest (two GABF medals), Bock (two GABF medals), Mai-Bock (three GABF medals and an honorable mention), Double Bock (GABF medal). *Seasonal:* Weizen (two GABF medals), Weizenbock, Spiced Ale, Holiday Bocks. 765-milliliter bottles and draft beer brewed on premises; 12-ounce bottles contract-brewed at The Lion.
The Pick: Just look at all those GABF medals! This is a tough call, but for me it has to be the Weizen. Ever since 1995 Stoudt's has nailed this beer solidly. It is richly refreshing, with classic clove and banana aromas and swirling flavors of peach and red plum. An

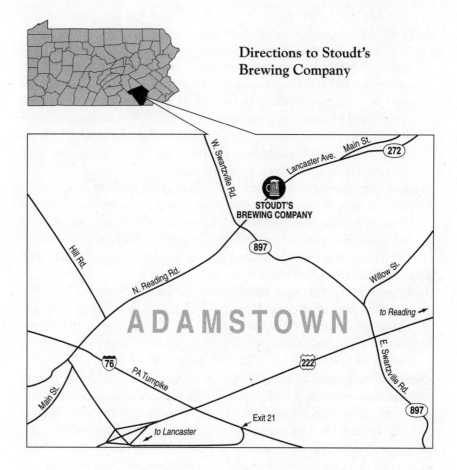

Directions to Stoudt's Brewing Company

unmatched after-the-fest beer. Abbey Triple is a powerful runner-up with its spicy, creamy, authentic profile.

Take-out beer: Four-packs (765-milliliter bottles), twelve-pack cases, and kegs. Not every beer is always available. All 765-milliliter bottles are unpasteurized and must be kept refrigerated.

Tours: Saturday at 3:00 P.M., Sunday at 1:00 P.M.

Brewpub hours: Monday through Thursday, 4:30 P.M.–11:00 P.M.; Friday and Saturday, noon–11:00 P.M.; Sunday, noon–9:00 P.M.

Food: Light fare at the pub—soup, sandwiches, and munchies. The *bockwurst* is exceptional! There's fine dining at the adjacent Black Angus restaurant, which is owned by Carol's husband, Ed Stoudt.

Extras: The country dancing nights and Bavarian Beer Festivals feature a variety of bands. Call ahead for bands and schedules. The Black Angus restaurant has a full liquor license.

Events: There's country dancing in the brewery hall every Friday and Sunday night starting at 6:30 (ages 21 and up). Great Eastern Invitational Microbrewery Festivals are in summer and fall (call for schedule and tickets). The Bavarian Beer Festival takes place in July and August (Saturdays starting at 5:00, Sundays starting at 2:00), and in October (Sundays starting at 2:00). On the five Sundays before Christmas, the Beer Hall becomes a traditional German *Christkindlsmarkt,* selling antique toys and Christmas items, and serving German holiday specialty foods.

Special considerations: In the brewery hall, kids are welcome except for Friday and Saturday nights, when there's country dancing (21 and up). The hall is handicapped-accessible, and cigars are allowed. The Black Angus restaurant is also handicapped-accessible. There is a special children's menu and cigars are allowed.

Parking: There is plenty of parking in the big side lot.

Lodging: Holiday Inn Lancaster County, Route 272, Denver (717-336-7541); Black Forest Inn, Route 272, Adamstown (717-484-0122); Adamstown Inn, 62 West Main Street, Adamstown (717-484-0800). Camping is available at Shady Grove Campground, Route 897, just north on Route 272, Adamstown (717-484-4225).

Nearby attractions: The antiques markets in Adamstown (including one in the same compound as the brewery) are regionally renowned. Stoudtburg, a planned European-style community started by the Stoudts, is an experimental shopping and living area behind the Black Angus complex. The Stoudts have constructed and sold buildings to artisans, who set up shops on the first floor and live on the second floor, much like in European towns. The Reading and Lancaster factory outlet stores are within easy driving distance. A guided tour of the restored buildings at the Ephrata Cloister gives tourists insight into a communal religious society founded in the 1730s. 632 Main Street, Ephrata (717-733-6600). The Green Dragon Farmer's Market and Auction takes place every Friday just north of Ephrata, where the area's Amish and Mennonite farmers mingle with antique hunters and grocery shoppers, while the song of the livestock auctioneer lifts over the din of the crowd.

Other good beer sites in the area: The Alpenhof, a traditional German *gasthaus*-type restaurant with a good stock of German beers, is two miles south of Shillington on Route 10 (610-373-1624.) Alexander's is an exceptional German deli and pizzeria at the east end of Pricetown Road in New Jerusalem that has seven outrageous taps and a selection of more than 200 bottled beers (610-682-2415). See also other good beer sites on pages 95 and 108.

Camelot Brewing Company

220 North Park Road
Reading
610-371-7700
www.camelot-ale.com

Long live the King! I half expect
someone to be shouting acclaim as I enter Camelot. The design intent
was to make the brewery resemble a medieval castle. It has succeeded
to varying degrees. The front doors are solidly built wood with sword-
styled handles, the bricked brewkettles have been given decorative
crenellations, and there is a colorful mural on one wall. The main dining room does suffer a bit from a dark, high ceiling. The unbroken
breadth of the room gives it a somewhat cavernous feel.

You forget that at the bar. There, the ceiling is lower, the brewhouse
is right before you in all its glory, and the taps, the taps are calling.

The beers needed only a little tuning up when I stopped in, six
weeks after opening. The business and technical support that Pugsley
Partners supplies enables brewpubs like Camelot to have good beer
right out of the gate. Alan Pugsley also provides the brewpubs with the
distinctive and robust Ringwood yeast. The use of Ringwood yeast can
make beers from different brewers similar, but always very good.

The Light Ale is pretty much perfect as is: quenching, dry, and
light in body. The Dry Irish Stout is almost ready for the big leagues, a
fine pint of black beer. The IPA is a bit unsettled but shows a lot of
potential, and the Pale Ale is a good standard Ringwood Pale. I hate
commenting on a brewpub this young, but given the track record of
Pugsley Partners, these beers will be sharp and in top form by the time
you read this.

Owner Vince Parisi has set up a very comfortable cigar lounge,
which is the only room where cigar smoking is allowed. Overstuffed
leather armchairs and couches create a smoker's haven that will be
hard to leave. Parisi has added an interesting personal touch; he sells
Camelot's own brand of cigars, made at a local cigar factory from
tobacco that's been steeped in Camelot's stout. That's got to be a
smoky smoke!

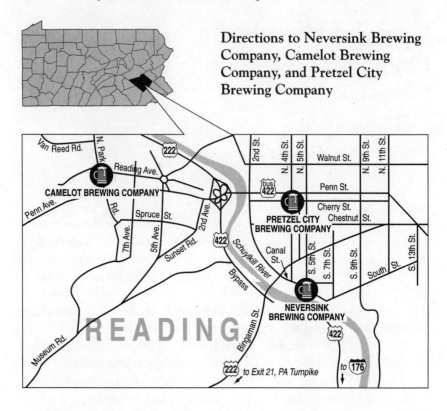

Directions to Neversink Brewing Company, Camelot Brewing Company, and Pretzel City Brewing Company

The location of Camelot is a huge draw for many people. Sited just over the bridge from the VF outlets, it's perfect for nonshoppers who simply want to sip from their own personal holy grail while someone else goes on a shopping quest.

Opened: October 1997.

Type: Brewpub.

Owner: Privately held corporation.

Brewers: Vince Parisi, Joe Klemmer, Matt Nuemeyer.

PA Microbrewers Guild: Not a member.

System: 25-barrel Pugsley Partners brewhouse. Potential annual capacity 10,000 barrels.

Annual production: No figures available yet.

Beers brewed: *Year-round:* Stonehenge Light Ale, Holy Grail Pale Ale, St. Patrick's Dry Irish Stout, IPA. *Seasonals:* Christmas Spice Ale, Honey Oatmeal Stout. All beers brewed on premises.

The Pick: St. Patrick's Dry Irish Stout. Pugsley system brewpubs almost always hit the ground running, and this was good beer less than two months after opening. It presents that paradox of the dryly malty beer: How can it taste so good, and quench your thirst, yet still leave you hankering for another as soon as you finish it?

Take-out beer: Growlers and kegs.

Tours: "Almost any time, upon request."

Brewpub hours: Sunday through Thursday, 11:00 A.M.–9:00 P.M.; Friday and Saturday, 11:00 A.M.–10:00 P.M. The bar will stay open until 2:00 A.M. on Friday and Saturday nights to accommodate bar customers already in the pub.

Food: Camelot's Cordon Bleu-trained chef has created a menu that has both English fare like bangers and mash and American standards like steaks and seafood. You won't come away from a meal hungry.

Extras: Separate cigar lounge with overstuffed armchairs and humidor.

Special considerations: Kids welcome. Handicapped-accessible.

Parking: Plenty of free parking.

Lodging: Country Inn & Suites, 405 North Park Road, Wyomissing (610-373-4444); Econo Lodge, 635 Spring Street, Wyomissing (610-378-5105); The Inn at Reading, 1040 Park Road, Wyomissing (610-372-7811); 9-Patch B&B, 726 Penn Avenue, West Reading (610-372-2711).

Nearby attractions: Let's be realistic. If you're at Camelot, you're in Reading for the outlets. Camelot is a two-minute walk from the VF Outlet Village. You can also shop at the Reading Outlet Center between Windsor and Douglass Streets, Reading Station at 951 North Sixth Street, and Designers Place, 801 Hill Avenue. See also nearby attractions on page 108.

Other good beer sites in the area: See other good beer sites on page 108.

Neversink Brewing Company

545 Canal Street
Reading
610-376-9996

Reading has always been a German
town. German immigrants worked in its factories along the Schuylkill
River. When I was growing up near there, some of the Reading
churches still held services in German. And German traditions, of
course, mean beer. Reading was home to a number of breweries, all of
which eventually died out. When that happened, German-Americans
took to drinking national brands and Yuengling like the rest of us. Few
would have thought that Reading would become a brewing town again.

Now there are three breweries in the city, and one of them, Neversink, is brewing lagers like its German forebears. It's enough to bring
a tear to a Dutchman's eye and a thirst to his throat. It has also been
more than enough to bring folks down to Canal Street in droves.

The Canal Street Pub is a lofty place filling the first floor of the
huge old Reading Hardware building. Original massive wood beams run
in pairs across the ceiling of the pub. This is a place for conversation
and laughter over a sandwich and a good lager beer. Those interested in
a more formal experience can walk through the pub to the dining room,
where white linen tablecloths and a wine bar with twenty wines by the
glass set the tone.

Neversink Brewing Company and the Canal Street Pub are actually separate businesses with separate addresses. The two, however, are
very close; you can see the top of the brewhouse poking up through the
floor in the front of the pub. Creating the pub to serve Neversink's beer
was a neat little stratagem to get around sections of the Pennsylvania
Liquor Code that forbade brewpubs from serving anything but those
malt beverages brewed on premises. Of course, the law changed just
before the pub and brewery opened. Oh, Pennsylvania, you trickster!

Neversink has enjoyed some critical acclaim when it has ventured
beyond the Canal Street Pub. They were very well received—the hit
of the show—at the Penn Fest in Pittsburgh in 1997.

The beers are almost all balanced toward malt rather than hops.
The IPA, dry-hopped with East Kent Goldings hops, is an exception.

But even it has only 36 IBU, which would be scarcely a tickle for a Pacific Northwest beer drinker. With all the other breweries around, though, who needs yet another hoppy beer? Neversink has found a popular niche with its malty, sometimes massive beers.

The food is exceptionally delicious, whether at the bar or in the dining room. Something as simple as clam chowder or chicken salad becomes an opportunity for the kitchen to excel. Reading's business and professional people have certainly discovered the place. I remember sitting at the bar one afternoon as a constant stream of judges, general contractors, and bankers walked into the place for lunch.

The brewery's name was inspired by the ridge behind Mt. Penn, Neversink Mountain. The name's a little unusual, but it's pure Reading, and it suits this brewery to a T.

Opened: June 1995.

Type: Brewery and associated pub (Canal Street Pub).

Owner: William G. McShane, president.

Brewer: Tom Rupp.

PA Microbrewers Guild: Not a member.

System: 15-barrel Pub Brewing System brewhouse (modified for step infusion or decoction brewing). Potential annual capacity 1800 barrels.

Annual production: 500 barrels in 5 months of 1996.

Beers brewed: *Year-round:* Kölsch, Pale Ale, Porter, Honey Nut Oatmeal Stout, Classic Lager, Fest, Mai-Bock, Bock (changes somewhat with the season), Doppel Bock. *Seasonals:* Hefe-Weizen, Wildberry Wheat, Winter Weizen Bock. All beers brewed on premises.

The Pick: Kölsch it is. Tom Rupp found a yeast strain that brings out the character in this fickle style. Most American-brewed Kölsch is light and foamy—a drink for customers who would really rather have a Coors Light. Not Neversink's! This is Kölsch with Khäracter! See that frothy white head, smell that mixed-fruit jammy nose, roll the sparkly liquid on your tongue, and savor this just-barely-bittered beauty of a beer. A close runner-up is the Mai-Bock.

Take-out beer: Half and quarter kegs, cases (12-ounce bottles in single-style and variety packs).

Tours: By appointment only, Monday through Saturday.

Pub hours: Monday through Saturday, 11:00 A.M.–1:00 A.M.

Food: The food at the Canal Street Pub comes in two styles, pub fare and fine dining. The fine dining menu features seafood, beef, duck, and vegetarian dishes, some of which are cooked with beer.

Extras: The pub has a full liquor license. Sixty to eighty wines are offered, along with single malts and a selection of bourbons and cognacs. There is live music in the pub on Thursday, Friday, and most Saturday nights.

Special considerations: Kids welcome. Handicapped-accessible. Cigars allowed in the pub after 9:30 P.M. Vegetarian meals available.

Directions: See map on page 104.

Parking: Large well-lit lot with security patrols.

Lodging: Sheraton Berkshire Inn, 422 West Papermill Road, Wyomissing (610-376-3811); Econo Lodge, 635 Spring Street, Wyomissing (610-378-5105); Country Inn and Suites, 405 North Park Road, Wyomissing (610-373-4444); Inn at Center Park, 730 Center Avenue, Reading (610-374-8557).

Nearby attractions: Reading is known for its outlets—VF Outlet Village, Reading Outlet Center, Reading Station and others. Just follow the signs. The Reading Public Museum has a planetarium and sculpture garden at 500 Museum Road (610-371-5850). For a great view of the city, make your way up to the Pagoda, a Japanese-style tower (albeit one trimmed in pink neon) that sits on Mt. Penn. It's breathtaking at night. The route to the Pagoda defies written description, so call 610-655-6374 for directions. The Daniel Boone Homestead is about nine miles east of town on Route 422 and includes the restored birthplace of Boone, a blacksmith shop, sawmill, and barn. The Mid-Atlantic Air Museum at the Reading Airport displays restored military and commercial aircraft, and puts on an annual air show. Call 610-372-7333 for information. Also contact the Visitors Bureau at 610-375-4085.

Other good beer sites in the area: The NorthEast Taproom is one of the best bars anywhere. Owner Pete Cammarano is devoted to beer and amusement. Witness his great selection of tap and bottled beer and events like the annual Spam-carving contest. Twelfth and Robeson Streets (610-372-5284). Third & Spruce is that rare find; a sports bar with great beer taps. They have thirty-six taps, twenty-three TVs, and five satellite dishes. Third and Spruce Streets, West Reading (610-376-5254). The friendly Douglassville Hotel serves huge dinners and has a hefty beer list. Route 422 East, Douglassville (610-385-2585). There are also a number of excellent old hotel bars in the small towns north of Reading: Fleetwood, Krumsville, Bowers, Virginville, and Kempton are the homes of some of my favorites. See also other good beer sites on page 102.

Pretzel City
Brewing Company

30 S. 4th Street
Reading
610-378-9477

Pretzel City has bounced back brilliantly from an early identity crisis. At
first it was going to be a brewery that would sell beer mainly to the
independently owned pub on the second floor and slowly build an outside business of other draft accounts. When the upstairs pub failed, the
brewery's plan was stood on its head. Outside sales suddenly became
crucial to survival. Fortunately, those sales grew, but now the brewery
finds itself *too* successful. The space, which would have been adequate
for supplying a pub and some local draft accounts, is wholly insufficient
for a growing microbrewery. Nothing's ever simple.

Still, Scott Baver could have worse problems. Pretzel City is making some excellent, out-of-the-ordinary beer, which is finally getting
the critical acclaim and industry respect it has always deserved. Scott
has also managed to pick up licensing deals with respected European
brewers to brew their beer in the United States. These include the
esteemed beers from the Belgian Brasserie la Binchoise, the fine Flem-
ish *witbier* Blanche de Charleroi, and Bolten Alt of Korschenbroich,
Germany. How did they get these licenses? It was probably because
they were already brewing great *witbiers* and *altbiers* of their own.

Pretzel City exemplifies what I consider most admirable in East
Coast breweries. East Coast brewers respect classic styles and their
characteristics. They demonstrate a judicious hand when it comes to
hopping rates and a more generous hand with malt. They exhibit
patience and a concern for balance. Pretzel City does all of this and it
shows. Just look at the beers . The only typical microbrewery beer style
is the Duke of Ale IPA. The Steam Horse Lager is what is called a
"California common" beer, since Anchor Brewing gets upset if anyone
else brews a "steam beer." True, *witbier* and bock are somewhat more
widespread, but Pretzel City's lineup is still a long way from the usual
Golden Ale, Pale Ale, Brown Ale, and Stout produced by most American brewers. Pretzel City has caught on to the secret of success in the
developing microbrew market. Stake out your territory and excel.

Make an appointment to tour the brewery. They've made some interesting adaptations to their surroundings. The tanks, for instance, soar up into the only openings available. It's a unique sight from the brewery and from the pub on the second floor, too. The pub, now reborn and welcoming visitors, is tucked under a rare "henhouse" roof with wooden bow trusses. It's worth a look, and it's a good place to sample some very fresh Pretzel City beer.

Opened: October 1995.
Type: Brewery.
Owner: S-Corporation under Pennsylvania laws.
Brewers: Scott E. Baver, Terry Ripple.
PA Microbrewers Guild: Member.
System: 15-barrel JV Northwest brewhouse. Potential annual capacity 3,000 barrels.
Annual production: 2,100 barrels in 1996.
Beers brewed: *Year-round:* Steam Horse Lager, Duke of Ale IPA, Wit Bier. *Seasonals:* Nor'Easter Ale, Dear Abby Dubble, Laures Bock, Xmas Bock. All draft beers brewed on premises; bottled beers currently brewed under contract at Independence Brewing. *Contracts:* Pretzel City also brews these European beers under license: Bolten Alt, La Binchoise Blonde, La Binchoise 1549, La Binchoise Biere des Ours, and Blanche de Charleroi.
The Pick: Nothing can stop the Duke of Ale. This IPA was intended to be a Brit-style, but Scott bowed to American tastes and threw in some Cascade hops. The result is an earthy, spicy, citrus-sharp hybrid that is incredibly tasty, particularly on the low-carbonation handpump. Some IPAs whip the tongue with hops, making for a bracing tonic. This beer gets in touch with all your senses and invites you to have another.
Take-out beer: Half and quarter kegs, cases.
Tours: By appointment only.
Food: The pub upstairs does not belong to the brewery, but like an unofficial house pub, it serves only Pretzel City beer. The food is standard pub fare, and the view of the brewery is great.
Special considerations: Kids welcome. Brewery tour is not handicapped-accessible.
Directions: See map on page 104.
Parking: On-street parking available.
Lodging, Nearby attractions, Other good beer sites: See page 108.

Old Lehigh Brewing Company

333 Union Street
Allentown
610-435-3331

Dick Cernok started out as a plumber, and he now runs Modern Plumbing in Allentown. Old Lehigh Brewing is located in the back of Modern Plumbing's offices, a solid old brick building that once stabled the horses for Allentown's trolleys. In an age when most microbrewers seem to be ex-stockbrokers, ex-investment bankers—people with more money than Rockefeller—I find a plumber opening a brewery to be downright refreshing.

It has turned out to be useful, too. Old Lehigh is studded with plumbing fixtures, pipe, and controls that Dick Cernok stocks and sells out front. "Hey," I said as we toured the brewery, "That's the control from my shower!" Dick uses these on-off temperature-control faucets to control the flow of cleaning water in the lagering room. This is probably one of the best-plumbed breweries in America. It has a nice homey feel, too.

One of Old Lehigh's first beers was its Cream Ale, decked out in a colorful covered bridge label. Allentown's Neuweiler Brewery used to make a cream ale that was very popular, and people here remember it fondly. It was soft, a little sweet, a touch tangy, and had a good malty grip to the body. But Old Lehigh has got this one dead to rights. It's one of the best cream ales in the country. Now to some people, that's probably a lot like saying "This is one of the best white breads in the country." I would only ask that they reserve judgment on this home-grown American beer style until they've tried Old Lehigh.

Brewer Bob Kort makes the beer in an all-Criveller brewery. Criveller is based in Niagara Falls, where Niagara Falls Brewing is its model facility. Criveller has the advantage of being within a reasonable drive of most of the Northeast. Niagara Falls is about six hours from Allentown, so if Bob absolutely had to have a part, someone could go get it and be back in a day. Criveller equipment has some interesting features, including a flying saucer-shaped bottle filler with an elevating platform that lifts the bottles up to the tubes. In full-speed operation it looks like the mothership heading for Planet X.

Old Lehigh is starting to find its way. The regular beers are where they want them now, and there are plans to expand the line with some seasonal labels. It's an exciting time at the brewery. The whiteboard outside the office is crowded with ideas for beer names, Bob is running pilot batches of new brews, and Dick is shepherding people through to take a look at the town's new brewery. Things are only getting better in back of the plumbing company.

Opened: May 1997.
Type: Brewery.
Owner: Private corporation. Richard P. Cernok, president.
Brewer: Bob Kort.
PA Microbrewers Guild: Not a member.
System: 15 barrel Criveller brewhouse. Potential annual capacity 10,000 barrels.
Annual production: No figures available yet.
Beers brewed: *Year-round:* Cream Ale, Amber Lager, Pale Ale, Nut Brown Ale, IPA. *Seasonals:* Buckwheat Oatmeal Stout, Kristall Wheat, Bock, Porter, Barleywine. All beers brewed on premises.
The Pick: I want to say the Oatmeal Stout, which was very good off the brewery tap, but this Cream Ale is driving me nuts. This is what people around here remember from brewers like Neuweiler: It's a soft, sweetish beer with just the slightest kiss of hop bitterness that draws you on and on into another glass. Old Lehigh has *nailed* that style.
Take-out beer: None available. Dick Cernok is "a firm believer in using the three-tier system only." (See *three-tier system* in the glossary.)
Tours: Saturday, 11:00 A.M.–1:00 P.M. Group tours during the week by appointment only.
Events: An Oktoberfest at the brewery is planned. Call for details.
Special considerations: Kids welcome. Handicapped-accessible.
Parking: Plenty of off-street parking.
Lodging: Allentown Comfort Suites, 3712 Hamilton Boulevard (610-437-9100); Days Inn, 2622 Lehigh Street (610-797-1234); Wydnor Hall Inn, B&B, 3612 Old Philadelphia Pike (610-867-6851).
Nearby attractions: Allentown is dominated by Pennsylvania Power and Light's midtown office building; you see it as soon as you cross the ridge from the south. Head for it and you'll be able to find the Liberty Bell Shrine at 620 Hamilton, in Zion's Reformed Church. The shrine marks the spot where the Liberty Bell and the bells of

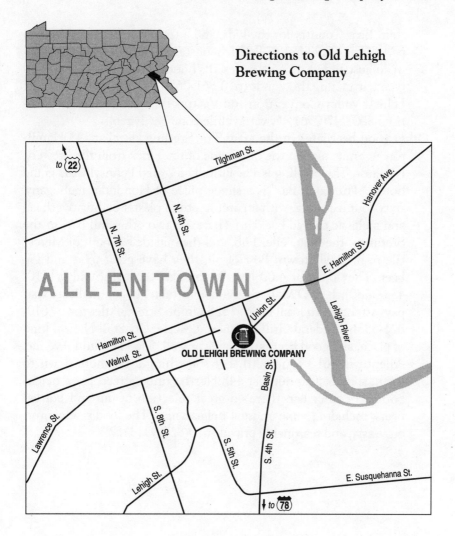

Directions to Old Lehigh Brewing Company

Christ Church were hidden when the British occupied Philadelphia in 1777. The Gross Memorial Rose Garden, especially pretty in spring and fall, is down by the riverside on Parkway Boulevard at Twenty-seventh Street (610-437-7627). The Allentown Art Museum has exhibits of European and American art, textiles, and the Fuller Gem Collection. Fifth and Court Streets (610-437-7627). For hoot'n'hollering fun, get out to Dorney Park and Wildwater Kingdom on Hamilton Boulevard west of town (800-386-8463). You'll find four roller coasters, including the new Steel Force coaster and the huge Hercules wooden coaster, Berenstain Bear Country for the kids, and a train ride between the two parks. The Musikfest in Bethlehem starts on the second Saturday in August and in nine days presents hundreds of musical acts of all types, attracting thousands (610-861-0678). Get in touch with the Lehigh Valley Convention and Visitors Bureau for more information: 800-747-0561, www.travelfile.com/ get?lvcvb

Other good beer sites in the area: The Sterling Hotel at 343 Hamilton Avenue, just on the other side of the block from the brewery, is a must. The Sterling is a beautifully restored Pennsylvania grand hotel. "The Long Bar" is a single piece of Honduran mahogany, sixty-four feet long, with an architectural plaster ceiling overhead and a classic carved backbar. There are two other full bars in the Sterling—the Neuweiler Pub, and the outside bar built of Mercer tile from Doylestown. Best of all, they have great food and tap beer. They open at 4:00 P.M. Wednesday through Sunday (610-433-3480). J. P. O'Malley's is a comfortable, happy multitap that pays attention to local beers. 1528 Union Street, Allentown (610-821-5556). Federal Grill is a more upscale, Cocktail Nation kind of place, and good beer is available as well. 536 Hamilton Avenue, Allentown (610-776-7600). For something a bit more down to earth, slide by Cannon's at 448 North Ninth Street. For a neighborhood corner bar, there's a great selection of tap and bottled beers, including some unusual Belgian ales. The food is adventurous, tasty, and reasonably priced (610-820-9313).

Weyerbacher Brewing Company

20 South Sixth Street
Easton
610-559-5561

Weyerbacher
Brewing Company, Inc.

Dan Weirback used to sell swimming pools. But when he got bit by the brewing bug, he just had to go with it. His choice of brewery name reflects his German ancestry. "The family name was Weyerbacher before the immigration officers got hold of it," Dan explains.

Weyerbacher Brewing is based in an old livery stable on Sixth Street in Easton. Dan recalls the Herculean task of cleaning this old building. "We'd be in here all day in the summer, vacuuming, washing, scrubbing, and at day's end it would look pretty good. Next morning we'd come in to find the air full of dust again! We finally just got gallons of sealant and doused every inch of wood. Now it's clean."

From start to finish, this is labor-intensive, hand-crafted beer. His brewing system was pieced together from several sources, but the brewers have learned every inch of it. The bottling system is a Meheen MicroMaster, a microchip-controlled, four-line filler run by compressed air. "It's capable of filling a hundred cases an hour," Dan says, "But anything more than fifty will drive you crazy pretty quick."

Weyerbacher has taken advantage of the quick decision-making allowed by a craft brewery. New beers can be formulated quickly, and expanded or dropped after a test run through the market. "We started out with the Easton Pale Ale as a major beer, then cut it back to being just a component of our Variety Packs," Dan explains. "There are a lot of Pale Ales out there." The ESB and IPA are the flagship beers right now.

Weyerbacher's seasonal beers, like the roasty, malty Prime Porter and Bavarian-style Hefe-weizen, are more adventurous. The most adventurous so far is the big, fat Raspberry Imperial Stout. This is a rich winter beer with plenty of body and malt sweetness, tamed by bitterness and a velvety tartness from the raspberries. "That's real fruit, too," Dan points out. "I don't use extracts!"

But big fat fruit beers don't always pay the bills, so Weyerbacher has taken an unusual step for a craft brewery. It's launched the Two Rivers Brewhouse bargain brand, which includes Golden Amber Ale and American Wheat. "They are popular in Easton," says Dan. "Easton

Directions to Weyerbacher Brewing Company

people want to support us, but the Weyerbacher beers were just a bit too much for some of them. The Two Rivers Brewhouse line features all-malt, microbrewed beers that are more easy-drinking." They're selling well, but as the Weyerbacher beers build, these lower-profit labels may get squeezed out.

Adaptation is essential for smaller craft breweries to survive. Dan Weirback has learned that lesson well. You can bet he'll be out selling beer and listening to what his customers tell him. Stop by and take the tour, and maybe you can give him a few suggestions too.

Opened: August 1995.
Type: Brewery and brewpub.
Owners: Dan Weirback and private investors.
Brewers: Dan Weirback, Curt Keck, Dave Danner, John Parsons.
PA Microbrewers Guild: Member.
System: 15-barrel VAFAC-sourced British brewhouse. Potential annual capacity 3,500 barrel.

Annual production: 1,700 barrels in 1996. 2,400 barrels projected for 1997.

Beers brewed: *Year-round:* Weyerbacher labels: ESB, IPA. Two Rivers Brewhouse label: Golden Amber Ale. *Seasonals:* Scotch Ale, Hefeweizen, Raspberry Imperial Stout, Winter Ale, AutumnFest, Prime Porter Belgian-style Ale. Two Rivers Brewhouse label: American Wheat. All beers brewed on premises.

The Pick: I love seasonals, and the Prime Porter is a winner. It's a chocolatey, roasty brew with a hint of molasses. You'll find it teetering on the fine line between stout and porter. I also have to "honorably mention" the Raspberry Imperial Stout—Belgian chocolate raspberry truffle in a bottle. It just keeps getting better, too.

Take-out beer: Case sales during tours; growlers and six-packs from pub.

Tours: Saturday, noon–2:00 P.M.

Pub hours: Tuesday and Wednesday, 4:00 P.M.–11:00 P.M.; Thursday and Friday, 4:00 P.M.–midnight; Saturday, noon–midnight.

Food: Limited menu of pub fare.

Special considerations: Kids welcome. Handicapped-accessible.

Parking: On-street parking is rarely a problem.

Lodging: Lafayette Inn, 525 West Monroe Street (610-253-4500); Days Inn, Route 22 and Twenty-fifth Street (610-253-0546, 800-329-7466).

Nearby attractions: Easton is home to Binney and Smith, makers of Crayola crayons. The Crayola Factory at Two Rivers Landing is their public face. Kids can draw on the walls, make crayons, and do other colorful stuff. 30 Center Square (610-515-8000). In the same building is the National Canal Museum, celebrating the history of America's canals. You can get a canal boat ride during the summer (610-515-8000). Easton's Shad Fishing Tournament and Festival is held in April and early May (call 610-258-1439 for precise dates) and ends with a big celebration of "planked" shad, lots of other good eats, and plenty of carnival fun. You'll find good canoeing opportunities on both the Delaware and Lehigh Rivers. Get the latest information on Easton happenings at www.easton-pa.org or by calling 610-515-1200.

Other good beer sites in the area: Pearly Baker's is a somewhat fancy but not snooty multitap, with first-class dining. Center Square (610-253-9949). Porter's Pub is a neighborhood bar that boasts twelve taps and a good selection of Belgian bottles at Seventh and Northampton Sreets (610-250-6561). Both have Weyerbacher beers on tap. Across the Delaware at 61 Bridge Street in Milford, New Jersey, is the Ship Inn, a brewpub with good British-style ales. (908-995-7007).

A word about . . .

Brewing Beer

You don't need to know much about beer to enjoy it. After all, I don't understand how the electronic fuel injection on my car really works but I know that when I stomp on the accelerator, the car's gonna go!

Knowing about the brewing process can help you understand how and why beer tastes the way it does. It's like seeing the ingredients used in cooking a dish and realizing where the flavors came from. Once you understand the recipe for beer, other things become more clear.

Beer is made from four basic ingredients: water, hops, yeast, and grain, generally barley malt. Other ingredients may be added, like sugars, spices, fruit, and vegetables, but they are extras. In fact, the oft-quoted Bavarian *Reinheitsgebot* (purity law), first promulgated in 1516, limited brewers to using only water, hops, and barley malt; yeast had not yet been discovered.

In the beginning, the malt is cracked in a mill to make a grist. The grist is mixed with water and heated (or "mashed") to convert the starches in the grain to sugars (see *decoction* and *infusion* in the glossary). Then the hot, sugary water—now called wort—is strained out of the mash. It is boiled in the brewkettle, where hops are added to balance the sweetness with their characteristic bitterness and sprightly aroma. The wort is strained, cooled, and pumped to a fermenter, where yeast is added.

A lager beer ferments slow and cool, whereas an ale ferments warmer and faster. After fermentation, the beer will either be force-carbonated or naturally carbonated and aged. When it is properly mature for its style, the beer is bottled, canned, kegged, or, in a brew-pub, sent to a large serving tank. And then we drink it. Happy Ending!

Naturally, it isn't quite that simple. The process varies somewhat from brewery to brewery. That's what makes beers unique. There are also major differences in the ways *micro* and *mainstream* brewers brew beer. One well-known distinction has to do with the use of nonbarley grains, specifically corn and rice, in the brewing process. Some micro-brewers have made a big deal of their *Reinheitsgebot*, proudly displaying slogans like "Barley, hops, water, and yeast—*and that's all!*" Mainstream brewers like Anheuser-Busch and Pennsylvania's regional brewers all add significant portions of corn or rice or both. Beer geeks howl about how these adjuncts make the beer inferior. Of course, the same geeks often rave about Belgian ales, which have a regular farrago of ingredients forbidden by the *Reinheitsgebot.*

Mainstream brewers boast about the quality of the corn grits and brewer's rice they use, while microbrewers chide them for using "cheap" adjunct grains and "inferior" six-row barley. Truth is, they're both right . . . and they're both wrong.

Barley, like beer, comes in two main types: two-row and six-row. The names refer to the rows of kernels on the heads of the grain. Six-row grain gives a greater yield per acre but has more husks on smaller kernels, which can give beer an unpleasant astringency. Two-row gives a plumper kernel with less husk, but costs significantly more. Each has its place and adherents.

When brewing began in America farmers and brewers discovered that six-row barley did much better than two-row in our climate and soil types. Two-row barley grown the same way as it had been in Europe produced a distinctly different malt. This became especially troublesome when the craze for pale lagers swept America in the mid-nineteenth century. The hearty ales they replaced had broad flavors from hops and yeast that easily compensated for these differences. But pale lagers are showcases for malt character, and small differences in the malt mean big differences in beer taste.

Brewers adapted and used what they had. They soon found that a small addition of corn or brewer's rice to the mash lightened the beer, smoothed out the husky astringency of the six-row malt, and gave the beer a crispness similar to the European pale lagers. Even though using these grains required the purchase, operation, and maintenance of additional equipment (cookers, storage silos, and conveyors), almost every American brewer did it. Some say they overdid it, as the percentages of adjuncts in the beer rose over the years. Is a beer that is 30 percent corn still a pilsner?

Microbrewers say adjunct grains are cheap substitutes for barley malt. In terms of yield, corn and brewer's rice are less expensive than two-row barley, but they are still high-quality grains. Similarly, six-row barley is not inherently inferior to two-row; it is just not as well suited to the brewing of some styles of beer. Mainstream brewers have adapted their brewing processes to six-row barley. The difference is in the beer those processes produce.

Another difference between micro and mainstream brewers is the practice of high-gravity brewing. The alcohol content of a beer is mainly dependent on the ratio of fermentable sugars to water in the wort, which determines the specific gravity of the wort. A higher gravity means more alcohol.

Large commercial brewers, in their constant search for ways to peel pennies off the costs of brewing, discovered that they could save money by brewing beer at a higher alcohol content and carefully diluting it later. To do this, a brewer adds a calculated extra amount of malt, rice, corn, whatever "fuel" is used, to boost the beer to 6.5 percent alcohol by volume (ABV) or higher. When the fermented beer has been filtered, water is added to bring the ABV down to the target level of 4 to 5 percent. You may remember an ad campaign in the early 1990s, in which Anheuser-Busch accused Coors of shipping "beer concentrate" across the country in tank cars for packaging at its Shenandoah facility. The so-called "beer concentrate" was this high-alcohol beer prior to dilution.

How does this method save money? It saves energy and labor costs during the brewing process by effectively squeezing 1,300 barrels of beer into a 1,000-barrel brewkettle. While 1,000 barrels are boiled, 1,300 barrels are eventually bottled. It also saves money by allowing more efficient use of fermentation tank space: 10,000-barrel fermenters produce 13,000 barrels of beer.

It sounds great, so why not do that with every beer? Because the high-gravity process can produce some odd flavor and aroma notes during fermentation. That's what brewers aim for in big beers like doppelbocks and barley wines. But these characteristics are out of place in a pilsner. I also feel that beer brewed by this high-gravity method suffers from a dulling phenomenon similar to "clipping" in audio reproduction: The highs and lows are clipped off, leaving only the middle.

With a studied nonchalance, big brewers keep this part of their brewing process away from the public eye. The only mainstream brewer who has ever mentioned it to me is the forthright Joe Gruss at Latrobe, and I salute him for his honesty. To tell the truth, of all beer styles, American mainstream lager is probably the style least affected by this process. It is mostly a practice that just seems vaguely wrong, and you won't see any microbrewers doing it.

So now you know how beer is made, and a few of the differences in how the big boys and the little guys do it. It's probably time for you to do a little field research. Have fun!

Beer from the Historic Triangle

How did I come to carve out this triangular area from York to Chambersburg to Harrisburg? To the east lies Pennsylvania Dutch country, and the Triangle isn't like that. To the north are mostly rural counties, and while the Triangle has plenty of farms, it encompasses the state capital and populous cities like York. To the northwest and west there are no breweries for 75 to 120 miles, and this area certainly isn't like that!

What *is* the Triangle like? The major industries are government—Harrisburg is the state capital—and tourism. Tourists are drawn to the area because of its history and its geography. There are significant historical sites from both the Revolutionary and Civil Wars. The Susquehanna River and the Appalachian Mountains, traced by the Appalachian Trail, appeal to outdoors lovers.

Harrisburg celebrates the Susquehanna with Riverfront Park, five miles of gardens and memorials along the river. The seat of government offers tourists the architectural glories of the State Capitol and a look at the history of the state at the State Museum of Pennsylvania. Once a year the state's farmers come to Harrisburg for the six-day Pennsylvania Farm Show, complete with animals, vegetables, crafts, and outstanding food.

Gettysburg is the foremost historical attraction in the Triangle, drawing thousands of visitors every day in the summer.

Carlisle is a beautiful little town with a history of its own. It was the home of two signers of the Declaration, and the location of the Carlisle Indian School where Jim Thorpe got his education. At Carlisle Barracks you can visit the Army's Military History Institute, a library with a huge collection of Civil War photographs.

York is still trying to find its way as a tourist attraction. The new Harley-Davidson plant and museum are helping, as are annual street rod and softball conventions. History buffs may know that York was the national capital for almost a year (1777–78), when the British occupied Philadelphia and drove out the Continental Congress.

The western reaches of the Triangle are liberally scattered with state game lands and stocked streams and lakes. Two of my favorite state parks, Colonel Denning and Gifford Pinchot, tempt the summer traveler with lakes perfect for swimming and canoeing.

The truth of the matter is that this area is more often driven through than driven to. With the Pennsylvania Turnpike and Interstate Routes 81 and 83 passing through, the Triangle area is continually criss-crossed by travelers. But take an exit, take a drive, then stop for a beer. You may just find something you like.

Gettysbrew Pub and Brewery

248 Hunterstown Road
Gettysburg
717-337-1001
www.gettysbrew.com

It's an oddly perfect situation at this pub and brewery, located near one of the nation's most revered historic battlefields, Gettysburg. It's housed in an historic building used as a field hospital by the Confederate army during the battle, and it's owned by a retired United States Army medical researcher. Dr. Paul Lemley loves Gettysburg, loves the building, loves his work, and loves to talk about it. A wiry bundle of energy, Paul is the reason this entry will need to be updated by the time you read it; he's always looking for ways to improve.

Paul brews his beer on a little extract system shoehorned into a historic brick-end barn, part of the Monfort Farm. During the battle of Gettysburg the Confederates brought casualties to the farm to be treated. After Lee's retreat, the Union Army's doctors continued to care for the hundreds of men who were too injured to travel. The only conditions treated at the Monfort Farm these days, of course, are hunger and thirst.

The pub has been minimally reconstructed. The dining room is under the soaring rafters of the barn overhead. Ventilation holes in the brick-end walls, common to Pennsylvania barns of that period, have been glassed over for comfort's sake. Underfoot are rough-hewn planks solid enough to hold a troop of Confederate cavalry. There are not many restaurants outside restored communities that offer this kind of simple, authentic, rustic beauty. In the summer you can take your ease out on the back patio, looking over the surrounding farmlands.

But you'll get more than fodder or bacon and beans here, don't worry. The small but efficient kitchen can handle everything from simple lunches to banquet dinners for 100 or more, and the ceramic tower taps will pour whichever brew you care to try.

Monfort Farm is an authentic piece of Gettysburg battlefield history. It's lucky that the man who built a brewpub here respects the history and the hallowed nature of this ground.

123

Opened: Brewery, August 1996; pub, July 1997.

Type: Brewpub.

Owner: Dr. Paul V. Lemley, Lt. Col., USA (Ret.).

Brewers: Paul Lemley, Mark Lemley.

PA Microbrewers Guild: Not a member.

System: 7-barrel Specific Equipment brewhouse (single vessel, extract-only); 3 14-barrel fermentors. Potential annual capacity 1,000 barrels.

Annual production: No figures available yet.

Beers brewed: *Year-round:* Pale Ale, Golden Ale, Hefe-weizen, Red Lager, Milk Stout. *Seasonals:* Festbier, Beer Cooler, Holiday Ale. All beers brewed on premises.

The Pick: Caveat: Gettysburg uses an all-extract system and no specialty grains at all. This is a limiting factor; you can make good beers with extracts, but you are going to have a hard time making excellent ones. That said, Paul's Golden Ale is not a bad drink. It's refreshing, has some nice banana and apple notes, and shows some spiciness, light clove, and a bit of sandalwood.

Take-out beer: Half-gallon growlers.

Tours: Every day during the first thirty minutes after opening.

Brewpub hours: Monday through Thursday, 4:00 P.M.–10:00 P.M.; Friday, 4:00 P.M.–midnight; Saturday, noon–midnight; Sunday, noon–10:00 P.M.

Food: Gettysbrew has recently upgraded its kitchen to provide a more sophisticated menu featuring entrees like salmon and prime rib. They can accommodate large groups, including bus tours.

Extras: Live music (call for schedule), big-screen TV sports, darts.

Events: Irregularly scheduled Civil War reenactment events based at the pub; call for information.

Special considerations: Kids welcome. (There are games for them and they can try the house root beer!) Handicapped-accessible. Cigars allowed on the deck. Vegetarian meals available.

Parking: Large, lighted free lot.

Lodging: Hampton Inn, 1280 York Road (717-338-9121); Comfort Inn, 871 York Road (717-337-2400); Holiday Inn Express, 869 York Road (717-337-1400). Lightner Farmhouse, historic B&B, 2350 Baltimore Pike (717-337-9508).

Nearby attractions: The Gettysburg National Military Park and Cemetery are naturally the main draws in Gettysburg. The Park Visitor Center is across from the Cemetery on Route 134 just south of town. Guided and self-guided walking and auto tours are available there, including private tours with licensed battlefield

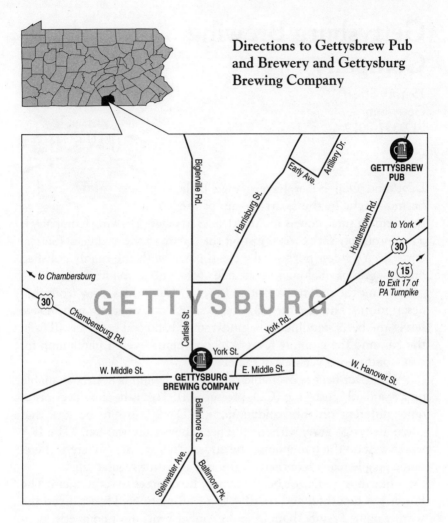

**Directions to Gettysbrew Pub
and Brewery and Gettysburg
Brewing Company**

guides. The Center also has a museum and the Electric Map, a large relief map of the area which uses colored lights to show the ebb and flow of the three-day battle. Another site of interest to military history buffs of a different era is Dwight D. Eisenhower's Gettysburg farm, preserved as the Eisenhower National Historic Site. There is a shuttle bus to the site from the National Park Visitor Center (717-334-1124).

Other good beer sites in the area: KClinger's is an excellent multitap beer bar with limited-release beers, vintage beers, and a whole boatload of attitude. It's a must-stop at 304 Poplar Street in Hanover, (717-633-9197).

Gettysburg Brewing Company

15 York Street
Gettysburg
717-337-0079

Dave and Gail Baker have a nice little business right in the heart of one of the best-known small towns in America. Gettysburg Brewing Company is a storefront on York Street, just off the square in the middle of Gettysburg. It's a modest but squeaky clean place, with the highly polished brewhouse ranked along the left side of the pub as you walk in.

I think the pub has a British feel, but Dave shies away from that description. "This is America," he says. "It's an American pub." Dave serves the beers standing up behind a small bar. Food service is all from the bar, and the comfort level is high. There's even a handpump for cask-conditioned versions of the beers.

Whatever beer is available on the handpump is always available on a standard "push" tap (CO_2 pressurized). This is because beer tastes quite different on the handpump, and Dave wants to be sure that guests never go away without the beer they really wanted. "The IPA works well on the handpump," he allows, "but it tastes different there. Some people really like the IPA the way it is on a regular tap."

I like most of Dave's beers any way he chooses to serve them. The Porter is a mouthful and the IPA is a well-mannered beast. Even the cornily named Amberham Lincoln Amber beats most competition in the middle-of-the-road amber ale category.

Though most of the beers have battlefield-derived names there are no other references in the pub to the battlefield. There are none of the seemingly obligatory Civil War pictures you find on the walls of nearly every other establishment in town. "Come on in," says Dave. "Take a break!"

It's a good place to take a break. Dave is very relaxed, and the pub is comfortably dark after a hot day spent tramping the battlefields from the Peace Memorial to Little Round Top. After a few of these good cool ales your head will no longer ring with the imagined roar of Union artillery. You'll be ready to think about other things, like how many souvenirs you still have to buy for your friends at work. Hmmmm . . . better have another Buford's Brown Ale first.

Opened: August 1996.

Type: Brewpub.

Owners: Dave Baker, Gail Baker.

Brewer: Dave Baker.

PA Microbrewers Guild: Not a member.

System: 4-barrel Elliott Bay Metal Fabricators brewhouse. Potential annual capacity 450 barrels.

Annual production: 300 barrels in 1996.

Beers brewed: *Year-round:* Gettysburg Golden, Amberham Lincoln Ale, Devil's Den Red IPA, Buford's Brown Ale, Pickett's Porter. *Seasonals:* Wheatfield Ale, Pumpkin Ale, Nutcracker Ale, Abbey Hoffman Abbey Ale (Tripel), Hap Baker Imperial Stout. All beers brewed on premises.

The Pick: Pickett's Porter is a beer with plenty of character: a mouthful of malt, balanced bitterness, and a long "drink me" finish. It's named Pickett's Porter, Dave explains, because it "valiantly charges across your palate . . . and then quietly retreats."

Take-out beer: Half-gallon growlers.

Tours: Brewhouse is in full sight of the pub; "talkthroughs" on request.

Brewpub hours: Thursday through Saturday, noon–11:00 P.M.; Sunday, noon–5:00 P.M.

Food: The food is simple but well crafted. The main items on the menu are handmade gourmet pizzas and toothsome deli sandwiches.

Extras: Real darts, pool table. Live jazz; call for schedule.

Special considerations: Kids welcome. Handicapped-accessible. No smoking. Vegetarian meals, including pizza, available.

Directions: See map on page 125.

Parking: On-street parking right in front can be tight, but there's a garage a block away at Carlisle Street and Racehorse Alley.

Lodging: Best Western Gettysburg Hotel, historic hotel on Lincoln Square, established 1797 (717 -337-2000); Herr Tavern and Publick House, 900 Chambersburg Road (800-362-9849); Quality Inn Larson's, on Seminary Ridge, 401 Buford Avenue (717-334-3141).

Nearby attractions: Within walking distance of the pub is Thistlefields, a quite authentic British tearoom on Chambersburg Street near Lincoln Square. There are a number of non-Civil War shops in town; Dave recommends Gallery 30 bookstore right across the street for a good selection of books and local artworks. In nearby Hanover, Utz Potato Chips at 900 High Street offers free tours showing the production of their delicious chips (717-637-6644). See also nearby attractions on page 124.

Other good beer sites in the area: See other good beer sites on page 125.

Rock Creek
Brewing
Company

1667 Orchard Drive
Chambersburg
804-649-9235
www.rcbrew.com

This is complicated. The brewery in Chambersburg was originally Arrowhead Brewing, a Peter Austin system brewery run by Fran Mead. Arrowhead started brewing in April 1990. The beers—Red Feather Pale Ale, Light Feather Golden Ale, and the now lamentably lost Arrowhead Brown Ale—were reasonably well received, but there did not seem to be enough capital to properly market them.

Rock Creek Brewing started as a contract brewery in Richmond, Virginia, in April 1995. Rock Creek's beer was contract-brewed at Arrowhead. When Arrowhead got into serious financial trouble, Jon Esposito of Rock Creek purchased the struggling brewery. That was in November 1996. Today the Chambersburg location produces all of the Rock Creek beers and, until recently, two of Arrowhead's beers (under the name Red Feather Brewing Company). So what that added up to was a contract brewer, now being the "brick and mortar" brewer, brewing the beers of a former brewery owner as a house name brand. Strange world.

Chambersburg is right on I-81, convenient to growing craft-brewed beer markets in Virginia and central Pennsylvania. Unfortunately, the area is not really craftbrew country. Rock Creek is just down the road from the local Anheuser-Busch wholesaler, which does big business.

The Rock Creek tour is nice. You'll get to see the hop percolator, where hop tea is brewed for addition to the hot wort, and the open fermenters ringwood yeast requires. It's a bright, open facility and the beer is well-crafted.

You'll find Chambersburg in the broad Cumberland Valley between the front ridges of the Appalachians, near extensive state game lands, trout-stocked lakes, the Appalachian Trail, and Michaux and Buchanan State Forests. The setting is quite impressive and a trip into the mountains on secondary roads takes you through beautiful scenery

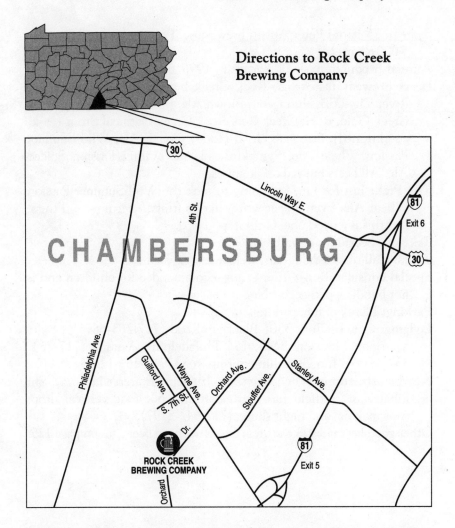

Directions to Rock Creek Brewing Company

and staid little towns with names like Dickey, Shimpstown, and Africa. Pack your rod and reel, get your backpack and camera ready, then drop in on Rock Creek before you head up into the mountains.

Opened: As Arrowhead Brewing, April 1990; as Rock Creek Brewing Company, November 1996.
Type: Brewery.
Owner: Jon Esposito.
Brewers: Sam Bell, Chris Russo.
PA Microbrewers Guild: Not a member.

System: 25-barrel Peter Austin brewhouse. Potential annual capacity 5,000+ barrels.

Annual production: 3,000 barrels in 1996. 5,000 projected for 1997.

Beers brewed: *Year-round:* Rock Creek brands: Devil's Elbow IPA, River City ESB, Nutrageous Brown Ale, Black Raven Porter, Rock Creek Gold, Rock Creek Red, Rock Creek Oatmeal Stout (cask-conditioned). *Seasonals:* Irish Honey Cream Ale, Wild Summer Passion Wheat Ale, Pumpkinhead Ale, Winter Passion Spiced Ale. All beers brewed on premises.

The Pick: Just for fun, I'm going to pick the Wild Summer Passion Wheat Ale. Even a beer writer likes a fruity fizzer now and then, and this is a good one. Chill it, pop it, do it!.

Take-out beer: None available.

Tours: Call to schedule tours, welcome at any time.

Special considerations: Tour is not recommended for children and is not handicapped-accessible.

Parking: Plenty of free parking.

Lodging: Comfort Inn, 3301 Blackgap Road (717-263-6655); Shultz Victorian Mansion B&B, 756 Philadelphia Avenue (717-263-3371); Days Inn, 30 Falling Spring Road (717-263-1288).

Nearby attractions: The Gettysburg battlefields aren't far away. Ski Liberty in Fairfield has fourteen trails, 606-foot vertical drop, snowmaking, and night skiing (717-642-8297).

Other good beer sites in the area: See other good beer sites on page 125.

Whitetail Brewing Company

111 North Hanover Street (rear)
Carlisle
717-258-9717

Wade Keech has been on a long odyssey. The journey began in 1994 in York, at the CyberCenter small business incubator. That's where Wade started Whitetail Brewing Company, at the prestigious address of 1600 Pennsylvania Avenue.

Whitetail is a Peter Austin brewery; it uses Austin's proprietary Ringwood yeast. In fact, Whitetail operates *the* Peter Austin brewhouse, the original one built by Austin about twenty years ago in the British brewery known as The Long Barn. The brewhouse was sold and shipped to a would-be brewer in America in the mid-1980s. But the buyer disappeared and the equipment sat in a warehouse in Philadelphia for ten years.

Whitetail, however, was never just another Ringwood yeast brewery. Wade brewed beer that transcended the commonalities of Ringwood beers. They were lively, sprightly, zesty beers. Wade's brightly light Maple Wheat surprised people with its delicious delicacy. Whitetail Ale's hypnotic appeal led you to consume pint after pint, smacking your lips all the while. Slow steady growth and critical acclaim became Whitetail's hallmark.

In the spring of 1996, Wade embraced The Dark Side and entered the world of big brewing. It started innocently enough with the idea of making a quaffable golden ale with a familiar name that would bring a whole new class of beer drinkers into the microbrewing camp. Wade brewed up a batch, designed a tap handle with a white pawprint on a blue background, and sold the beer as Nittany Ale.

Almost any Pennsylvanian can guess what happened. Sports bars bought the beer, Penn State fans bought the beer, and everyone started calling Whitetail. Wade was in a Red Queen's race, running as fast as he could just to keep up. Demand for the beer outstripped the capacity of the brewery and he was forced to go to Rock Creek Brewing in Chambersburg to have the beer brewed under contract. I remember calling

131

Wade during that time to ask if he had any news for my *Ale Street News* column. "Oh, the Nittany Ale's doing really, really well," said Wade. "But do me a favor: Don't mention it. I can't keep up with it now!"

In the midst of this madness, Whitetail's tenure at Cyber Center ended. The small business baby was being turned out to make it in the real world. That is how Whitetail Brewing Company wound up in a space behind Market Cross Pub in Carlisle. Market Cross had always been a good customer, and Wade had even brewed a house beer for them. The brewhouse sat for some months, unassembled, while Wade set up a new contract brewing arrangement; demand for Nittany Ale had overwhelmed Rock Creek as well.

The last time I talked to Wade, he was planning to renovate the brewery space in Carlisle and have operations underway again in August 1998. He was in negotiations with larger breweries to determine the future of Nittany Ale, considering further contract brewing or licensing of the brand. Either option had the potential to make enough Nittany Ale to satisfy every Penn State fan.

Best of all, Wade was thinking about new beers. "I'd like to try some Belgians," he said wistfully. "We have a closed room for different fermentations so we can keep the Ringwood yeast uncontaminated." It sounded like Wade had finally, and happily, come home to being a small brewer again.

Opened: October 1994.
Type: Brewery.
Owner: Wade Keech.
Brewer: Wade Keech.
PA Microbrewers Guild: Member.
System: 10-barrel Peter Austin brewhouse. Potential annual capacity 3,000 barrels.
Annual production: 1,300 barrels in 1996.
Beers brewed: *Year-round:* Whitetail Ale, Brown Ale, Maple Wheat, Stout, Nittany Ale. *Seasonals:* Vanilla Wheat, Honey Cream Ale; more are planned. Draft Whitetail beers brewed on premises. Bottled Nittany Ale is contract brewed.
The Pick: Wade's Maple Wheat is one of the few maple beers I can stomach, and this I can drink by the pint. It's light, sweet, and has that woodsy, smoky, unique maple flavor high in the mouth.
Take-out beer: Not available.
Tours: Weekdays 11:00 A.M.–5:00 P.M., whenever Wade's in. You can

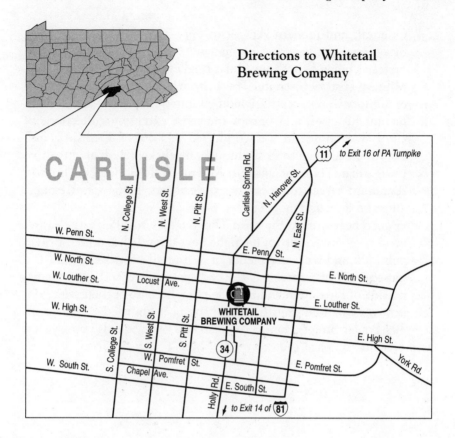

Directions to Whitetail Brewing Company

get a quick tour while you're waiting for your lunch at Market Cross Pub.

Special considerations: Kids welcome. Handicapped-accessible.

Parking: On-street parking is easy to find.

Lodging: Rodeway Inn Carlisle, 1239 Harrisburg Pike (717-249-2800); Econo Lodge Carlisle, 1460 Harrisburg Pike (717-249-7775); Jacob's Resting Place B&B, 1007 Harrisburg Pike (717-243-1766); Yellow Breeches House B&B, 213 Front Street, Boiling Springs (717-258-8344).

Nearby attractions: Carlisle is well known for an annual series of automobile flea markets, where car enthusiasts buy and swap car parts from vintage autos and hot rods. There is a different market each month from April to October. Call Carlisle Productions for current information on schedules and locations (717-343-7855). The Trout Art Gallery on High Street on the Dickinson College campus, has a variety of art including classical Greek, African,

Oriental, and modern American (717-245-1711). Carlisle Barracks, one of the oldest permanent Army posts in the United States, is home to both the Omar Bradley Museum and the Army's Military History Institute. The Institute houses a deep collection of military history texts, including United States and foreign regimental histories, and one of the most extensive collections of Civil War photos in the world (717-245-3611). Carlisle is also simply a nice town to stroll through, nicely kept with an attractive town square. Not far away in Mount Holly Springs, T. Jimmy's restaurant serves some pretty exotic meats: buffalo, rattlesnake, alligator, lion, and more (717-486-5542).

Other good beer sites in the area: The Market Cross Pub is the easiest good beer site to get to; it's right next door. It has a nice British pub look and feel, and plenty of Whitetail beer. KClinger's is a must-stop. This is probably the best spot for beer in Pennsylvania, outside of Pittsburgh and Philadelphia, because of their selection, how they handle their beer, and the beer knowledge of its staff. 304 Poplar Street, Hanover (717-633-9197). See also other good beer sites on page 140.

Appalachian Brewing Company

50 North Cameron Street
Harrisburg
717-221-1080
www.abcbrew.com

Old and worn but beautiful. That describes the Appalachian Mountains. These folded ridges, eroded remnants of sky-piercing peaks, thrust north into the state from Maryland and then make a bend to the northeast, curving around the state capital at Harrisburg. Compared to mountain chains in the West, and even to New Hampshire's Presidential range, Pennsylvania's mountains stand head and shoulders below the rest in terms of sheer altitude. In my view they bow to no mountains when it comes to the beauty of their vistas and foliage.

Appalachian Brewing Company is strangely similar to its namesake. Although it's newly opened, it is in some ways old and worn. The brewhouse is recycled from Vancouver Island Brewery in British Columbia. The Canadian brewery sold Appalachian the equipment when it upgraded to a substantially larger system. The Harrisburg building is a print shop dating from 1890 that took two years to renovate. Appalachian's bottler is a used German classic, a Holdefleiss long-tube filler. Even brewmaster Artie Tafoya is recycled in a way, though I'd be the last to call him old. Tafoya built his reputation in the Colorado brewing scene and has relocated to Harrisburg.

Like the Appalachians, this brewery is also eye-catching. The building was designed for function, to hold massive machinery, and yet there is a beauty in its solid construction, huge timbers, glowing hardwood floors, and wide-swinging front doors. The brewhouse is distinctive—bulbous unitanks look like a formation of great aluminum balloons straining to take flight.

Appalachian has become a sponsor of the Appalachian Trail Conference, a nonprofit organization promoting the use and maintenance of the Appalachian Trail. The Appalachian Trail runs from Maine to Georgia and that, not coincidentally, is the potential market for this beer. The Purist Pale Ale is named for "purist" hikers who hike every inch of the trail and don't skip the tough parts. Water Gap Wheat recalls the water gaps along the trail, where rivers cut through the ridges.

Officials in Harrisburg evidently did some research and saw the positive effect that a brewpub can have on its neighborhood. They courted Appalachian and sold them the building for $1. Considering the amount of restoration that was necessary, it was just barely a bargain, but it made the project possible for the brewers. The city viewed the brewpub as the cornerstone of its Paxton Commons project. Reclamation of the area is already starting to ripple outwards.

This is one of the biggest places you'll ever feel comfortable in. With its high ceiling, the great depth of its main room, and the massive tanks behind the glass wall to the right, one thing Appalachian has is plenty of room. The total floor space is 53,000 square feet, making Appalachian possibly the largest brewpub in the United States. Once the third floor is completed, they'll have more than enough room to do whatever they want. With the record these people already have for renovation, I'm looking forward to seeing what they do next.

Opened: January 1997.

Type: Brewpub and brewery.

Owners: Shawn Gallagher, Jack Sproch, Matt Smith, Bill Habacivch.

Brewers: Artie Tafoya, Joe Scheffey.

PA Microbrewers Guild: Not a member.

System: 36-barrel Alliance brewhouse. Potential annual capacity 15,000 barrels.

Annual production: Projected 1997 production 3,000 to 4,000 barrels.

Beers brewed: *Year-round:* Purist Pale Ale, Water Gap Wheat, Jolly Scot Scottish Ale, Susquehanna Stout. *Seasonals:* Bavarian Pilsner, Hefe-Weizen, Octoberfest. More are in the works. All beers brewed on premises.

The Pick: The Hefe-Weizen, for sure. Artie Tafoya was the hefe-king of the GABF when he was brewing in Colorado, and he hasn't lost a step. This hefe has every bit of cloudiness and cloviness that you're looking for. *Prost!*

Take-out beer: Half-gallon growlers and six packs.

Tours: Saturday at 1:00 P.M.

Brewpub hours: Sunday through Thursday, 11:00 A.M.–11:00 P.M.; Friday and Saturday, 11:00 A.M.–midnight.

Food: Stone-oven pizzas and calzones, soups, salads, and two-fisted sandwiches make up most of the menu.

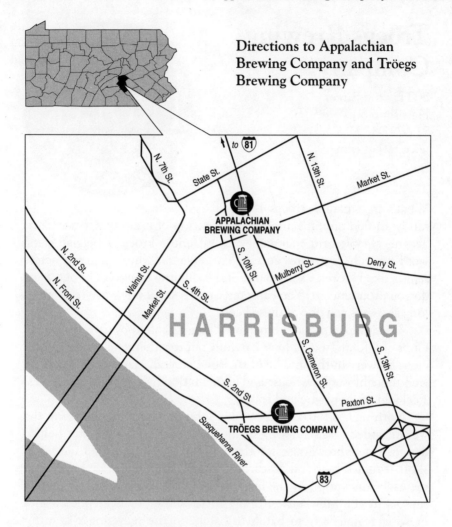

Directions to Appalachian Brewing Company and Tröegs Brewing Company

Extras: Liquor license, Sunday BrewJam featuring acoustic and jazz music, billiards, darts, foosball, pinball, video, sportspub, outdoor deck seating.

Special considerations: Kids welcome. Handicapped-accessible. Cigars allowed and sold. Vegetarian meals available.

Parking: Off-street lot behind building.

Lodging: Holiday Inn Express Riverfront, 525 South Front Street (717-233-1611); Ramada Inn on Market Square, 23 South Second Street (717-234-5021); Comfort Inn East, 4021 Union Deposit Road (717-561-8100).

Nearby attractions, Other good beer sites: See pages 139–140.

Tröegs Brewing Company

800 Paxton Street
Harrisburg
717-232-1297
www.troegs.com

What's in a name? Tröegs is certainly an odd one. It's a loose combination of brewery partner Chris Trogner's adolescent nickname "Trogs" and a kroeg, a Belgian slang word for pub. Even in central Pennsylvania, where you run across names like Hocker, Ochtemaier, and Fishburn, Tröegs sticks out. How do you pronounce it? You can pretty much say it any way you want as long as it gets you one of these beers!

Tröegs's logo proudly proclaims "Hand Crafted by Two Brothers." Chris and John Trogner have carefully put together a technically proficient brewery in the middle of the state capital, Harrisburg. There's a well-thought-out brewhouse and fermentation hall, spotless in stainless steel and white plastic and epoxy.

Nothing less is to be expected of John Trogner, who brewed at the well-regarded Oasis Brewing Company in Colorado and later helped design a new brewhouse for them. John is neatly turned out, with short-trimmed hair and an earnest face. With quiet pride he showed me each innovation in the brewery, from the electronic temperature sensors in the brewkettles, designed to allow precise replication of brewing regimens from batch to batch, to the recycling system for recapturing used cleaning caustic.

But don't worry: Your tour won't be strictly a walk through Beer Geek Town. Chris, the marketing and sales half of this partnership, charms visitors in the brewery's attractive tasting room. The room is decorated with an impressive collection of beer bottles and cans and artfully draped sacks of malt. Chris points out with mock despair that the brothers have no license to sell their beer in the tasting room, "so we have to *give* it all away!" Such sacrifices are part of the brewers' hard life.

It may well be hard; Tröegs comes late to a somewhat saturated market and faces formidable barriers. The brewery has low name recognition, and consumers already feel overwhelmed by beer choices. Tap and shelf space at bars and distributorships is shrinking. But John and Chris hope to overcome these hurdles with exceptional beer and as much exposure as they can stand.

It sounds like a good plan to me. They sure do have good beer and a lot of energy. And there's a lot to be said in this industry for John's commitment to consistency. Get lucky and try some of the brothers' beer soon.

Opened: June 1997.
Type: Brewery.
Owners: Chris Trogner, John Trogner.
Brewers: Head Brewer John Trogner, Assistant Brewer Blair Trogner.
PA Microbrewers Guild: Member.
System: 20-barrel JV Northwest brewhouse. Potential annual capacity 5,000 barrels.
Annual production: No figures available yet. 1,000 barrels projected for 1997.
Beers brewed: *Year-round:* Tröegs Pale Ale, Tröegs ESB, Tröegs Nut Brown Ale. *Seasonals:* Seasonals are planned. All beers brewed on premises.
The Pick: I refuse to pick between Pale Ale and ESB, because picking will deny me the opportunity to note how wonderfully differentiated these two rock-solid beers are. When I heard that the first two beers from Tröegs were going to be an ESB and a pale ale, I thought "These beers are too similar to live!" I happily admit my error. The ESB is fuller, more solid, and a touch more bitter than the Pale Ale; the Pale Ale is brighter, livelier, and fruitier than the ESB.
Take-out beer: Cases and kegs.
Tours: Saturday at noon and 2:00 P.M., or by appointment. (Tour includes a tasting room with large collection of beer bottles and cans; room can be rented for catered events.)
Special considerations: Kids welcome. Handicapped-accessible.
Directions: See map on page 137.
Parking: Large off-street lot.
Lodging: Hilton Harrisburg & Towers, 1 North Second Street (717-233-6000); Allenberry Resort Inn 1559 Boiling Springs Road, Boiling Springs (717-258-3211); Holiday Inn Express Riverfront, 525 South Front Street (717-233-1611); Hotel Hershey, 1 Hotel Road, Hershey (717-533-2171).
Nearby attractions: The State Museum of Pennsylvania has a wide range of exhibits on industry, art, science, archeology, and of

course, Pennsylvania history. Third Street between North and Forster, north of the Capitol (717-787-4978). The State Capitol offers free tours every day of the week to view the grand architectural features of this massive stone structure. Riverfront Park hosts a number of festivals; call the mayor's office for more information (717-255-3040). You may want to time your visit for January to catch the Pennsylvania Farm Show, a huge and friendly display of the state's agricultural bounty from fancy chickens to butter sculptures to draft horse pulling competitions—and the food is fantastic! Fair warning, though—Pennsylvanians have a superstition about "Farm Show Weather." Winter often seems to save its worst for that week. (717-255-3040). Nearby Hersheypark is a treat for roller coaster fans (800-437-7439). Hershey's Chocolate World offers a tour ride that exhibits the chocolate manufacturing process in a nonfactory setting. 800 Park Boulevard (717-534-4900).

Other good beer sites in the area: Zembie's was one of my farthest-flung regular stops when I lived in Lancaster. It has a great marble bar and is very cool and soothing in the summer. 226 North Second Street, Harrisburg (717-232-5020). Nick's 1014 Cafe, at 1014 North Third Street, in Harrisburg, probably has the best selection of beer in town, including cask-conditioned ales on their hand-pump (717-238-8844).

York Brewing Company

140 Roosevelt Avenue
York
717-846-PINT
www.yorkbrewing.com

York Brewing Company has one of the best-built steam generation systems of any microbrewery I've ever seen. That's a roundabout way of letting you know that the brewery is run, and was largely built, by John Humphries and Tom Hafera, two former nuclear engineers. John told me that the local inspectors were hassling him about the steam plant, assuming that he and Tom knew nothing about it. "I told them that Tom and I had worked with more pounds of steam in the last two years than they would ever see in their lives!" he chuckled.

The brewery shows evidence of the owners' background. Anchored in concrete, over-engineered at times, this brewery is *solid*. John and Tim also indulged their fondness for technology; there are some nice bells and whistles on the brewhouse, and the labels are sharp-looking glossies with original art.

Those labels reveal York Brewing's aim to stand out in the increasingly crowded market. Ruffed Grouse Stout and Susquehanna Ale are names that will make an immediate connection with any Pennsylvanian. The Ruffed Grouse is the state bird, a wily gamebird that "drums" the air in courtship displays and bursts from cover like feathered fireworks to confound even experienced hunters. The Susquehanna is the state's heartflow, providing sport, power, irrigation and life itself.

York Brewing has created beers fit for these labels. The stout is bold for a first effort, an unabashedly dry oatmeal stout that challenges you to take it or leave it. Susquehanna Ale is the session ale; drinkable yet never boring, a sustaining beer. It's nice to see a new brewery willing to step out so strongly.

York lacks the ready-made tourist attractions of Amish country, and it's cursed by odd highway and street configurations. It has been overlooked as a destination in the past, but the White Rose city is working hard to change that. There's a big softball tournament on Labor Day weekend, street rod shows in early June, and the Harley-

Davidson open house and the York Fair in September. These events have attracted thousands; perhaps the new brewery will bring more.

Opened: July 1997.

Type: Brewery.

Owners: John Humphries, Cindy Humphries, Tom Hafera, Mary Hafera.

Brewers: John Humphries, Tom Hafera.

PA Microbrewers Guild: Not a member.

System: 30-barrel Criveller brewhouse. Potential annual capacity 5,000 barrels.

Annual production: No figures available.

Beers brewed: *Year-round:* Susquehanna Ale, Ruffed Grouse (oatmeal) Stout, Longbeard Lager, Black Bear Porter. All beers brewed on premises.

The Pick: The Ruffed Grouse oatmeal stout is all you could ask from a start-up microbrewery. It's dark, roasty, full-bodied, and smooth, but possesses a nice backbite of roasted barley dryness.

Take-out beer: None available.

Tours: Call ahead. "If we're here, you can have a tour."

Special considerations: Tour is not suitable for children and is not handicapped-accessible.

Parking: Pull in between 150 and 160 Roosevelt Avenue for lots of off-street parking. Go to the front of the building and see the receptionist.

Lodging: Barnhart's Hospitality Inn, 3021 East Market Street (717-755-2806); Holiday Inn East Market, 2600 East Market Street (717-755-1966); Yorktowne Hotel, historic hotel, 48 East Market Street (717-848-1111). York hosts some heavily attended events during the year. Lodging can be scarce, so you might want to schedule a visit for some other time!

Nearby attractions: Harley-Davidson's Rodney C. Gott Museum is on the grounds of the Harley-Davidson assembly plant at Route 30 and Eden Road, about one mile east of I-83. Combined plant-and-museum tours are given Monday through Friday at 10:00 A.M. and 1:30 P.M.; museum-only tours are given weekdays at 12:30 P.M. On Saturday's there are museum-only tours at 10:00 and 11:00 A.M., and at 1:00 and 2:00 P.M. The museum is closed on long weekends (717-848-1177, ext. 5900). York was the capital of America for nine months in 1777 and 1778 while the British occupied Philadelphia. The York County Colonial Courthouse, where the Congress adopted the Articles of Confederation, has been reconstructed at

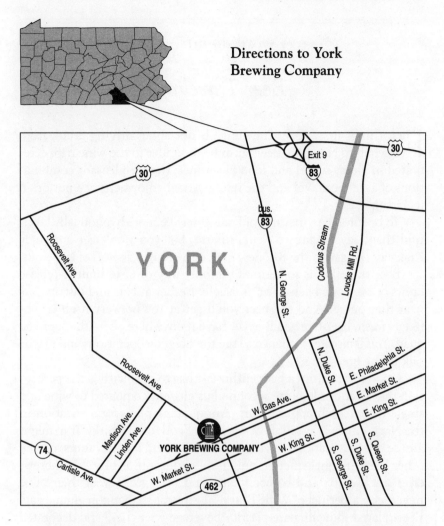

Directions to York Brewing Company

West Market and Pershing Streets. It can be toured Monday through Saturday, 10:00 A.M.–4:00 P.M. There is a cluster of restored buildings open for visit at 157 West Market Street: The Golden Plough Tavern, the General Gates House, and the Bobb Log House all date from the eighteenth century (717-848-1587). Call the York Visitors Information Center for more ideas (717-843-6660).

Other good beer sites in the area: Roosevelt Tavern—good bar, good staff, good food—is right across the street from the brewery. KClinger's, an outstanding multitap beer bar, features limited-release and vintage beers. 304 Poplar Street, Hanover. Call 717-633-9197 for directions.

Beer Traveling

First things first: "Beer traveling" is not about driving drunk from brewpub to brewpub. Beer outings are similar to the wine trips celebrated in glossy travel and food magazines; they're pleasant combinations of carefree travel and the semimystical enjoyment of a potion in its birthplace.

To be sure, the vineyards of France may be more hypnotically beautiful than, say, backtown Wilkes-Barre, but you won't get any juicy Krakauer sausage in the Rhône valley, either. Life's a series of trade-offs.

Beer traveling is sometimes the only way to taste limited-release brews or brewpub beers. Beer is usually fresher at bars and distributors near the source. And the beer you'll get at the brewery itself is sublimely fresh, beer like you'll never have it anywhere else—the supreme quaff. You'll also get a chance to see the brewing operations and maybe talk to the brewer.

One of the things a beer enthusiast has to deal with is the perception that beer drinkers are second-class citizens compared to wine and single-malt scotch connoisseurs. Announcing plans for a vacation in the Napa Valley or a couple of weeks on Scotland's Whisky Trail might arouse envious glances. A vacation built around brewery tours, on the other hand, might generate only mild confusion or pity. Microbreweries sell T-shirts and baseball caps, and beer geeks wear them. I've never seen a Beringer "Wine Rules!" T-shirt or a Chandon gimme cap. Beer-related souvenirs are plastic "beverage wrenches" and decorated pint glasses. Wine paraphernalia tends to be of a higher order: corkscrews, foil cutters, tasting glasses.

How do you as a beer enthusiast deal with this problem of perception? Simple: *Revel* in it. The first time my family went on a long camping trip with an experienced camper friend, we were concerned about wearing wrinkled clothes and sneakers all the time. Our guide had one reply to all our worries: "Hey! You're campers! Enjoy it!" It worked for us, it will work for you: "Hey! I'm traveling to breweries!" How bad can that be?

When you're planning a beer outing, you need to think about your approach. If you want to visit just one brewery, or perhaps tour the closely packed breweries in Philadelphia or Pittsburgh, you can first settle in at a nearby hotel. Get your cab fare or your walking shoes ready, and you're set to work your way through the brewery offerings. If you plan to visit several breweries in different towns, it is essential that you travel with a nondrinking driver.

You should know that the beer at brewpubs and microbreweries is sometimes stronger than mainstream beer. Often brewers will tell you the alcohol content of their beers. Pay attention to it. Keep in mind that most beers are between 4.5 and 5.0 percent ABV, and judge your limits accordingly. Of course, you might want to do your figuring before you start sampling.

Beer traveling is about enjoying beer and discovering the places where it is at its best. You could make a simple whirlwind tour of breweries, but I'd suggest you do other things too. Beer is only part of life, after all. I've always enjoyed trips to breweries more when we mixed in other attractions.

Upstate Beer
Adventure

Upstate Pennsylvania has a natural beauty to make most states envious. It's graced by the high lakes and birches of the Poconos, the "Grand Canyon of Pennsylvania," the gamelands of Potter County, the ridges and ravines of the Allegheny Forest and the crashing surf of Lake Erie. Anglers and hunters will find the state a rich preserve of fish and game in a tranquil setting of pine, oak, and mountain laurel, the state flower. For information on seasons, licenses, state game lands, and stocked lakes, call the Game Commission (717-787-4250) or the Fish and Boat Commission (717-657-4518).

Hikers and campers enjoy Pennsylvania's extensive system of trails and state campgrounds. The Appalachian Trail runs west along the front ridge of the Appalachians, then heads south between Gettysburg and Harrisburg. There are short hikes to scenic sites at Dingmans Falls in the Delaware Water Gap National Recreation Area and at Hawk Mountain Sanctuary. In the skies over Hawk Mountain, autumn migration routes converge, making the sanctuary an ideal spot for observing migratory hawks, eagles, and other birds of prey.

Pennsylvania has an extensive state park system, largely thanks to Governor Gifford Pinchot, a Reform governor who was a well-known conservationist and one of the Commonwealth's great politicians. (Pinchot was also an ardent prohibitionist who presided over the creation of the byzantine regulations of Pennsylvania's Liquor Code, but nobody's perfect.) You can get information about Pennsylvania's state parks from the Bureau of State Parks (800-637-2757). Be forewarned that drinking is forbidden in state parks and the rangers take it pretty seriously.

Upstate Pennsylvania also offers canoeing on rivers like the Allegheny, the Clarion, the Delaware, and the Susquehanna. For the more experienced whitewater aficionado, Pine Creek runs the Grand Canyon of Pennsylvania and is rated as a Class III trip. If you're traveling in winter, take your skis. Pennsylvania has more than thirty downhill ski areas, some with vertical drops of over 1,000 feet.

If you're a more sedentary type, upstate Pennsylvania offers many miles of scenic driving. Beyond the ridges of the Appalachian front lies the ravine and plateau country of the northwest. The fiery fall foliage of the northern tier rivals that of New England but draws far fewer people, leaving roads clear of leaf peepers. Along the way, well-kept small towns like Montrose, Emporium, Warren, and St. Marys, the home of Straub Brewing, shine with quiet beauty.

Potter County has been calling itself "God's Country" for years. I think it's safe to say that *all* of upstate Pennsylvania is pretty close to Heaven.

Hoppers Brewpub and Erie Brewing Company

123 W. 14th Street
Erie
814-452-2787

It's lonely up in the northwest corner by Lake Erie, especially when you're the only brewpub around. Hoppers has its work cut out for it, bringing the gospel of good beer to a dry land. It is miles and miles to another Pennsylvania brewery. Straub in St. Marys is closest, about two hours away. How does a brewery survive up here with no other brewers around to prime the pump for people's tastes?

Pretty well, actually. Part of it has to be the location. Hoppers is in a portion of the old train station, and it has been beautifully restored. Dark green paint and beige marble complement the dark wood paneling and fixtures, making this a soothing spot to relax and have a beer.

Bob Shaffer's little kingdom of tanks and kettles is tucked in the back of the brewpub, off the station's big central rotunda with its arching dome overhead. It's compact but neat in the brewhouse, a well-designed arena for mashing and fermentation. This is where Hoppers' beers are created, where the beloved Railbender was born.

There's no doubt about it: Erie loves Hoppers' Railbender Ale. Described by Bob as falling somewhere between an English old ale and a wee heavy, this big malty beer has more than a touch more alcohol than regular beers. At 6.8 percent ABV, it's one of the two best-sellers at the bar. The other is Mad Anthony's Red, a beer named for Revolutionary War hero General "Mad" Anthony Wayne (also known to regulars as "Crazy Tony"). In an era in which most brewpub patrons ask for "whatever's your lightest beer," Railbender is strongly bucking the trend.

That's why Railbender and Mad Anthony's Red are in bottles. Hoppers is, after all, also known as Erie Brewing Company. Bob sees an opportunity to jump into the market with beers that already meet the local tastes. And currently there are no competing local brewers.

Some might say that Hoppers doesn't have a ghost of a chance, but Hoppers is familiar with those, too. One of the serving staff swears she saw a man walking up a stairway that led to nowhere in the closed off section of the train station. Bob himself has heard odd noises during off hours, but he tries not to think about them…

There is a forties feel to Hoppers bar as you sit with your beer by the Arrivals board. (These days the board is chalked up with beers coming on tap, not trains coming into the station.) Maybe if you put on a fedora and a trenchcoat, Lauren Bacall just might come tap-tap-tapping across the marble floor to join you for a Railbender.

Opened: January 1994.

Type: Brewery and brewpub.

Owners: Phil Eden, Bill Miller, Mark Armbruster.

Brewer: Bob Shaffer.

PA Microbrewers Guild: Not a member.

System: 10-barrel JVNW brewhouse. Potential annual capacity 2,300 barrels.

Annual production: 1,100 barrels in 1997.

Beers brewed: *Year-round:* Railbender Ale, Mad Anthony's Red, Gold Spike Wheat, Presque Isle Pale Ale, Drake's Crude Ale, Kolsch-bier. *Seasonals:* IPA, Oatmeal Stout, Maibock, Hazelnut Porter. All beers brewed on premises.

The Pick: It's Drake's Crude, but don't think it was an easy choice. The big Railbender came in a close second with its hypnotic maltiness. But I picked Drake's Crude because it's a hefty brown ale with some real flavor. I've tasted brewpub porters with less character than Drake's Crude. This weighty ale may be flagrantly outside the style parameters, but so what? It's a good beer.

Take-out beer: Growlers, Railbender and Mad Anthony's Red in bottles. Two more beers to be bottled in 1998.

Tours: Saturday, 4:00 P.M.–5:00 P.M., and by appointment.

Brewpub hours: Monday through Saturday, 11:30 A.M.–2:00 A.M.; closed Sunday.

Food: Southwestern cuisine.

Extras: Hoppers has a full liquor license, darts, pinball, and pool tables. You can enjoy live music every week, Wednesday through Saturday.

Events: Oktoberfest and a St. Patrick's day party with special stout.

Special considerations: Kids welcome. Handicapped-accessible. Cigars allowed and sold. Vegetarian meals available.

Parking: Plenty of parking out front in the park.

Lodging: Spencer House B&B, 519 West Sixth Street (814-454-5984); Glass House Inn, 3202 West Sixth Street (800-956-7222); Red Roof Inn, 7865 Perry Highway (814-868-5246).

Nearby attractions: Presque Isle State Park on Lake Erie is the closest

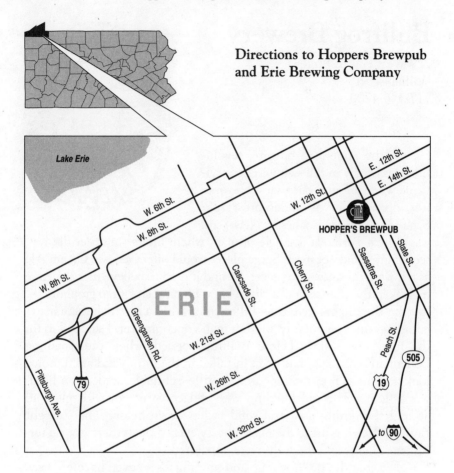

Directions to Hoppers Brewpub and Erie Brewing Company

thing Pennsylvania has to a seashore. This sand spit has some beautiful beaches undisturbed by boardwalks or hotels. It is a wildlife conservation area with trails, swimming, boating, fishing, and picnicking areas (814-833-7424). Right at the entrance to the park is Waldameer Amusement Park and Water World (814-838-3591). There is a minor league baseball team and hockey team in town; ask at the brewpub for schedules.

Other good beer sites in the area: Sullivan's Pub and Eatery has the best Guinness in town. 301 French Street (814-452-3446 or 814-459-3222). Oscar's is Erie's relaxed and comfortable multitap bar at Twelfth and Pittsburgh Streets in the plaza (814-454-4325).

Bullfrog Brewery

229 West Fourth Street
Williamsport
717-326-4700

I knew the American brewing revolution was finally in full swing in Pennsylvania when I found out that a brewpub was opening in Williamsport. From Scranton to Erie to Rochester, New York, was a great Bermuda Triangle of malt, where interesting beer did not, seemingly could not exist. Some places would offer Genesee Cream Ale as if it were the answer to prayer. I found it hard to believe that someone had taken the chance of planting a brewpub on such barren ground.

But the rumors were true; Billtown now has a brewpub. One man's barren ground is evidently another man's open market. I stopped in for the first time shortly before Bullfrog opened, when the gleaming Bohemian brewhouse had been installed in the front windows. I took a look around as brewmaster-to-be Charlie Schnable sanded the hardwood floors. The old building was well constructed, with glass all around the dining area and solid beams down below. The sunlight through the glass made the place cheery even though there was no furniture or lights and the walls were unpainted.

Now that the Bullfrog is up and running it's an even happier place. Williamsport seems to love it, and business is good. Brewpubs often brew lighter beers to get people in the door. After they're in, the bartender works his will on them and lures them on to Amber, Porter, Stout...That's the primrose path Williamsport's beer drinkers are treading now, courtesy of Mr. Schnable and Company.

Bullfrog has a series of good beers. Marzen's maltiness is autumnally appropriate and Susquehanna Stout is a smooth dry stout. Bullfrog also offers pure fruit flavorings for customers to add to the light-bodied wheat beer.

The Bullfrog is a friendly oasis of variety and character. You might even consider a trek into the old "Beermuda Triangle" just to check it out.

Opened: August 1996.

Type: Brewpub.

Owners: Bob Koch, Harriet Koch, Steven Koch, Charles Schnable, Barbara Whipple, Marjorie Hynson, John Hynson.

Brewer: Charles Schnable.

PA Microbrewers Guild: Not a member.

System: 10-barrel Bohemian brewhouse. Potential annual capacity 1,500 barrels.

Annual production: 610 barrels in 1997.

Beers brewed: *Year-round:* Billtown Blonde, Fruit Wheat, Red Ale, Susquehanna Stout, IPA. *Seasonals:* Sailfrog Ale, Marzen, Christmas Warmer, Elderberry Stout, Dunkelweizen, Dunkel, Williamsporter, Brown Ale, Oktoberfest, Anniversary Ale, Bavarian Weiss. All beers brewed on premises.

The Pick: I'll pick my second-favorite beer, and I'll give you the reason. Bullfrog's IPA is served too cold for its own good; let it warm up and it has a beatiful spicy hop aroma that is one of the best around. My favorite Bullfrog beer, though, was the Anniversary Ale, a big chewy beer that straddled the point where old ale, strong ale, and barleywine come together. Make it again, Charlie!

Take-out beer: Half- and 1-gallon growlers, quarter and half kegs (call ahead for keg availability).

Tours: Call ahead; tours are available whenever the brewer is in.

Brewpub hours: Monday through Thursday, 11:00 A.M.–midnight; Friday through Saturday, 11:00 A.M.–2:00 A.M.; Sunday, 9:00 A.M.(brunch)–midnight.

Food: Bullfrog's menu features brewpub staples like nachos, burgers, and a range of sandwiches, but they also have vegetarian dishes, pasta entrees, and seafood.

Extras: Darts, live music several times a week (call for schedule), and "goofy dance theme" evenings. (I don't make this stuff up, I just report it.)

Special consideratons: Kids welcome. Handicapped-accessible. Cigars allowed. Vegetarian meals available.

Parking: On-street parking. Parking garage one block away.

Lodging: Genetti Hotel & Suites, 200 West Fourth Street (717-326-6600); Econo Lodge, 2401 East Third Street (717-326-1501). Reighard House B&B, 1323 East Third Street (717-326-3593).

Nearby attractions: Williamsport is the birthplace of Little League baseball and home of the annual Little League World Series in August. Call the Chamber of Commerce for information (717-326-1971). The Peter J. McGovern Little League Museum, next to the

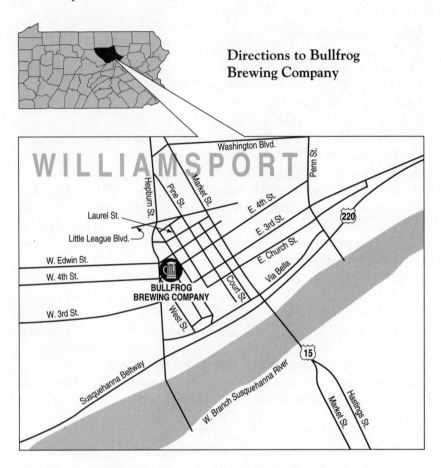

Directions to Bullfrog Brewing Company

World Series field on Route 15, has batting cages, Little League history, and major leaguers' Little League uniforms and equipment. Take a Susquehanna River ride on the *Hiawatha*, a paddle-wheel riverboat (800-358-9900). In nearby Woolrich, you'll find the Woolrich Mills factory outlet and some outstanding bargains (717-769-7401). If you go south from Williamsport on Route 15, stop at the scenic overlook where you can see the whole valley stretching out for miles. Further down the road is Clyde Peeling's Reptiland, a reptile zoo with snakes, lizards, tortoises, frogs, and alligators. It's a Pennsylvania classic (800-REPTILAND).

Other good beer sites in the area: Russell's, at 117 West Main Street in Bloomsburg, is an outstandingly civilized restaurant and bar with excellent beer and whiskey. Call 717-387-1332 for directions. Selin's Grove and Russell's are both over half an hour away, but they're worth the trip. See also other good beer sites on page 158.

Selin's Grove
Brewing Company

119 N. Market Street
Selinsgrove
717-374-7308

"What do you think of this one?" "Maybe I'll try one of those." "Look at that!" "How about a little more?" "This one's pretty good." "Is that one ready yet?" *You* try sitting at the bar at Selin's Grove without hearing other people's conversations!

One of the reasons I like this little basement brewpub is the low-volume background music and lack of television. Steve Leason and Heather McNabb say they want people to "practice the art of communication," something that all too many pubs make impossible.

Steve and Heather are like that. Maybe a touch of hippie is in these two; it seems that anyone who lives in Colorado picks up some of that. But don't think it's all "wow, man" and starry eyes in Selin's Grove. These folks work for a living. And they do good work, too.

The beer is knock-your-socks-off stuff. Heather and Steve both brew, and it's impossible to tell who brews which beer. I tried nine beers when I was last at Selin's Grove and seven of them were exceptional. My notes have phrases like "reaches out and grabs you" (Old Trail ESB), "real beer" (Cream Ale), and "intensely flavored, a knockout beer" (Shade Mountain Oatmeal Stout). All this good beer comes from a classic "Frankenstein" brewhouse, pieces from here and there cobbled together by Steve and Heather and family and friends.

Financial reasons forced the two to locate in Selinsgrove, but they have made the best of it. The brewpub occupies the basement of the Snyder mansion, which belongs to Heather's parents. "We're here because we could afford it," Heather cheerfully admits.

Any qualms they may have had about their new location were settled early by a little thing Heather saw in a local church cookbook. "We realized the brewpub would be within 100 feet of a church," Heather recalls. This proximity would allow the church to block the brewpub. "We went over to see if we could talk to them about it," she continued, "and I saw the church cookbook, one of those community projects. I opened it and on the first page was a homebrew recipe. We thought that looked like we had a pretty good chance!"

The couple delved into Selinsgrove history, looking for evidence of a brewing heritage. They came across a few mentions, but were more interested in something else they found. It seems a man named Mathias App had a distillery in Selinsgrove in the early 1800s. He had a water pump at the distillery that was powered by stray dogs in a wheel, and he paid small boys to catch dogs for him. Heather and Steve liked this image of a dog-powered distillery so much they made it the symbol of the brewery.

Selin's Grove is very much out of the ordinary for a brewpub. Its intimate size, fireplace, vegetarian entrees, smoke-free environment, and wide range of excellent beers help set it apart. That's precisely why I like it.

Opened: December 1996.

Type: Brewpub.

Owners: Heather McNabb, Steven Leason.

Brewers: Heather McNabb, Steven Leason.

PA Microbrewers Guild: Not a member.

System: 3-barrel self-designed brewhouse, built from scratch. Potential annual capacity 300 barrels.

Annual production: Projected 1997 production is 175 barrels.

Beers brewed: *Year-round:* Shade Mountain Oatmeal Stout, White Horse Porter, Stealth Triple, Old Trail ESB, Priestly Pale Ale, Smooth John Scottish Ale. *Seasonals:* Fruit beer (fruit changes seasonally), Wilder's Weissbier, St. Fillan's Wee Heavy, Barleywine Ale. This list is still growing; call for current taps. Selin's Grove has two beer engines and cask-conditions some of its beers for hand dispense. All beers brewed on premises.

The Pick: This is an outstanding selection of beers for such a tiny, young brewpub. I have two favorites. The Shade Mountain Oatmeal Stout is a lighter-bodied yet intensely flavored stout, possessed of smooth body with a real roasted barley bite—a great all-around stout. The Barleywine Ale is very broad and full of malt, with a pleasing touch of butterscotch, fruitiness, and alcohol heat.

Take-out beer: Half-gallon and 2-liter growlers.

Tours: "Anytime we are not too busy we are happy to give tours."

Brewpub hours: Wednesday and Thursday, 4:00 P.M.–11:00 P.M.; Friday and Saturday, noon–midnight. (Expanded hours are planned. Please call ahead.)

Food: Sandwiches, soups, and salads make up the bulk of the menu, along with two weekly hot entree specials. The emphasis is on

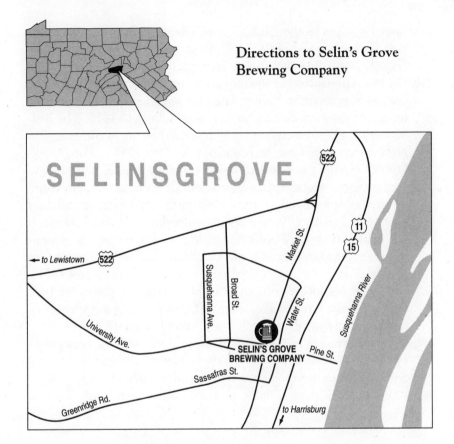

healthy, vegetarian items. (In a brewpub? Amazing!) Good, house-made root beer, organic coffees and teas round out the menu for kids and nondrinkers.

Extras: Live music every other week—bluegrass, swing, folk, blues, and much more. Call for schedule. Assorted books, magazines, tavern puzzles, backgammon, and chess. "We're too small for darts," says Steve Leason. Now that's a *microbrewery!*

Special considerations: Kids welcome. Handicapped-accessible. Interior is completely smoke-free, but in the outside beer garden, cigars and cigarettes are allowed. Many vegetarian meals available, including selections to suit full vegans.

Parking: The entrance to the brewpub is actually in the rear, not on Market Street. Parking is available on Market; then you simply walk through the side garden to the rear entrance. There is also a parking lot off Strawberry Alley.

Lodging: Potteiger House B&B, 8 West Chestnut Street, half a block from brewpub (717-374-0415); Comfort Inn, 710 South Route 11/15 (717-374-8880); Hampton Inn, 3 Stettler Avenue (717-743-2223).

Nearby attractions: Small museums and restored homes abound in the central Susquehanna Valley. The brewpub itself is in the restored home of Governor Simon Snyder, which dates to 1816. The Mifflinburg Buggy Museum at 523 Green Street in Mifflinburg displays carriage-making techniques (717-966-1355). The Joseph Priestly House, the home of a wide-ranging thinker who discovered oxygen, founded the Unitarian Church in America, and influenced the writing of the Constitution, has been restored for visits. 472 Priestley Avenue, Northumberland (717-473-9474). If you're as nuts about Woolrich clothing as I am, run up the river to Route 44, head over Bald Eagle Mountain, and follow the signs to Woolrich and the huge Woolrich factory store (717-769-7401). For more outdoorsy fun, the Susquehanna has plenty of boat ramps, Middle Creek Lake, south of Selinsgrove, is a stocked fishing lake, and state game lands are scattered along the river.

Other good beer sites in the area: BJ's, one block from the brewpub at 17 North Market, is a steak and rib restaurant with several micros on tap. There's not much else within thirty miles.

The Franconia Brewing Company

Pocono Mountains Business Park
(off Route 940)
Mt. Pocono
800-367-2348
www.franconia-beer.com

Franconia was not yet brewing when I finished this book in January of 1998. The beautiful copper Huppmann brewhouse was still being refurbished and plumbed, the refrigeration units sat unassembled on the floor, the lagering tanks were not in place, and welders were still fabricating some of the fittings. But I know there will be beer, and I know it will be good, because I know Guy Hagner.

Guy has been working toward this for a long time. He went to Germany back in 1980 as part of obtaining a degree in economics. Before he left, his dad gave him a copy of Michael Jackson's *World Guide to Beer*. It became a malty *Guide Michelin* for Guy and his friends as they sampled Germany's best beer while they learned about Deutschebank policy. As Guy drank nectar at the small *hausbrauerei* of Bavaria, Franconia, Austria, and Czechoslovakia, he grew convinced that small, local breweries would work in the United States. He decided to learn about brewing so he could become part of it.

After working a few years for Pabst and learning all he could, Guy attended the Siebel Institute in Chicago, America's premier brewing school. His first job as a brewer was as an assistant to the brewmaster at Dixie Brewing in New Orleans. It was a fateful appointment; four months later the brewmaster died of a heart attack and Guy was given the job "because they could get me really cheap!" He was there four years, during which time he helped formulate Dixie's Blackened Voodoo beer, a beer that spread Dixie's name throughout the country.

New Orleans was fun, exotic, and delicious. "I gained fifty pounds there!" Guy laughs. But he and his wife decided to move closer to home, and in 1990 Guy became brewmaster at The Lion in Wilkes-Barre. After four years brewing under the financial constraints of a brewery struggling to survive, he struck out on his own with the Franconia project. Now, almost eighteen years after Guy first had the idea of a small American brewery making high-quality German-style lagers, his journey is about to come to an end in the beginning of Franconia.

Guy intends Franconia to be the most authentic producer of German-style beers in America. The brewery's German brewhouse was originally installed in the Dietz brewery in Weismain, in Franconia. Guy will use all German malt, almost all of it from Bamberg, milled in a German four-roller mill. He has worked with the Keesmann brewery of Bamberg and will be brewing their Herren Pils under contract. Everything possible is being done to brew true-to-style lagers and other German beer types.

The proof is in the drinking, of course. By the time you read this, Franconia's beer will be on the market and you'll be able to judge for yourself.

Opened: Projected for April 1998.

Type: Brewery.

Owner: Pennsylvania C-Corporation with approximately 2,300 shareholders. Guy Hagner, president.

Brewer: Guy Hagner.

PA Microbrewers Guild: Not a member.

System: 60-barrel Huppmann brewhouse. Potential annual capacity 10,000–12,000 barrels.

Annual production: No figures available yet.

Beers brewed: *Year-round:* Herren Pils, Helles, Dunkles, Braunbier Lager. *Seasonals:* Weiss (amber, hearty type), Doppelbock, Rauchbier, Festbier, Altbier. All beers brewed on premises.

The Pick: At the time I visited Franconia, the Herren Pils was the only beer available. That was fine with me, because even at the end of a big 25-ounce mug, I wanted more. This is sublimely German pilsner with a steady malt base and a bitter hop snap to it, a dry combination that leaves you ready for another.

Take-out beer: Kegs and cases.

Tours: Call for seasonal schedule of tours.

Brewpub hours: Call for hours.

Food: Simple fare, just enough to tide you over and keep you from getting too tipsy.

Events: Events planned for now are an Oktoberfest and the occasional Trainfest. The rail line from Scranton's Steamtown runs less than fifty yards from the back of the brewery. Trainloads of people have already come up for brats, blues, and beer.

Special considerations: Kids welcome. Handicapped-accessible.

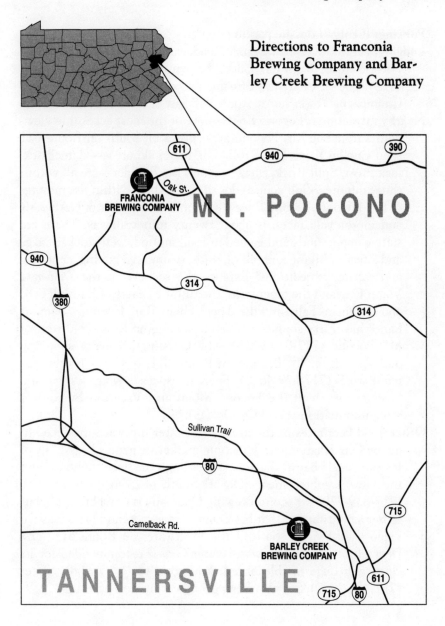

Directions to Franconia
Brewing Company and Bar-
ley Creek Brewing Company

Parking: Plenty of on-site parking.

Lodging: Farmhouse B&B, Grange Road, east of town (717-839-0796); Pocono Super 8 Motel, south of town on Route 611 (717-839-7728); Caesar's Paradise Stream, Poconos resort with the famed Champagne Tower suites, Route 940 east of town (717-839-8881).

Nearby attractions: Pocono Knob is one of the most accessible viewpoints from the Mt. Pocono area, just a bit south on Route 611 then east on Knob Hill Road. The major ski areas—Camelback, Jack Frost, Split Rock, Shawnee, and Big Boulder—are all within thirty minutes. Golf courses dot the area, three within ten minutes of Mt. Pocono. Pocono Raceway, home to a number of NASCAR and motorcycle races, is about twenty minutes away. There are state campgrounds and game lands all around, well-stocked lakes and streams, hiking and biking trails, swimming, golfing, canoeing and rafting expeditions. Explore the scenery of the Delaware Water Gap and the mountains, the rushing beauty of Bushkill Falls and Dingmans Falls, and the Appalachian Trail. If it rains, Summit Lanes has thirty-six lanes of great bowling on Route 940 west of Mt. Pocono (717-839-9635). The Crossings, a major shopping outlet south of Mt. Pocono on Route 611, has over 100 brand-name stores (717-629-4650). There is also a yearly jazz festival and blues festival; call the Pocono Mountains Vacation Bureau for more information (800-POCONOS).

Other good beer sites in the area: Swiftwater Inn was introduced to me by Guy Hagner and Franconia marketing genius Rick Maisto. It's the classic bar in the area. Yuengling's the beer of choice, and the view is subterranean. Dig it! South of town on Route 611 (717-839-7206). Pocono Brewing Company is not a brewpub, but rather a multitap bar that books major blues acts and has a massive video wall TV. It's south of the Swiftwater on Route 611. The Deer Head Inn in Delaware Water Gap is recommended for its classically huge marble urinal. You gotta see it! 5 Main Street (717-424-2000). See also other good beer sites on page 165.

Barley Creek
Brewing Company

Sullivan Trail and Camelback Road
Tannersville
717-629-9399
www.barleycreek.com

Trip Ruvane claims that Barley Creek Brewing Company is housed in a renovated nineteenth century farmhouse. If you press him on that, he will laughingly admit that the farmhouse was "renovated with extreme prejudice." What he means is that he and his crew intended to restore the building, but once they got into the job they realized it had to be *seriously* renovated . . . as in torn down. That's the source of the ball peen hammer tap handle for Barley Creek's excellent Renovator Stout.

But the structure you see is authentically old, at least in part. The stone foundation and cellar remain, making an attractive office wall for Trip and his wife, Eileen. Upstairs, where you and I drink Trip's beer and eat his delicious food, much of the exposed wood—solidly thick beams and paneling—was salvaged from old buildings.

Barley Creek is one of the most attractive new-construction brewpubs around. It's designed like a tall-peaked wooden ski chalet, airy and open with miles of overhead space. Glass walls at either end let the sun shine on the dining room and provide passing motorists a striking view of the brewery's tanks. More than a few of them have stopped.

Visitors to the area abound. The Poconos may not have the biggest vertical drops or the deepest powder (or any powder) but they are the heart of a gorgeous region located close enough to several urban areas to be an easy weekend trip for many people. You can ski in the Poconos without fighting your way through an airport with your skis or white-knuckling it up the interstate to New England with one ear cocked for the radar detector's whine. You can relax, get in your skiing, and still have time for a trip to the brewpub.

What a place for a pub to be situated, halfway between a major ski area (Camelback) and a major outlet mall (the Crossings). The mind happily waffles: Should we go up the mountain and ski, down the mountain and shop, or just stay here on the side of the mountain and have a few more of these delicious beers?

Barley Creek doesn't just serve excellent beer. Trip hired a great chef away from a country club and put him to work conjuring up out-of-the-ordinary fare. My favorite is Crane's Crazy Chip Dip, the recipe for which Trip claims to have won in a drunken, late-night game of Blockhead. Served in a hot crock surrounded by a variety of corn chips, Crane's dip is a cheesey, spicy, appealingly gooey mess that is just the thing on a cold day. Or a hot day. Or a rainy day. Any day, so long as you're at the bar with a glass of Renovator or the new SuperHOP.

After working hard in banking and public relations, Trip and Eileen Ruvane appear to have found their niche. They run an outstandingly clean, fun, and satisfying brewpub with great food and beer. That it is perched in the Poconos, where they love to be, is a happy bonus.

Opened: December 1995.

Type: Brewpub.

Owners: Trip Ruvane, Eileen Ruvane.

Brewers: Tim Phillips, Rico Gallo.

PA Microbrewers Guild: Member.

System: 10-barrel Peter Austin brewhouse. Potential annual capacity 3,000 barrels.

Annual production: 1,900 barrels in 1996.

Beers brewed: *Year-round:* Brown Antler Ale, Renovator Stout, Aussie Gold, IPA, and ESB. *Seasonals:* SuperHOP, J. B.'s Irish Red, Albee Bock, Strawberry Wheat, Hefe Weizen, Cranberry Bog Wheat, Jenkins Woods Lager, Dunkelblitzen Lager, Deacon Dortmunder, Black Widow Lager, Barley Black & Brown, Wahoo Wheat, Chestnut Mountain Lager, Export Ale, Atlas Ale, Apple Creek Ale, Khunnermann's Cream Ale, Blackberry Porter, "and more to come." All beers brewed on premises.

The Pick: It's Renovator Stout for the dark full body, to the pleasant dryness of the finish, even the hammerhead tap handle. I pretty much love everything about this beer. Renovator is the reason I go to some beer festivals. It is the best stout I've ever had from a Ringwood yeast brewery. Every now and then a keg finds its way down here to Bucks County; otherwise I have to find an excuse to head up to Tannersville to get an occasional fix.

Take-out beer: Kegs and half gallon growlers.

Tours: Monday through Friday, 12:30 P.M. and 4:00 P.M.; Sundays at 12:30 P.M.; and by appointment.

Brewpub hours: Seven days a week, 11:30 A.M.–"late night."

Food: It's all pretty good. They offer homemade soups, imaginative appetizers, hearty sandwiches, pub grub, fresh desserts, big steaks and a kids' menu.

Extras: Gift shop. Live music on weekends. Outdoor deck. Two full bars (one on deck). Pool tables, foosball, and skiing machine. Ping-Pong Monday nights. Bar games and metal ring puzzles. Summer Brewgrass festival, Great Pocono Wing-Off (August) and Chowder-Off (spring), Malt Masters Invitational Micro-brew Fest (early ski season). Far Side comics in the bathrooms. Eileen Ruvane says, "If you can't find something to do at Barley Creek, seek therapy."

Special considerations: Kids welcome. Handicapped-accessible. Cigars allowed. Vegetarian meals available.

Directions: See map on page 161

Parking: Plentiful on-site parking.

Lodging: Pine Knob Inn B&B, Route 447, Canadensis (717-595-2532); Holiday Inn, Route 611, Bartonsville (717-424-6100); The Chateau Resort, Camelback Road, Tannersville (717-629-5900); Comfort Inn, Route 611, Bartonsville (717-476-1500).

Nearby attractions: Tannersville is right in the middle of the Poconos. See nearby attractions on page 162.

Other good beer sites in the area: Pocono Brewing Company is not a brewpub, it's a multitap bar that books major blues acts and sports a massive videowall TV. It's about five miles north on Route 611. Cooper's Seafood House is one of the original beer bars and still has a selection big enough to satisfy any thirsty beer geek. 701 North Washington Avenue, Scranton (717-346-6883). Pearly Baker's is an elegant multitap with a fine dining menu, right on Center Square in Easton (610-253-9949). See also other good beer sites on page 162.

A *word about . . .*

The Pennsylvania Microbrewers Guild

A number of Keystone State breweries have formed the Pennsylvania Microbrewers Guild to promote Pennsylvania's own beers to Pennsylvanians. "It's primarily a business and marketing organization," according to Dan Weirback, first guild president and principal of Weyerbacher Brewing Company in Easton. "The two goals are to promote awareness of fine Pennsylvania micros to the public and to support more modern brewery laws in Pennsylvania."

Membership in the guild currently stands at fouteen: Barley Creek (Tannersville), Church Brew Works (Pittsburgh), Independence (Philadelphia), Lancaster Malt (Lancaster), Pennsylvania (Pittsburgh), Pretzel City (Reading), Red Bell (Philadelphia), Sly Fox (Phoenixville), Stoudt's (Adamstown), Tröegs (Harrisburg), Valley Forge (Wayne), Weyerbacher (Easton), Whitetail (Carlisle), and Yards (Philadelphia).

According to Tom Kehoe, co-owner of Yards and 1997 guild vice president, membership is limited to "brewers who have a Pennsylvania brewing license and have their own equipment and those who brew true to style; that is, no adjuncts unless they're true to the style of the beer." It all started in September 1996, when Carol Stoudt sent a letter to some of the brewers about starting an organization. Meetings followed, and the guild incorporated and adopted rules and by-laws in April of 1997. That's when things took a bad turn. The sticking point appears to have been defining membership eligibility.

The problem concerned contract brewing, which surely comes as no surprise to anyone who has followed the contentious wrangling over this aspect of the brewing industry. Disagreement on this issue led to Victory Brewing's withdrawing from the guild. Victory's Bill Covaleski warned the group that requiring members simply to own brewing equipment and hold a Pennsylvania brewing license was not enough: "As a group, with significant investment in your own brewing facilities, you have chosen to validate the labels of others who may choose to undertake as little as the investment of packaging and a single barrel brewhouse."

In other words, a brewer who has beer made under contract is still allowed to become a member of the guild, provided he or she owns a brewhouse, however small. This rankled some who viewed membership in the guild as a kind of certificate or guarantee of good beer and craft-brewing practices.

Tom Kehoe said, "It seems to be calming down. We're just saying, 'Look, we're not trying to be real exclusive, we're trying to promote ourselves.' Our competition shouldn't be each other; it's the bigger guys." The eligibility issue took up a lot of the guild's energies in its first year. They still managed to get a promotional brochure printed and distributed to the state's visitor centers and beer distributors. The guild also held its first beer festival, at Barley Creek, in November 1997. The comfortable atmosphere of the festival seemed to go a long way toward ironing out difficulties.

Current guild president David Biles, of Valley Forge Brewing Company, said that the guild has set its sights on Harrisburg and points west. The major legislative goal is to influence Project 2000, the total overhaul of the state liquor code by the Pennsylvania Liquor Control Board. The guild is working with the Pennsylvania Beer Wholesalers Association on common goals. "Our main aim is to open the marketplace on package sales," Dave explained. "We're also working on forming a relationship with the state's small wineries to cross-promote each other's products." The Guild is addressing the distance problem of the western brewers by starting a western chapter. "We have a major membership initiative this year," Dave said. "Most of the new brewers in Pennsylvania are interested, as are the new brewpubs in the southeastern part of the state. We had some birthing problems, but now we're a cute toddler and everyone likes us."

Pittsburgh:
(Not Just) Iron City

Pittsburgh has come a long way from the days of Carnegie and Frick. The steel mills are silent—or leveled—and the coke furnaces no longer loft their foul stench on the breeze. Pittsburgh went through hard, hard times in the 1970s and 1980s. The population dropped and thousands lost high-wage jobs as the American steel production industry collapsed under the pressure of subsidized overseas competition. Major regional brewer Pittsburgh Brewing—and its Iron City beer—fell into the hands of Australian investors. This city, once a symbol of American industrial might, was turning into a rusty ghost town.

I went to grad school in Pittsburgh in 1982. I treasured visits to Homestead to drink at Chiodo's Tavern. I drank my share of I.C. Light and Straub on my student budget. During that time and in subsequent visits over the next years I watched the city sink into a malaise as dreary as the faded old yellow brick homes peculiar to the city. I didn't know how Chiodo's would survive the demolition of the Homestead Steel Works, a massive structure right behind the bar that was a source of its business and pride.

One of the first harbingers of a turnaround was Tom Pastorius's return to town from Germany in 1985 with his idea for a microbrewery. After testing the waters by having Pittsburgh Brewing contract brew their beer for a couple years, they started work on their restaurant and Pennsylvania Brewery. Hard work and tight budgets began to slowly pay off.

Similarly, the city started a slow return to health. Pittsburgh gradually let go of the idea that big steel would return, bringing high wages and union power with it, and started to search for its future in other directions. The citizens began to realize their strengths: smaller specialty steel industries, health care, excellent universities, river trade, and tourism. Local businesses found innovative ways to compete, and employees and city government cooperated to persuade companies to stay in the 'Burgh.

Today Pittsburgh is a hardworking town with its eyes on a new future. This city of 1,500 bridges has built on the strength of its past—its museums, fine architecture, and revived industries—to span the abyss left by the departed steel industry. The South Side is a bustling center of nightlife and the suburbs are growing and sprouting new businesses.

I was happy to return to Pittsburgh in 1997, after five years away, and see a cleaner, more confident city with new growth sparking all over. Pittsburgh Brewing was locally owned once more, and Tom Pastorius's lagers were nationally recognized for their excellence. There are new breweries in town too: Church Brew Works, the Foundry, the Strip, Valhalla, and a John Harvard's out in the eastern suburbs. There are new beer bars with lots of great taps, and the Sharp Edge—just two blocks from where I used to live—has one of the best selections of draft Belgian beers in the country.

Best of all, Joe Chiodo's tavern survives and thrives. This consummate neighborhood bar still has the vine-shaded deck, the Mystery Sandwich, the best fries (real potatoes, no spices, no funny cuts), and a great selection of import beers at reasonable prices. Chiodo's is Pittsburgh for me; whether it's up, down, or struggling, it's always friendly, sincere, and open-hearted.

Go to Pittsburgh as a beer traveler, but don't miss all the other things the city has to offer.

To avoid lots of repetition, I have decided to consolidate the **Nearby attractions, Lodging,** and **Other good beer sites in the area** sections for the Pittsburgh breweries. The entry for John Harvard's Brew House in Wilkins Township includes information specific to that area. The other breweries are all very close to one another. (My sincere thanks to Tom and Mary Beth Pastorius of Pennsylvania Brewing for their significant help with this section.)

Attractions: You may want to come to Pittsburgh just to look at its architectural glories. This city is full of beautiful buildings, both industrial and residential. The Carnegie Museums house just about everything: dinosaurs, Egyptian artifacts, gems and minerals, wind tunnels and earthquake simulations, and Impressionist art. Surely something will interest you or your family. Call 412-622-3131 for the Carnegie Museum of Art and the Carnegie Museum of Natural History at 4400 Forbes Avenue and 412-237-3400 for the Carnegie Science Center at 1 Allegheny Avenue. Another Carnegie Museum is dedicated entirely to a famous Pittsburgh native's work: The Andy Warhol Museum is at 117 Sandusky Street (412-237-8300). The Frick Art and Historical Center includes the restored mansion of Henry Clay Frick, the Carriage Museum with sleighs and vintage automobiles, and the Frick Art Museum. 7227 Reynolds Street (412-371-0606).

Point State Park, where the Allegheny and Monongahela Rivers meet to form the Ohio River, is a beautiful green spot right beside downtown. The 150-foot spray of the fountain is one of the largest in the country. Don't miss the Duquesne Incline, a Victorian solution to Pittsburgh's steep south shore hills. Ride the incline's hill-hugging cable car up to the aptly named Grandview Avenue for a spectacular view of the Golden Triangle (412-381-1665).

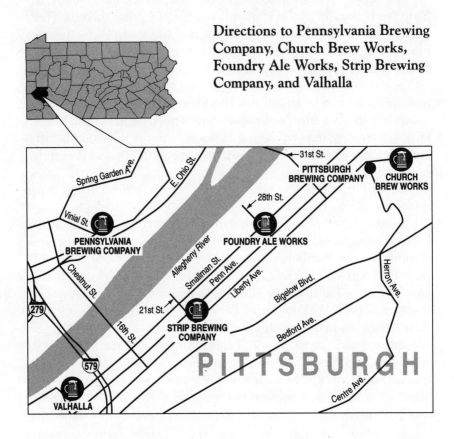

Directions to Pennsylvania Brewing Company, Church Brew Works, Foundry Ale Works, Strip Brewing Company, and Valhalla

For just walking around and having fun while maybe buying a few things, you have two great choices: the Strip District and South Side. The Strip District is Pittsburgh's produce and meat market, north and south of the 2000 block of Penn Avenue This is a busy, bustling, fun place during the day. At night things shift to the South Side, on Carson Street around Fat Head's and Smokin' Joe's. This is a younger, more fringe scene, but a lot of fun, and you can find some great casual food and drink here.

The Pittsburgh Zoo has Siberian tigers, zebras, elephants, and the AquaZoo's shark tank and living coral reef. There is a special kids' zoo with a sea lion pool (412-665-3640). For more rousing recreation, Kennywood Amusement Park, 4800 Kennywood Boulevard, West Mifflin, has four roller coasters, thirty other rides, and fourteen children's rides (412-461-0500). There's also Sandcastle, a water park on the

Monongahela with water slides, a huge hot tub, a lazy river, and go-karts (412-462-6666).

Pittsburgh celebrates in the summer. The Shadyside Summer Arts Festival in July and August starts the ball rolling, followed by the Three Rivers Art Festival and the ten-day Mellon Jazz Festival in June. The Three Rivers Regatta is on the first weekend in August, a wild time in this river city. For further information on these events and other attractions, call the Greater Pittsburgh Convention and Visitors Bureau (412-281-7711).

Lodging: The Priory–A City Inn, historic B&B, 614 Pressley Street (412-231-3338); Doubletree Hotel, 1000 Penn Avenue (412-281-3700 or 800-222-TREE), Best Western, Parkway Center Inn, Parkway Center Mall, 875 Greentree Road (412-922-7070).

Camping: Ohiopyle State Park (412-329-8951), Raccoon Creek State Park (412-899-2200).

Other good beer sites in the area: Headwaters Cafe is located in Three Rivers Stadium and serves Penn Brewing beers during sports events. The Sharp Edge has great bar food and probably the best selection of Belgian taps in the United States outside of Philadelphia. It alone is worth a visit to Pittsburgh. 302 South Saint Clair Street (412-661-3537). Kaya has a funky menu of Caribbean fusion and vegetarian dishes and great beer. It's a cool place at 2000 Smallman Street in the Strip (412-261-6565). Smokin' Joe's has a wall o' taps going, and the bartenders were very beer savvy the night I was there. East Carson and Twentieth on South Side (412-341-6757). When you go to Fat Head's, get a Headwich and wash it down with any of the great beers available. Fat Head's has an excellent selection in bottles and twenty taps. 1805 East Carson Street (412-431-7433). The Squirrel Hill Cafe, known as the "Squirrel Cage," is a bit bright, loud, and young in the evenings, but the beer is top-notch and reasonably priced. They have a broad selection of nonlocal microbrews at 5802 Forbes Avenue (412-521-3327). Chiodo's is the must-see, must-go, must-drink bar in Pittsburgh. I love this place, it's a bar's bar. 107 West Eighth Street, Homestead (412-416-3113).

Pennsylvania Brewing Company

800 Vinial Street
Pittsburgh
412-237-9400
www.pennbrew.com

Tom Pastorius once told me a very simple truth about why he opened a microbrewery and why it brews the kinds of beers it does. "Pennsylvania Brewing exists to make beers that I like," he said. Those beers are German-style lagers, and Tom's brewery makes some of the best in the United States.

Lagers are underappreciated by most American beer geeks, though, and that's part of the reason Pennsylvania Brewing has had such a hard time becoming popular. This lack of appreciation is a mystery to me. Carol Stoudt blames it on "Budweiser backlash." "Budweiser is the beer that micro lovers hate—for whatever reasons—and it's a lager. They throw all lagers together as dull beers."

That makes it particularly tough on microbrewers who want to brew lagers, for not only are lagers less popular, but they are substantially more expensive to brew. They are more labor-intensive than ales, use more energy (cooling costs for the lagering), and they stay in the tanks longer, which means the same amount of tankage produces less lager than ale in a year. And yet a brewer cannot charge more for lagers. The customers don't see or care about the extra costs, so they won't pay more for the beer.

What's more, lager brewers often feel that they brew to higher standards than ale brewers do. Ales are generally more complex and somewhat more eccentric in character than lagers. That gives ale brewers a bit of wiggle room. Lager brewers have very little leeway; their brews are by nature cleaner, purer of essence, a simple yet subtle interplay of hops and malt. As Tom Pastorius says, "A lager brewer is hanging right out there with nowhere to hide!"

Tom has nothing to worry about from what I've tasted of his beer, and I've tasted my share. His flagship Penn Pilsner is brewed under contract because of the sheer volume it represents. Tom first contracted Pittsburgh Brewing to make the beer in 1986, and introduced

174

it to the market in his multi-great grandfather's hometown of Philadelphia (his ancestor founded Germantown).

After two years of selling, scrimping, saving, and sweating, Tom opened his brewery pub at 800 Vinial Street, in part of the old Eberhardt and Ober brewery. Lots of family work went into the brewery; Tom built the sturdy, simple furniture himself. The pub is a beauty of German style and functionality, and Tom has indoctrinated his staff in the Teutonic obsession with having everything just so, *alles in ordnung*. The place settings, tablecloths, and food presentation are uniformly excellent. I can vouch for the food itself; it is definitely *not* a matter of style over substance. I'd like to eat at Tom's table often, say once or twice a day.

The beer is outstanding. The thing I like most about Penn's beers is their balance. They do not go overboard on anything. Even the doublebock, malty though it is, is kept in a tenuous dynamic balance by malt dryness. That's the mark of a true brewmaster.

My hat's off to Tom and his gracious wife, Mary Beth. They have built an honest business and a beautiful one. The service is competent and friendly; the food is fresh and praiseworthy. The beer is clean, pure, and delicious. I don't know what more you can ask of a brewer.

Opened: March 1986.

Type: Brewpub and brewery.

Owners: Thomas V. Pastorius, Mary Beth Pastorius.

Brewers: Alexander Deml, Peter Boettcher.

PA Microbrewers Guild: Member.

System: 45-barrel Jacob Carl GmbH brewhouse. Potential annual capacity 20,500 barrels (plus 8,000 barrels contracted Penn Pilsner).

Annual production: 15,000 barrels in 1996.

Beers brewed: *Year-round:* Penn Pilsner*, Penn Gold* (GABF gold, 1990 and 1993), Kaiser Pils, Penn Dark*, Penn Hefeweizen* (GABF silver, 1997). *Seasonals:* Oktoberfest*, St. Nikolaus Bock*, Maerzen, Altbier, Maibock, All Star Lager, Pastorator Double Bock. (* denotes beers in bottles and on draft.) All beers except Penn Pilsner brewed on premises; Penn Pilsner also contract-brewed at Jones Brewing Company.

The Pick: The entire Penn line is excellent, but the Pick is easy: St. Nikolaus Bock. Tom Pastorius makes one of the best bocks in the United States. The St. Nikolaus is creamy smooth, chocolatey, and just rich enough, without stepping over the line into double-bock territory. A beer hearty enough for German food, yet smooth enough to quaff. *Ausgezeichnet!* Excellent!

Take-out beer: Six-packs, cases, quarter and half kegs.

Tours: Tours are by appointment, for groups of twenty or more. (The brewery is visible from the dining room and the ratskellar.)

Brewpub hours: Monday through Saturday, 11:00 A.M.–midnight; closed Sundays and major holidays.

Food: Penn makes some great German food, but you can also get American food. There is a full lunch and dinner menu of appetizers, soups, salads, sandwiches, and entrees. All desserts are made on premises. Tom and Mary Beth are just a bit fanatic about the quality of ingredients—you can taste it.

Extras: Full liquor license. Selection includes German schnapps such as Jagermeister and Himbeerngeist. Live entertainment four nights a week; call for schedule.

Events: Penn hosts the Pennsylvania Microbrewers Fest on the first Saturday of June—a friendly accessible fest I highly recommend—and its own Oktoberfest the last two weekends of September. There are also ceremonial tappings of seasonal beers; call for dates.

Special considerations: Kids welcome. Handicapped-accessible. Cigars allowed. Vegetarian meals available.

Directions: See map on page 172.

Parking: Free off-street parking.

Church Brew Works

3525 Liberty Avenue
Pittsburgh
412-688-8200
www.churchbrew.com

Prepare yourself for a shock when you first walk into the Church Brew Works. At least, it was something of a shock to me. Intellectually I *knew* that the Church Brew Works was located in a church. (As far as I'm aware, this is the only brewpub in America in such a setting.) It's in the former St. John the Baptist Roman Catholic Church, to be specific, just up the street from Pittsburgh Brewing in Pittsburgh's Lawrenceville neighborhood. I had actually seen the church being renovated some months before the brewpub opened. Even so, it was strange to walk into the place the first time and see a brewhouse, tanks and all, sitting right up on the altar of what was obviously, definitely, for sure a church. Don't get me wrong. I saw nothing particularly heinous about the fact that it was a brewery. I would have had the same reaction if I had found, say, a beauty salon or a McDonald's.

What's also surprising is that the people who grew up with St. John's as their church seem to be pretty happy about the brewpub in general. That's mostly because the parish had shrunk so much that the diocese had closed it and deconsecrated the church. The building was headed for the wrecking ball when Sean Casey and other local investors bought it to convert it into the brewpub. The friends of the church, people who had been baptized, confirmed, and married there, figured that having the building and their memories intertwined with a brewpub was better than seeing the church leveled to make room for another professional building or mini-market.

Their new faith has been rewarded. The Church Brew Works has brought some excitement to Lawrenceville. Colorful banners fly outside the spruced-up building. People are slowing down to look and stopping to have a drink. Everyone is doing a little better, including the employees at Pittsburgh Brewing, who now have someplace cool to go for lunch.

And the Church is pretty cool. The stained glass and gold decorations were retained and refurbished, as was the church's lectern, which serves as a hostess station. The ceiling is immensely high, all the way up to the organ loft in the rear.

The Church has a selection of beers ranging from good to excellent. There is a strong lager component in response to local tastes. Many Pittsburghers are of Eastern and Central European descent, and those folks do love their lagers. You can get a *dunkel* anytime, Festbier in the fall, bock in the winter. That's a nice break from the usual unending brewpub parade of ale, ale, ale.

Some Pittsburghers have already become faithful Church-goers. It has been a blessing to this neighborhood.

Opened: August 1996.

Type: Brewpub.

Owner: Corporation. Sean Casey, president.

Brewer: Bryan Pearson.

PA Microbrewers Guild: Member.

System: 15-barrel Specific Mechanical brewhouse. Potential annual capacity 1,500 barrels.

Annual production: 500 barrels in six months of 1996.

Beers brewed: *Year-round:* Celestial Gold, Pipe Organ Pale Ale, Pious Monk Dunkel, Bell Tower Brown Ale. *Seasonals:* Up to twelve varied seasonal beers per year. All beers brewed on premises.

The Pick: I'll give the nod to the Pipe Organ Pale Ale. There's a nice malt flavor, a good balance with the British hops (East Kent Goldings). It's clean, it's proper, it's the one to have by the pint during meals or relaxation. (The Pious Monk Dunkel was pretty good, too.)

Take-out beer: Growlers, kegs by prior arrangement.

Tours: Monday through Friday at 5:00 P.M.

Brewpub hours: Monday through Thursday, 11:30 A.M.–11:45 P.M.; Friday and Saturday, 11:30 A.M.–1:00 A.M.; Sunday, noon–10:00 P.M.

Food: An eclectic American regional menu that is very popular with the lunchtime crowd. Some heart-healthy selections.

Extras: Full liquor license. Offers a selection of malts, bourbons, and cognacs. Occasional live music; call for information. There is an outside patio and hop garden for warm weather.

Events: Oktoberfest.

Special considerations: Kids welcome. Handicapped-accessible. Cigars allowed on outdoor patio only. Vegetarian meals available.

Directions: See map on page 172.

Parking: Large off-street lot and plenty of on-street parking.

Foundry Ale Works

2816 Smallman Street
Pittsburgh
412-338-9050

How could a brewery called the Foundry be anywhere but Iron City? Images of gargantuan Bessemer converters come to mind, blasting through a brew with a shower of malt sparks. Overhead cranes carrying huge vats of steaming wort to massive tanks. Brewery workers, muscled like Soviet tractor heroes and sporting welders' goggles, pouring fermented beer into carbonation crucibles.

Okay, I've got an active beer imagination. You should hear my theory on malto-geology and drilling for beer sometime. The fact is, the Foundry does have a serious overhead crane left over from when the building really was a foundry. When the brewery got its tanks and vessels, the crane worked just fine and brought the vessels to the back of the brewhouse. It remains in the brewhouse as a conversation piece, but I wouldn't want to upset my waitress too much as long as that thing's working!

The Foundry has a high central ceiling with a broad mezzanine overlooking the main floor below. The brewery is in the back, visible through glass from the entire pub. It's another version of the ever-popular Theater of Brewing: Watch the brewer make your beer right before your eyes!

The Foundry had just opened as I was finishing this manuscript. I got to taste two of their beers, the IPA and the Dry Oatmeal Stout. The IPA was not good; it may have been stale. I took the stout, therefore, without much enthusiasm, but it was a marvel, full of flavor and chewy body. I finished it and licked my lips. That's what I call a good omen.

Add this brewpub to your list posthaste.

Opened: December 1997.
Type: Brewpub.
Owners: Blaze Katich, Paul Williams, Bill Rodgers.
Brewer: John Zangwill.
PA Microbrewers Guild: Not a member.
System: 8-barrel New World brewhouse. Potential annual capacity 1,250 barrels.

Annual production: No figures available.

Beers brewed: The Foundry's madly rotating beers include IPA, Foundry Light, Golden Ale, American Pale Ale, Robust Porter, Nut'n'Honey, Brown Ale, Dry Oatmeal Stout, Irish Red, Belgian Wit, Razwheat, ESB and Old Ale (both on beer engine; both cask conditioned), Kölsch, Dunkelweizen, Blueberry Ale, El Niño Ale... and that's just in the first six weeks. All beers brewed on premises.

The Pick: Dry Oatmeal Stout. I tried this before the brewpub opened, and it stopped me in my tracks—astonishingly good. A whole skein of flavors rolled over my tongue: cookies, malt, toffee, coffee, and a touch of chocolate, like a really good pastry without the fat. Health stout!

Take-out beer: Not available yet. Call for more information.

Tours: On request during normal hours.

Brewpub hours: Sunday through Thursday, 11:00 A.M.–1:00 A.M.; Friday and Saturday, 11:00 A.M.–2:00 A.M.

Food: American wood-grill cuisine. "As extensive and good as the beer," partner Blaze Katich promises. Wood-fired brick pizza oven, meat cooked on wood-burning grill, steamed clams, mussels, and shrimp. Rotating general menu.

Extras: Liquor license pending. Darts, shuffleboard, and foosball. Live music; call for schedule.

Special considerations: Kids welcome (special menu and games). Handicapped-accessible. Cigars allowed and for sale. Vegetarian meals available.

Directions: See map on page 172.

Parking: Free parking lot behind building.

Strip Brewing Company and Restaurant

2106 Penn Avenue
Pittsburgh
412-338-BEER
www.stripbrewing.com

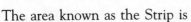

The area known as the Strip is
four or five blocks of Penn Avenue east of the Sixteenth Street Bridge.
What is The Strip? Think Ninth Street Market in Philadelphia, or
maybe Faneuil Hall in Boston with the roof torn off. The bustling
Strip is the heart of Pittsburgh's produce, meat, and seafood markets.
Many of the buildings display signs that go back for years, proclaiming
them as this or that terminal, co-op, or market. There are delis, fruit
stands, seafood shops with the catch of the day laid out on ice, Asian
groceries of several different ethnicities, and gadget emporiums. Cafes,
restaurants, and sandwich shops are crowded in between them.

You can get most any kind of good food down here, but until
recently you couldn't get a good beer. That changed when Strip Brewing Company opened. This attractive brewpub has made the Strip a
part of its ambiance (as well as a part of its name); a glass wall sepa-
rates the bar and dining room from the outside world, and the show on
the Strip is often the best in town.

You can sit at the window and watch the action, or you can go to
the bar and sample the beer. These brewers are not afraid to try ales,
lagers, and Bavarian hefe-weizens, a style that has taken Pittsburgh by
storm in the past year. Bartenders will be happy to suggest all kinds of
beer mixes, and experimentation is encouraged. As at Bullfrog in
Williamsport, you can make custom fruit-wheat beers by adding natural
raspberry, peach, and cherry flavors to the light, crisp Stripped Wheat.

If experimenting at the bar is too much work, there's a nice living-
room kind of lounge with couches and armchairs. It's like drinking at
home with a waiter to get your beer for you.

The brewpub does a booming lunch business, which is no surprise
given its ideal location. Sit near the windows and people-watch as you
munch a lunch made with ingredients that were probably bought that
day no more than two blocks from where you're sitting.

That's the whole idea of the Strip and Strip Brewery. If you want good things, go to the source. For produce, fish, cheese, and meat, go to the Strip. For beer, go to Strip Brewery. Seems pretty simple to me.

Opened: June 1997.

Type: Brewpub.

Owner: SLAM Corporation.

Brewers: Bill Ehlert, Dave Achkio.

PA Microbrewers Guild: Not a member.

System: 10-barrel Saaz Brewing Equipment brewhouse. Potential annual capacity 1,400 barrels.

Annual production: Estimated 1997 production 300 barrels.

Beers brewed: *Year-round:* Redhead Ale, Pale Gal Ale, Hopus Maximus, Porter O'Call, Wüggleundstrip Hefe-weizen, Ye Olde Golde, Hazelnut Porter, Stripped Wheat, Cellar Conditioned Ale. *Seasonals:* Love Stout No. 9, Scandalous Scotch Ale, Downtown Brown, Quaker Stout. All beers brewed on premises.

The Pick: Hopus Maximus. I generally hate picking the hoppy beer at any brewery, just because it's so easy to pick the beer that sticks out. There's no thought or subtlety involved. But the five hop varieties blend in Hopus into a powerful roar that is not dominated by any one variety and synergistically creates a flavor and aroma profile all its own. Hopheads rejoice!

Take-out beer: Half-gallon growlers, kegs.

Tours: "Just ask."

Brewpub hours: Monday through Thursday, 11:00 A.M.–midnight; Friday, 11:00 A.M.–1:00 A.M.; Saturday, 8:30A.M.–1:00 A.M.; Sunday, 11:00 A.M.–9:00 P.M.

Food: Strip's menu is pub fare and American bistro. It is prepared with the city's freshest provisions bought at the markets right on the Strip.

Extras: Full liquor license, darts. They also have a 110-seat banquet area for dinners, meetings, or private parties. Late night menu, with discounts after 9:00 P.M. on weekdays and 10:00 P.M. on weekends.

Special considerations: Kids welcome. Handicapped-accessible. Cigars allowed. Vegetarian meals available.

Directions: See map on page 172.

Parking: On-street parking, which can get hairy at lunchtime in the Strip. Things thin out quickly after 4:00 P.M.

Valhalla

1150 Smallman Street
Pittsburgh
412-434-1440

I've seen a lot of goofy themes for   V ∧ L H ∧ L L ∧

restaurants and brewpubs. There
are the fifties joints with booths made from the back seats of '57 Chevys and poodle-skirted waitresses dancing on the tables. There's the infamous Burp Castle in New York, where hooded "monks" serve Belgian beer. I've eaten in railway cars, airplanes, and rain forests. But I must admit, until I went to Valhalla I'd never had a beer in Asgard, mythical home of the Norse gods.

A little background information on Norse mythos is in order. Valhalla, the Hall of Heroes, is where the heroic dead were brought from the field of battle. They were brought there by the Valkyries, the daughters of Odin Allfather, ruler of the Norse gods and one mean SOB. The Valkyries would ride over a battle, watching for acts of heroism by a doomed warrior. They would then swoop down on the hero as he died and carry him away to Valhalla. (Brave warriors who lived apparently weren't worth the trip.) The lucky dead in Valhalla would fight each other every day and be magically healed up just in time for dinner and drinks every night. It's the Viking version of *The Peter Principle*: be brave, screw up, get promoted.

Come to think of it, this brewpub is aptly named. Most of us perform heroic acts during the day, suffering the slings and arrows of outrageous fortune working for the Man. Then 5:00 comes and we are miraculously restored by the food and drink at Valhalla.

Enough mythology; let's talk brewpubs. Valhalla really does take the Viking stuff semi-seriously, from the swords and shields on the walls right down to the curiously comfortable Danish-design backless barstools. There's an attractive mural in authentic Viking style over the north bar, and the tap handles are carved in artful Sutton Hoo fashion.

The whole pub soars dramatically through an open two stories with casually asymmetrical balconies ringing the main floor. The brewhouse itself is on a suspended platform in the middle of the pub, visible from everywhere. The fermentation/aging tanks are stacked behind glass at the far end of the pub, letting everyone see where the beer comes from. There's an upper-story deck outside overlooking Smallman Street and the Allegheny River. The deck is surrounded by a railing hung with more Viking symbols; all it needs is a mast and dragonhead to look like a longboat rowing downtown.

The beers are mainly lagers, a manly sort of northern beer. The *dunkel*, pilsner, and Vienna lager that make up Valhalla's regular offerings are solid beers. The hefe-weizen is ready for prime time, breadfresh and ripe with bananas.

Fortunately you don't need a Valkyrie—or a heroic death—to get to this Valhalla. Just hail a cab.

Opened: June 1997.

Type: Brewpub.

Owner: Smallman Brewing Company.

Brewer: Patrick O'Neill.

PA Microbrewers Guild: Not a member.

System: 15-barrel Pub Brewing System brewhouse. Potential annual capacity 1,500 barrels.

Annual production: No figures available.

Beers brewed: *Year-round:* Pillage Pilsner, Eric the Red (Vienna lager), Big Olaf (*dunkel*). *Seasonals:* Thor's Wild Wheat (Bavarian-type), Honey Wheat, Winterbock; more coming. All beers brewed on premises.

The Pick: The Bavarian-style Thor's Wild Wheat. Fresh, yeasty, almost bread-like, it's easy to see why this style of beer is so popular in Pittsburgh. It does well here at Valhalla, too.

Take-out beer: None available yet. Call for information.

Tours: First Saturday of the month; call for times. Also given by appointment for groups of twelve or more.

Brewpub hours: Kitchen is open Monday through Thursday, 11:00 A.M.–10:00 P.M.; Friday and Saturday, 11:00 A.M.–midnight. The bar will stay open longer, depending on business, until 2:00 A.M. Closed Sunday.

Food: Not what you'd expect at a place with a Viking theme and swords on the walls. There is a Cajun-Mediterranean feel to the menu, with a jarring but very welcome Teutonic element. Good-looking appetizers.

Extras: Full liquor license. Selection of single malts. Projection TV for sports. Outside deck overlooking the Allegheny River.

Special considerations: Kids welcome. Handicapped-accessible. Cigars allowed and for sale. Vegetarian meals available.

Directions: See map on page 172.

Parking: Free parking in back. Large pay lot across the street.

John Harvard's Brew House, Wilkins Township

3466 William Penn Highway
Wilkins Township
412-824-9440
www.johnharvards.com

It's another John Harvard's Brew House! This one was the first brewpub to open in Pittsburgh's suburbs. Like the Springfield Brew House, the Wilkins Township Brew House is boldly staking out nontraditional brewpub space. It is tucked into a shopping center and seems to be doing well there.

You can get the John Harvard's story from the earlier entry for the Wayne Brew House (page 73). I got to the Wilkins Township Brew House just two months after Pete Seaman first fired up his Pub Brewing System kettle. It came as no surprise that things were running smoothly. "They [John Harvard's management] have it pretty well figured out," Pete says.

This is one of the neatest brewpub breweries I've ever seen. Every hose is coiled or snaked along the edge of the floor, every delivery tube is fastened securely to the wall, and the brewing vessels gleam behind the glass barrier separating them from the customers. It's no show brewery, though. Pete's beers stand up to inspection as hale and hearty, and they pass the all-important customer quaffability test as well.

This Brew House seems more open than the other two, thanks to a glass front wall that came with the storefront space. In a rainy area like this, it is probably a good idea to get as much light as you can when it's out there.

If you're headed into Pittsburgh from points east, the Wilkins Township Brew House is a good place to break your beer fast. Monroeville residents must appreciate being able to get fresh, real beer without a trip down to Pittsburgh.

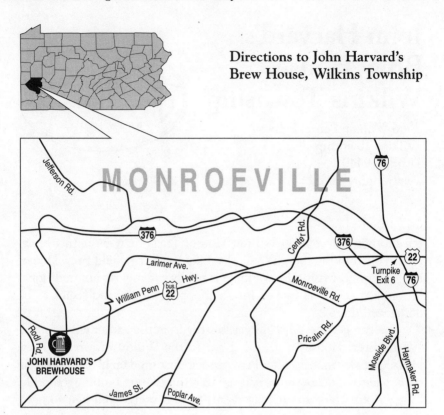

Directions to John Harvard's Brew House, Wilkins Township

Opened: August 1997.

Type: Brewpub.

Owner: John Harvard's Brew House, Boston.

Brewers: Head Brewer Peter Seaman, Sean McIntyre.

PA Microbrewers Guild: Membership pending.

System: 15-barrel Pub Brewing brewhouse. Potential annual capacity approximately 2,500 barrels.

Annual production: No figures available.

Beers brewed: The following beers or types of beers are on at all times: John Harvard's Pale Ale, Nut Brown Ale, All-American Light Lager, some sort of fruit-wheat beer (the fruit varies), varying golden or amber hoppy beers, a varying porter or stout. *Seasonals:* Mid-Winter Strong Ale, Presidential Ale, Celtic Strong Ale, Big Bad Bock, Crystal Pilsner, Harvard Hefe-Weizen, Smokin' Joe's Lager, Summer Ale, Oktoberfest, Harvest Spiced Ale, Christmas Ale. All beers brewed on premises.

The Pick: What I sampled was an exceptional John Harvard's Nut Brown Ale. It was round and full, not watery, with just that touch of nuttiness that makes you wonder if it's real or suggestibility. Who cares? It's a good jar of beer, and that's all that matters.

Take-out beer: Growlers.

Tours: Upon request during daytime hours.

Brewpub hours: Monday through Thursday, 11:30 A.M.–midnight; Friday and Saturday, 11:30 A.M.–1:00 A.M.; Sunday, 11:30 A.M.–10:30 P.M.

Food: Upscale pub fare: mixed grill, chicken pot pie, grilled meatloaf, calamari, etc.

Extras: Full liquor license. Beer dinners once a month, call for information.

Special considerations: Kids welcome. Handicapped-accessible. Vegetarian meals available.

Parking: Off-street lot.

Lodging: Days Inn Monroeville, 2727 Mosside Boulevard (412-856-1610); Radisson Hotel Pittsburgh, by the Monroeville Mall, 101 Mall Boulevard, Monroeville (412-373-7300); Harley Hotel, 699 Rodi Road, Monroeville (412-244-1600).

Nearby attractions: You'll see the Sri Venkateswara Temple as you drive along the Penn Lincoln Parkway, and you might as well take a closer look. This gleaming white structure is one of ten Hindu temples in the United States. South McCully Road, Monroeville. See the introduction to this section for other Pittsburgh attractions (pages 171–173).

Other good beer sites in the area: See the introduction to this section (page 173).

New Arrivals

These Pennsylvania breweries opened after the manuscript was completed in early 1998.

Bethlehem Brew Works

569 Main Street
Bethlehem
(610) 882-1300

Type: Brewpub.
Owners: Dave Fegley, Dick Fegley, Jean Fegley, Jeff Fegley, Peg Fegley, Rich Fegley.
Brewer: Jeff Fegley.
Beers brewed: Valley Golden Ale, South Mountain Hefe-weizen, Old Gal Pale Ale, British ESB, Mountain Hawk Brown Ale, Steelworker's Stout.
Tours: Available upon request during brewpub hours.
Brewpub hours: Monday through Thursday, 11:00 A.M.–10:00 P.M., bar until midnight; Friday and Saturday, 11:00 A.M.–2:00 P.M.; Sunday, 11:00 A.M.–9:00 P.M.

Brew Moon, King of Prussia

160 North Gulph Road
King of Prussia
(610) 230-BREW
www.brewmoon.com

Type: Brewpub.
Owner: Elliot Fiener.
Brewer: Brion Boyer.
Beers brewed: Munich Gold, Prussia's Pride ESB, Planetary Porter, Granite Pale Ale, Oktoberfest, Obsidian Stout, Grasshopper IPA, Boston Scotch, Mayberry Wheat R.F.D., Moonlight American Ale, Eclipse Stout, Blonde Ale, Beanpot Bitter, Belgian Tripel, Belgian Dubble.
Tours: Night and day, at customer's request.
Brewpub hours: Sunday–Wednesday, 11:30 A.M.–midnight; Thursday–Saturday, 11:30 A.M.–2:00 A.M.

Jack's Mountain Restaurant and Brewery
9074 U.S. Highway 522 South
Lewistown
(717) 242-6483

Type: Brewpub.
Owners: David White, Karen White, Craig Ake, Sandra Ake.
Brewer: David White.
Beers brewed: Pale Ale; plans to brew six beers on a regular basis.
Tours: To be announced.
Brewpub hours: Weeknights, 11:00 A.M.–midnight, Weekends, 11:00 A.M.–1:30 A.M., closed Sundays. Kitchen open weekdays until 9:00 P.M. and weekends until 10:00 P.M.

Mount Nittany Brewing Company
200 Shady Lane
Philipsburg
(814) 342-2118
www.mtnittanybrew.com

Type: Brewery.
Owner: Mark Bloom.
Brewer: Mark Bloom.
Beers brewed: Jed Red Ale; more are planned.
Tours: Available upon request.

Red Star Brewing Company
Ehalt and Harrison Streets
Greensburg

Type: Brewpub.
Owners: Majority partners: Ernie Valozzi, Al Spinelli.
Brewer: Mike Escourt.
Beers brewed: Golden, American Pale Ale, English Brown Ale, Irish Dry Stout.
Tours: To be announced.
Brewpub hours: To be announced.

GLOSSARY

ABV/ABW. Alcohol by volume/alcohol by weight. These are two slightly different ways of measuring the alcohol content of beverages, as a percentage of either the beverage total volume or its weight. For example, if you have 1 liter of 4 percent ABV beer, 4 percent of that liter (40 ml) is alcohol. However, because alcohol weighs only 79.6 percent as much as water, that same beer is only 3.18 percent ABW. This may seem like a dry exercise in mathematics, but it is at the heart of the common belief that Canadian beer is stronger than American beer. Canadian brewers generally use ABV figures, whereas American brewers have historically used the lower ABW figures. Mainstream Canadian and American lagers are approximately equal in strength. Just to confuse the issue further, most American microbreweries use ABV figures. This is very important if you're trying to keep a handle on how much alcohol you're consuming. If you know how much Bud (at roughly 4.8 percent ABV) you can safely consume, you can extrapolate from there. Learn your limits.

Adjunct. Any nonbarley malt source of sugars for fermentation. This can be candy sugar, corn grits, corn or rice syrups, or any number of specialty grains. Wheat, rye, and candy sugars are considered by beer geeks to be "politically correct" adjuncts; corn and rice are generally taken as signs of swill. Small amounts of corn, however, used as a brewing ingredient for certain styles of beer, is slowly gaining acceptance in craft-brewing circles.

Ale. The generic term for warm-fermented beers. (See "A word about ... Ales and Lagers" on page 87.)

Anheuser-Busch. Anheuser-Busch (A-B) is the world's largest brewer, with approximately 45 percent of the U.S. market and 8 percent of the world's market. Its flagship beer, Budweiser, is the world's best-selling beer. Because of this, A-B is often the whipping boy of the microbrewers, but A-B has taken its share of shots at the micros as well. No one disputes the quality control and consistency of brewers like A-B. I've met Augie Busch; he is sharp, devoted to his company and its beers, and driven to improve the company's standing. A-B has over 100 highly trained and qualified brewmasters who are fanatical about quality in ingredients and process.

Barley. A wonderfully apt grain for brewing beer. Barley grows well in relatively marginal soil and climate. It has no significant gluten content, which makes it unsuitable for baking bread and thereby limits market competition for brewers buying the grain. Its husk serves as a very efficient filter at the end of the mashing process. And, of course, it makes beer that tastes really, really good. Barley comes in two types: two-row and six-row, named for the rows of kernels on the heads of the grain. In days past, two-row barley was plumper and considered finer. Six-row barley was easier to grow, had a better yield per acre and higher enzymatic power, but had a somewhat astringent character. These differences have been lessened by cross-breeding. Most North American barley is six-row, for reasons of soil and climate. (Incidentally, the grain's kernels or corns are the source of the name "John Barleycorn," a traditional personification of barley or beer.)

Barrel. A traditional measure of beer volume equal to thirty-one U.S. gallons. The most common containers of draft beer in the United States are half and quarter barrels, or kegs, at 15.5 gallons and 7.75 gallons respectively.

Beer. A fermented beverage brewed from grain, generally malted barley. "Beer" covers a variety of beverages, including ales and lagers, stouts and bocks, porters and pilsners, lambics and altbiers, cream ale, kölsch, and wheat beer.

Beer geek. A person who takes beer a little more seriously than does the average person. Often homebrewers, beer geeks love to argue with other beer geeks about what makes exceptional beers exceptional. That is, if they've been able to agree on which beers are exceptional in the first place. A beer geek is the kind of person who would buy a book about traveling to breweries ... the kind of person who would read the glossary of a beer book. Hey, hi there!

Bottle-conditioned. Describes a beer that has been bottled with an added dose of live yeast. This living yeast causes the beer to mature and change as it ages over periods of one to thirty years or more.

Brewhouse. The vessels used to mash the malt and grains and boil the wort. The malt and grains are mashed in a vessel called a mash turn. Brewhouse size is generally given in terms of the capacity of the brewkettle, where the wort is boiled. A brewery's annual capacity is a function of brewhouse size, fermentation, and aging tank capacity, and the length of the aging cycle for the brewery's beers.

Brewpub. A brewery that sells the majority of its output on draft, on premises. Or, a tavern that brews its own beer. Until recently,

Pennsylvania law forbade brewpubs to sell anything but their own beer, brewed on premises. That law has been changed, and now brewpubs may obtain a tavern license and serve a full range of alcoholic beverages.

Brewer. One who brews beer for commercial sale.

CAMRA. The CAMpaign for Real Ale. A British beer-drinkers' consumer group formed in the early 1970s by beer drinkers irate over the disappearance of cask-conditioned ale. They have been very vocal and successful in bringing this traditional drink back to a place of importance in the United Kingdom. CAMRA sets high standards for cask-conditioned ale which only a few brewers in the United States match.

Carbonation. The fizzy effects of carbon dioxide (CO_2) in solution in a liquid (e.g., beer). Carbonation can be accomplished artificially by injecting the beer with the gas, or naturally by trapping the CO_2, which is a by-product of fermentation. There is no intrinsic qualitative difference between beers carbonated by these two methods. Brewer's choice, essentially. Low carbonation will allow a broader array of flavors to come through, while high carbonation can result in a perceived bitterness. Most American drinkers prefer a higher carbonation.

Cask. A keg designed to serve cask-conditioned ale by gravity feed or by handpump, not by gas pressure.

Cask-conditioned ale. An unfiltered ale that is put in a cask before it is completely ready to serve. The yeast still in the beer continues to work, and ideally brings the beer to perfection at the point of sale. The flip side to achieving this supreme freshness is that the ale will continue to "work," and will become sour within five to seven days. Bars should sell the cask out before then or remove it from sale. If you are served sour cask-conditioned beer, send it back! Cask-conditioned ale is generally served at cellar temperature (55-60 degrees Fahrenheit) and is lightly carbonated. Some American brewers, Stoudt's among them, are experimenting with cask-conditioned lager beers.

Cold-filtering. The practice of passing finished beer through progressively finer filters (usually cellulose or ceramic) to strip out microorganisms that can spoil the beer when it is stored. Brewers like Coors and Miller and also some smaller brewers use cold-filtering as an alternative to pasteurization (see below). Some beer geeks complain that this "strip-filtering" robs beers of their more subtle complexities and some of their body.

Contract brewer. A brewer who hires an existing brewery to brew beer on contract. Contract brewers range from those who simply have a different label put on one of the brewery's existing brands to those who maintain a separate on-site staff to actually brew the beer at the brewery. Some brewers and beer geeks feel contract-brewed beer is inherently inferior. This is strictly a moral and business issue: Some of the best beers on the market are contract-brewed.

Craft brewer. The new term for microbrewer. Craft brewer, like microbrewer before it, is really a code word for any brewer producing beers other than mainstream American lagers like Budweiser and Lite. (See "A word about ... Micros, Brewpubs, and Craft Brewers" on page 53.)

Decoction. The type of mashing often used by lager brewers to wring the full character from the malt. In a decoction mash, a portion of the hot mash is taken to another vessel, brought to boiling, and returned to the mash, thus raising the temperature. (See Infusion.)

Dry-hopping. Adding hops to the beer in post-fermentation stages, often in porous bags to allow easy removal. This results in a greater hop aroma in the finished beer. A few brewers put a small bag of hop cones in each cask of their cask-conditioned beers, resulting in a particularly intense hop aroma in a glass of the draft beer.

ESB. Extra Special Bitter, an ale style with a rich malt character and full body, perhaps some butter or butterscotch aromas and an understated hop bitterness. An ESB is only noticeably bitter in comparison to a Mild Ale, a style not often seen in America.

Esters. Aroma compounds produced by fermentation that gives some ales lightly fruity aromas: banana, pear, and grapefruit, among others. The aromas produced are tightly linked to the yeast strain used. Ester-based aromas should not be confused with the less subtle fruit aromas of a beer to which fruit or fruit essences have been added.

Extract. More specifically, malt extract. Malt extract is kind of like concentrated wort (see below). Malt is mashed and the resulting sweet, unhopped wort is reduced to a syrup. This is important to know because some breweries brew with malt extract. In extract brewing the extract is mixed with water and boiled. Specialty grains (black patent or chocolate malts, wheat, roasted barley, etc.) can be added for flavor notes and nuances. It is actually more expensive to brew with extract, but you need less equipment, which can be crucial in cramped brewing areas. The quality of the beer may suffer as well. Some people claim to be able to pick out extract brews. I've had extract brews that had a common taste—a kind of thin, vegetal sharpness—but I've regularly had excellent extract brews at the Samuel Adams Brew House in Philly. My advice is to try it yourself.

Fermentation. The miracle of yeast; the heart of making beer. Fermentation is the process in which yeast turns sugar and water into alcohol, heat, carbon dioxide, esters, and traces of other compounds.

Final gravity. See Gravity.

Firkin. A cask or keg holding nine gallons of beer, specially plumbed for gravity or handpump dispense.

GABF. The Great American Beer Festival. Since 1982 America's breweries have been invited each year to bring their best beer to the GABF in Denver to showcase what America can brew. Since 1987 the GABF has awarded medals for various styles of beer; fifty styles were judged in 1997, three medals for each style. To ensure impartiality, the beers are tasted blind, their identities hidden from the judges. GABF medals are the most prestigious awards in American brewing because of the festival's longevity and reputation for fairness.

Gravity. The specific gravity of wort (original gravity) or finished beer (terminal gravity). The ratio of dissolved sugars to water determines the gravity of the wort. If there are more dissolved sugars, the original gravity and the potential alcohol are higher. The sugar that is converted to alcohol by the yeast lowers the terminal gravity, and makes the beer drier, just like wine. A brewer can determine the alcohol content of a beer by mathematical comparison of its original gravity and terminal gravity.

Growler. A jug or bottle used to take home draft beer. These are usually either simple half-gallon glass jugs with screwtops or more elaborate molded glass containers with swingtop seals. The origin of the name is from the old phrase "rushing the growler," which referred to the practice of buying beer by the pail at the local tavern or brewery for home consumption. Unfortunately, why this was called "rushing the growler" has not yet yielded to etymological scholarship. Stay tuned.

Handpump. A hand-powered pump for dispensing beer from a keg. Either a handpump or a gravity tap is always used for dispensing cask-conditioned beer; however, the presence of a handpump does not guarantee that the beer being dispensed is cask-conditioned.

Homebrewing. Making honest-to-goodness beer at home for personal consumption. Homebrewing is where many American craft brewers got their start.

Hops. The spice of beer. Hop plants are vines (humulus lupus), whose flower has a remarkable effect on beer. The flower's resins and oils add bitterness and a variety of aromas (spicy, piney, citrus, and others) to the finished beer. Beer without hops would be more like a fizzy, sweet, "alco-soda."

IBU. International Bittering Unit, a measure of a beer's bitterness. Humans can first perceive bitterness at levels between 8 and 12 IBU. Budweiser has 11.5 IBU, Heineken 18, Sierra Nevada Pale Ale 32, Pilsner Urquell 43, and a monster like Sierra Nevada Bigfoot clocks in at 98 IBU. Equivalent amounts of bitterness will seem greater in a lighter-bodied beer, whereas a heavier, maltier beer like Bigfoot needs lots of bitterness to be perceived as balanced.

Infusion. The mashing method generally used by ale brewers. Infusion entails heating the mash in a single vessel until the starches have been converted to sugar. Infusion mashing is simplier than decoction mashing and works well with the right types of malt.

IPA. India Pale Ale, a British ale style that has been almost completely co-opted by American brewers, characterized in this country by intense hop bitterness, accompanied in better examples of the style by a full-malt body. The name derives from the style's origin as a beer brewed for export to British beer drinkers in India. The beer was strong and heavily laced with hops—a natural preservative—to better endure the long sea voyage.

Kräusening. The practice of carbonating beer by a second fermentation. After the main fermentation has taken place and its vigorous blowoff of carbon dioxide has been allowed to escape, a small amount of fresh wort is added to the tank. A second fermentation takes place and the carbon dioxide is captured in solution. General opinion is that there is little sensory difference between kräusened beer and beer carbonated by injection, but some brewers use this more traditional method.

Lager. The generic term for all cold-fermented beers. Lager has also been appropriated as a name for the lightly hopped pilsners that have become the world's most popular beers, such as Budweiser, Ki-Rin, Brahma, Heineken, and Foster's. Many people speak of pilsners and lagers as if they are two different syles of beer, which is incorrect. All pilsners are lagers, but not all lagers are pilsners. Some are bocks, hellesbiers, and Märzens.

Malt. Generally this refers to malted barley, although other grains can be malted and used in brewing. Barley is wetted and allowed to sprout, which causes the hard, stable starches in the grain to convert to soluble starches (and small amounts of sugars). The grains, now called malt, are kiln-dried to kill the sprouts and conserve the starches. Malt is responsible for the color of beer. The kilned malt can be roasted, which will darken its color and intensify its flavors like a French roast coffee.

Mash. A mixture of cracked grains of malt and water, which is then heated. Heating causes starches in the malt to convert to sugars, which will be consumed by the yeast in fermentation. The length of time the mash is heated, temperatures, and techniques used are crucial to the character of the finished beer. Two mashing techniques are infusion and decoction.

Megabrewer. A mainstream brewer, generally producing five million or more barrels of American-style pilsner beer annually. Anheuser-Busch, Miller, and Coors are the best-known megabrewers.

Microbrewer. A somewhat dated term, originally defined as a brewer producing less than fifteen thousand barrels of beer in a year. Microbrewer, like craft brewer, is generally applied to any brewer producing beers other than mainstream American lagers. (See "A word about ... Micros, Brewpubs, and Craft Brewers" on page 53.)

Original gravity. See Gravity.

Pasteurization. A process named for its inventor, Louis Pasteur, the famed French microbiologist. Pasteurization involves heating beer to kill the microorganisms in it. This keeps beer fresh longer, but unfortunately it also changes the flavor because the beer is essentially cooked. "Flash pasteurization" sends fresh beer through a heated pipe where most of the microorganisms are killed and the beer is only hot for twenty seconds or so, as opposed to the twenty to thirty minutes of regular "tunnel" pasteurization. (See Cold-filtering.)

Pilsner. The Beer That Conquered The World. Developed in 1842 in Pilsen (now Plzen, in the Czech Republic), it is a hoppy pale lager that quickly became known as "pilsner" or "pilsener," the German word meaning simply "from Pilsen." Pilsner rapidly became the most popular beer in the world, and now accounts for over 80 percent of all beer consumed worldwide. Budweiser, a less hoppy, more delicate version of pilsner was developed in the Czech town of Budejovice, formerly known as Budweis. Anheuser-Busch's Budweiser, the world's best-selling beer, is quite a different animal.

Pitching. The technical term for adding yeast to wort.

PLCB. The Pennsylvania Liquor Control Board. The PLCB enforces the Pennsylvania Liquor Code. The PLCB is not always popular with consumers and retailers, but it is sometimes the only agency regulating the sanitary standards of your local taps. (See "A word about … The Pennsylvania Liquor Code & Regulations" on page 25.)

Prohibition. The period from 1920 to 1933 when the sale, manufacture, or transportation of alcoholic beverages was illegal in the United States, thanks to the Eighteenth Amendment and the Volstead Act. (Pennsylvania just barely approved the measure, I'm proud to say.) Prohibition had a disastrous effect on American brewing and brought about a huge growth in organized crime and government corruption. Repeal of Prohibition came with ratification of the Twenty-first Amendment in December 1933. Beer drinkers, however, had gotten an eight-month head start when the Volstead Act, the enforcement legislation of Prohibition, was amended to allow sales of 3.2 percent ABW beer. The amendment took effect at midnight, April 7. According to Will Anderson's *From Beer to Eternity*, over one million barrels of beer were consumed on April 7; 2,323,000 six-packs each hour. By the way, Pennsylvania is still waiting for the full fruits of Repeal: Ask your state legislator why you can't buy beer by the six-pack from distributors. Ask today!

Quaff and Quaffability. Quaff means to drink large quantities. With craft brews, this usually means a pint or more. A pale ale generally is quaffable; a doublebock generally is not. A good, truly quaffable doublebock would be dangerous, given the style's usual alcohol levels!

Real ale. See Cask-conditioned ale.

Regional brewery. Somewhere between a micro and a megabrewer. Annual production by regional breweries ranges from thirty-five thousand to two million barrels. They generally brew mainstream American lagers. However, some microbrewers—Boston Beer Company, Pete's, and Sierra Nevada, for instance—have climbed to this production level, and some regional brewers, like Anchor, Matt's, and August Schell, have reinvented themselves and now produce craft-brewed beer. The Lion seems to be trying this strategy with its Brewery Hill beers. (See "A word about … Micros, Brewpubs, and Craft Brewers" on page 53.)

Reinheitsgebot. The German beer Purity Law, which has its roots in a 1516 Bavarian statute limiting the ingredients in beer to barley malt, hops, and water. The law evolved into an inch-thick book and was the cornerstone of high-quality German brewing. It was deemed anticompetitive by the European Community courts and overturned in 1988. Most German brewers, however, continue to brew by its standards; tradition and the demands of their customers ensure it.

Repeal. See Prohibition.

Ringwood yeast. The house yeast of Peter Austin and Pugsley System breweries. A very particular yeast, which requires an open fermenter, it is mostly found on the East Coast. Some well-known examples of Ringwood-brewed beers are Geary's, Wild Goose, Oliver's, Shipyard, and Red Feather. Ringwood beers are often easily identifiable by a certain nuttiness to their flavor. A brewer who isn't careful will find that Ringwood has created an undesirably high level of diacetyl, a compound that gives a beer a buttery or butterscotch aroma.

Swill. A derogatory term used by beer geeks for American mainstream beers. The beers do not really deserve the name, since they are made with pure ingredients under conditions of quality control and sanitation some micros only wish they could achieve.

Terminal gravity. See Gravity.

Three-tier system. A holdover from before Prohibition, the three-tier system requires Pennsylvania brewers, wholesalers, and retailers to be separate entities. The system was put in place to curtail financial abuses that were common when the three were mingled. Owning both wholesale and retail outlets gave unscrupulous brewers the power to rake off ungodly amounts of money, which all too often was used to finance political graft and police corruption. The three-tier system keeps the wholesaler insulated from pressure from the brewer and puts a layer of separation between brewer and retailer. Pennsylvania's regional brewers generally credit the state's strong three-tier laws with their survival.

Wort. The pre-beer grain broth of sugars, proteins, hop oils and alpha acids, and whatever else that was added or developed during the mashing process. Once the yeast has been pitched and starts its jolly work, wort becomes beer.

Yeast. A miraculous fungus that, among other things, converts sugar into alcohol and carbon dioxide. The particular yeast strain used in brewing beer greatly influences the aroma and flavor of the beer. An Anheuser-Busch brewmaster recently told me that the yeast strain used there is the major factor in the flavor and aroma of Budweiser. Yeast is the sole source of the clovey, banana-rama aroma and the taste of Bavarian-style wheat beers. The original *Reinheitsgebot* of 1516 made no mention of yeast. It hadn't been discovered yet. Early brewing depended on a variety of sources for yeast: adding a starter from the previous batch of beer; exposing the wort to the wild yeasts carried on the open air (a method still used for Belgian lambic beers); always using the same vats for fermentation (yeast would cling to cracks and pores in the wood); or using a "magic stick" to stir the beer. (The stick would, of course, have the dormant yeast from the last batch dried on its surface.) British brewers called the turbulent, billowing foam on fermenting beer *goddesgood*—"God is good"—because the foam meant that the predictable magic of the yeast was making beer. And beer, as Ben Franklin said, is proof that God loves us and wants us to be happy. Amen.

INDEX